KLAUS KOCH

The Prophets

VOLUME ONE

The Assyrian Period

FORTRESS PRESS PHILADELPHIA

Translated by Margaret Kohl from the German *Die Propheten* I: *Assyrische Zeit* by Klaus Koch, copyright © 1978 Verlag W. Kohlhammer GmbH, Stuttgart, Berlin, Köln, and Mainz, The Federal Republic of Germany, in the series Urban-Taschenbücher, no. 280.

Published in the United Kingdom by SCM Press, London

First Fortress Press Edition 1983

Library of Congress Cataloging in Publication Data

Koch, Klaus, 1926-
The prophets
Translation of: Die Profeten.
Bibliography: v. 1, p.
Contents: v. 1. The Assyrian period
1. Prophets. I. Title.
BS1198.K6313 1983 224'.06 79-8894
ISBN 0-8006-1648-0 (v. 1)

Printed in the United States of America 1-1648

99 98 97 9 10

CONTENTS

INTRODUCTION

The intention of the present study is to introduce readers to the thinking of Israel's prophets. The prophets whose words have been collected in the writings of the Old Testament are not simply the charismatically endowed recipients of visions and spoken messages. Nor are they merely writers to whom we owe splendid examples of Hebrew poetry. It is not even enough to see them as preachers who, filled with a profound faith, proclaim as the word of God a kerygma which awaits the faith of its hearers. The prophets – at least the prophets who have given their names to scriptural books – were at the same time independent thinkers who, in a process of what I should like to term 'subsequent insight', give a rational form to what they have already become certain of intuitively. They demand similar reflection from their listeners, too. They maintain that the evidence for what they put forward is convincing if it is seen against the background of the traditions and the historical experiences which they share with their listeners. To grasp *the prophets as thinkers* – to work out the distinctive intellectual profiles of these mighty figures – has not as yet been systematically undertaken. To this extent, the two volumes presented here explore new ground.

I cannot save the reader the labour of considering semantic investigations in the context of an ancient Semitic language, even though the results may seem strange to us in our twentieth century of the Christian era. In order to make it easier to approach the material and to bring out the contemporary significance which, in my view, prophecy still has today, I shall first develop a preliminary aid to understanding, drawn from the problems of our own day, under the heading, 'In Search of the Future'. However, what I have written here can easily be omitted without affecting the subsequent historical account.

At present, anyone who describes the ideas and effects of the prophetic movement in Israel cannot draw on a broad scholarly consensus. The wide spectrum of opinion in contemporary studies will immediately be evident to the reader who compares recent German surveys of the subject (e.g. those of Gerhard von Rad or

Georg Fohrer, see the bibliography) with the corresponding sections of the present book. On subjects of central importance I have touched on the theories of other scholars where they differ from my own – as far as was possible in a general account. I have put forward the reasons for my own methods of interpretation in my book on Amos (1976), and would ask the specialist to look at that. The same structural, form-critical and semantic methods underlie my treatment of the other prophetic writings here, although I have been unable to justify these methods in the space available.

What the prophets wrote was passed down through the centuries in manuscript, with additions and topical glosses, so that it is sometimes difficult to discover the original wording. In the dispute about the authenticity of prophetic texts, some colleagues will find me too conservative. The reason is that I do not consider the literary criticism which has again become fashionable today (though it has in fact been dug out of the drawers of the nineteenth century) to be a historical method, when it is simply pursued in isolation. The assertions of the literary critic only become more than a subjective judgment founded on personal taste when they are linked with investigations into the language of the text, the history of its transmission, and semantics.

To keep the book within bounds, I have been forced to assume some knowledge of Israel's history and the religion of the Old Testament. Non-theologians should turn to standard works of reference for additional explanations. Biblical names have been given in their more familiar forms. In translating the prophetic texts I have laid more stress on semantic accuracy than on a smooth style. At the same time, I have tried to preserve the poetic structure where this is part of the original text. The half-lines which are characteristic of this poetry are therefore separated by diagonal strokes (/). Where the Massoretic text has corrupt readings, I have indicated conjectures on the original by means of square brackets. These are also used to show the earlier stages of a prophetic text where this has been discovered by a study of its transmission. The different structural elements of the prophecy (if 'prophecy' is seen formally, as the most common literary genre or type of prophetic language) are indicated by capital letters (A, B, C). (For the significance of these letters see section 3.3. below and my remarks in *The Growth of the Biblical Tradition,* ET New York and London 1969, sections 15–18.) In case of doubt the reader may find a scholarly commentary of help: see the bibliography.

I should like here to express my special thanks to Margaret Kohl, who has once again translated a complicated text into comprehensible English.

TRANSLATOR'S NOTE

The biblical quotations have been taken from the Revised Standard Version; but its wording has been modified where this was necessary for a correct reading of the author's text.

In a quotation, a Hebrew word followed by the RSV reading in brackets and inverted commas indicates that the English reading is only approximate, and that the correct meaning of the Hebrew is explained in the text.

I

Towards a Preliminary Understanding

1. In Search of the Future: The Longing for a Moral World Order

1.1 A prophet addresses himself to the future. He is not alone in this. Wherever people begin thinking today, whenever they prod their minds into new awareness, at least one motive, if not *the* motive, is the striving to acquire some knowledge about impending developments and possibilities. As soon as we begin to talk about our work, our family, politics or the church, this becomes obvious. But doesn't the question 'What are things going to be like tomorrow?' press in on us even when, perhaps defensively, we are trying to take our minds off things and to amuse ourselves, or are basking in our memories? The anxieties of men and women revolve round their future, whether they are conscious of it or not. Unlike animals, human beings are not determined by patterns of behaviour which have been passed down to them; so in their thinking they continually try to divine what is lying in wait for them, in the form of action or suffering. Hovering between fear and hope, they try to distinguish the real from the possible and the impossible, what is really the case from what is desirable. They even press forward in the light of what the philosopher Ernst Bloch called the principle of hope.

Because of this, earlier centuries often made the intellectual attempt to give the future a structure and a theme. They developed doctrines about heaven and hell to lend significance to behaviour now and offer rules for action. Modern men and women, schooled by science, can see this as no more than groundless speculation. The exact sciences have indoctrinated them as to what 'correct' thinking means. They break people of dreaming and a wanton search for the future. The only dreams permissible are the ones that are properly channelled, to which we give the name of working hypotheses; or at most science fiction, as a type of fairy tale. It is true that once upon a time modern science started out with the aim of emancipatory enlightenment, which was supposed to be going to lead mankind to undreamed of heights. But the belief in progress which the sciences themselves evoked has been destroyed again by those sciences. For them, planning has replaced utopia, so that the future may be brought under our control, whether short-term, medium-term or long-term. But scientific planning is an undertaking that has many ramifications. All too often the layman feels compelled to meet the statements of the experts with suspicion. Hardly anyone is still prepared to risk his life for planned targets, as the utopians of past centuries did often enough. So for us the horizon of the future has closed in, and no longer offers any comprehensive goals for human action. The new futurology makes no difference here, for it is limited to extrapolations of what can be shown to exist already, here and now.

No one will deny the usefulness of the modern sciences and the technologies that have emerged from them. External living conditions have been decisively improved by them. But have they made human hopes more certain, or fear less compelling? Today anything that goes beyond the narrowly circumscribed framework of scientific forecast 'isn't a question of knowledge; it's a matter of belief', as the phrase goes. The Christian faith which is appealed to for this has withdrawn from any claim at this point. Where the future of men and women is concerned, it has no theories, and confines itself to resignation to God's will.

The prophets, on the other hand, only believed on the basis of what they already knew.

1.2 Not everyone who says something definite about the future is a prophet. Prophets are distinguished from mere soothsayers in that they base what is impending on the present, drawing their conclusions from the moral behaviour of the people round them. Their moral futurism is founded on a need which, ultimately speaking, is deeply rooted in everyone. A reflective search for the future is generally bound up with a longing that from now on things will be better: in personal life, in society, and in the world. Better, not merely in the economic and technological sector, but in the sense that life will become more in accord with human dignity. People are bothered not only by the transitoriness of the present but also by the discrepancy between *moral behaviour and what happens in the world*. Only rarely, when we look at the present, do we have the comforting feeling that things go well for the good and badly for the wicked. Generally the reverse seems to be true. Good is vanquished and evil triumphs. But then the human mind clings to the expectation that the future will bring juster conditions. The reflective search for the future becomes the search for a better time, or at least one when things will balance out.

Are there arguments in favour of this? Is there any certainty? The history of religion offers a wealth of different patterns as solutions, from India's notion of karma to Islamic and Christian eschatology. In past centuries philosophers have puzzled over this complex. For Kant, as we know, the cleavage between moral behaviour and the course of nature was *the* ultimate problem of practical reason, and its solution only seemed possible by postulating 'God'. J. G. Fichte maintained that the moral order of the world was the highest philosophical wisdom (thereby introducing a concept which for a time played a large part in the study of Israelite prophecy). It is true that the philosophy of our own time – and its theology too, to a large extent – has capitulated before the task of offering any solution for the triple problem: moral action – present conditions – future time. According to the common view, the course of nature is not concerned with what men and women call good or evil, and the movement of historical and social processes is blind to the risks to the individual life. After two world wars, with their appalling results, is it possible seriously to maintain the opposite, and to talk about the progress of individuals, or nations, or humanity?

Only Marxism is still capable of sustaining hope here, because it shifts the agent's interest from his personal life to the future of the working class. But where Marxism is dismissed as ideology, what remains seems to be nothing more than an enormous mental and spiritual deficit, where the fundamental desire of every individual person for a better future is concerned. For the average man or woman, the abstract assertion of human responsibility is no longer plausible, even by way of some kind of success in future life; so the moral norms threaten to become mere rules-of-the-road, if not actually manipulations. This can even be seen from the way our proverbs have changed. Our ancestors used to weave into what they said phrases like 'Honesty is the best policy' or 'Pride goes before a fall'; and these phrases were perhaps even given a metaphysical justification: 'The mills of God grind slowly but they grind exceeding small.' What one hears on the street nowadays are only sayings like 'Do what you like – just don't get caught', because 'You have to look after number one'. The only metaphysical echo is at most, 'There's no gratitude in this world.'

Of course no reasonable person would deny that in daily practice we can still, thank God, come across countless humane acts in our present civilization, and that many of our contemporaries do feel responsible for the common good. But this practice is no longer accompanied by any cogent theory. The sceptic may well ask how long this can go on, and whether in the long run humane action that is purely practical is not bound to break down in times of crisis. Doesn't the breakdown of a moral order in the world call in question the point of any conduct that is not purely selfish?

1.3 At this moment in history it is worth turning to Israel's prophets. For they were able to develop a view of mankind's future which sustained succeeding centuries, if not millennia. Behind the prophets was a language and civilization in which the validity of a kind of moral order had for centuries belonged to the very foundations of people's interpretation of existence. Men and women were, of course, aware that in individual cases this order did not prevail. Many of the psalms of lament complain of this very thing, and complain of it with grief, but without surrendering a total view of existence.

This traditional conviction was transformed by the authors of the prophetic books in a highly individual way. When they appear for the first time in the eighth century BC, they do not maintain that the present is characterized by the melancholy fact that good people have a bad time of it and therefore God will give them a better future (though by general feeling and opinion this was probably considered the obvious solution, at that time as in our own). The prophets' primary concern was not the sufferings of the righteous: decent men and women. On the contrary. The first thing we find them saying is that far too many people are getting on far too well, and that in the near future this is going to lead to inescapable catastrophe. Such a radical criticism of society and such a pessimistic expectation of the future is new and unique in the ancient world. If we are to understand prophecy as a whole, however, it must be added that during the period of the Exile, the later prophets made an about-turn, establishing that in their own day there was a surplus of suffering on the part of the innocent. These people were now consoled with encouraging and affirmative statements about the future, though this does not mean that these prophets now called in question the truth of earlier prophecy.

How are these two things connected? In both cases something like a moral order in the world is not merely postulated; it is explained and justified. What makes the prophets interesting is not the mere assertion of a connection between human action, what goes on in the world, and future developments; it is the nature of the justification. This is of such a kind that people have talked about the futurism of the prophets, which here means a theory about the essential connection between the present and the future. Every prophet has his own way of illuminating this connection, as the following pages will show. This is only a brief anticipation of what awaits the reader.

Ethical conduct only appears to have a point at all if it is based on the presupposition that there is an essential link between present moral behaviour and a harmonious, satisfactory life in the future. If this link does not exist, all that remains, logically speaking, is the selfishness and practical nihilism which the prophets occasionally attribute to their opponents: 'Let us eat and drink, for tomorrow we die' (Isa. 22.13). But how can this moral connection between cause and effect be conceived of? Only by presupposing God. The prophets emerge against the background of Israel's conviction that the one God – as the foundation of the nation's existence and the background to its Palestinian homeland – allows every member of this people to achieve his or her appropriate destiny. Contrary to a widespread Western interpretation of the God of the Old Testament, the Hebrew did not conceive of his God as the other-worldly judge, who continually keeps a watch on people from some outside point, intervening if necessary to punish or reward. On the contrary, Yahweh (or El or Elohim, to use other names for God) directs land and people from within and sees to it that a connection is evident between action and outcome for everyone on earth. From this viewpoint a picture of a total historical or supra-historical process emerges, to which we might give the name of 'metahistory'. *Metahistory* is a modern term for what Isaiah calls 'Yahweh's work' and Jeremiah 'Yahweh's way'. It covers a multiplicity of interactions between God, human beings and the course of the world. Theoretical elements play their part, although the prophets are not particularly interested in the theory. What they are concerned about is that people should recognize the meaning of history and should comprehend and apprehend their future in that light.

The prophets assume that the world has an underlying meaning which goes beyond normal perception; yet they cling obstinately to a resolute this-worldliness. A supernatural, eternal life as the goal for men and women (which appears later in apocalyptic), or rebirth, or anything of the kind, is not under discussion here. It is their stress on the underlying meaning of this present which gives the prophets' ideas their splendour – and also their limitation.

1.4 What we have at our disposal in written form as the words of the prophets – and even more what they at one time proclaimed by word of mouth – does not purport to be the result of empirical analysis. It is preserved in God-given *visions and spoken messages*. 'The vision of Isaiah which he saw' is the heading of the Book of Isaiah, and the headings of all the other prophetic books are similar. Their inspiration is by no means confined to revelations of the future; it is also the illumination of present conditions. But the prophets do not see either of these things as representing a fundamental contradiction to the knowledge gained from normal experience. They put forward knowledge based on underlying truths, but not mysteries. They therefore require their readers and themselves to follow up the inspiration and to verify in a process of *subsequent insight* what seems to have been revealed to them by the divine forerunner. The normal Israelite is incapable of meeting with what the prophet undergoes as private experience, but he is able to enter into it through a subsequent process of perception, and to accept it as true. The prophets do not aim to proclaim a mystery which could only be accepted by surrendering reason. But they do take to task the foolish people who do not trust God's inspiration and do not permit themselves to be moved to subsequent insight. In this way the prophet is like an astronaut who, having landed on the moon, has now returned to earth and expects his contemporaries to trust his observations, even if they can never travel to the moon themselves.

It is the achievement of the prophets that they absorb into their thinking anything that linguistic heritage, everyday events and private, secret experience provide them with on their way. They do not let go until all this has been fused into a unity and – in pre-exilic times at least – can be poured out in poetic form. To trace how this is done is the aim of the following chapters.

II

Prelude

2. Inductive and Intuitive Divination in Antiquity and its Connection with Monotheism and Monanthropology in Israel

2.1 Israel's prophets were the heralds of a future springing from a simple responsibility on the part of their audience on the one hand and a simple divine ground of reality on the other. As such, they tower above all comparable figures of ancient times. Nevertheless, they do not suddenly appear on the stage of religious history like Melchizedek, without father, mother or genealogy. Prophecy is one trend among many in the manticism which was so immensely widespread in the ancient world.

Manticism (or divination, as I shall now call it) means clairvoyance or soothsaying, the private or professional enquiry into the future against the background of a religious or magic view of the world. Enlightened people from the northern hemisphere are accustomed to sweep such things aside as superstition. But it would be unduly hasty to draw conclusions about the ancient world from the clairvoyants and charlatans of our own time, who get along without any well-founded theory. In antiquity, divination was largely pursued against the background of a model of the world and of life which was utterly convincing to contemporaries.

Cicero already distinguished two types of divination, and religious studies still employ his categories today: 1. inductive or instrumental divination, which interprets given omens; 2. intuitive or mediated divination, where a human medium passes on some direct divine inspiration through his voice. Both types are represented on the outskirts of biblical religion, but the part they play varies in importance in different civilizations and cultures.

2.2 Inductive or *omen divination* is rooted in experiences we still have today, in a dim way. Anyone who sees a red sky at sunset expects fine weather the next day; if he sees a swallow swooping low over the ground, he thinks it is going to rain. Rules of this kind have come to be part of our linguistic heritage; they have entered the language out of the experience of many generations. Only a few people are capable of explaining why the one phenomenon points to the other. Subsequently, scientific reasons may be added; these point to the breaking of rays of light, or to humidity, and so forth. Ancient oriental inductive divination started from similar observations. The only difference was that it then sought systematically in all events for analogies with future developments – developments affecting not merely nature but human society as well. The assumption was that impending fate had already arrived at certain sectors on earth or in heaven before it had come to affect human beings. The swallow is already oppressed by the drop in atmospheric pressure before the rain falls on human beings; in the same way, numerous spheres offering portents were discovered, with phenomena which 'got wind' of impending developments before men and women perceived them. It was *the Babylonians and Assyrians*, more than any other ancient peoples, who, during the second and first millennia before Christ, developed an extensive 'science' of omens. Exceptional natural phenomena, either in the sky (eclipses of the sun or moon, storms, and so forth) or on earth (the birth of deformed children or animals, etc.) became *ittum* (Hebrew *'ōt*), divinely appointed signs that something extraordinary was impending. The professional interpreter of the future, who was called a *baru*, understood how to draw conclusions from these observations for king, city and country. The *baru* was also able to acquire additional information by means of an omen which he himself induced; this was called *tertum* (= Heb. *tōrāh*?). The examination of entrails played a special part here. An animal was slaughtered after a question had been whispered into its ear, and from the form taken by certain parts of its body, especially the liver, future destiny was deciphered. The Babylonians studied the anatomy of the sheep's liver and discovered in it a microanthropos, with a mouth, fingers and so forth; indeed a microcosm, with chariot and palace. They composed textbooks with omens like the following:

> Supposing that the path is on the right lobe of the liver, on the left side the fissure is straight, and the orifice of the path opens towards the stomach, then your enemy will be taken prisoner with the help of your God and will be turned away.[1]

Equally significant are the movements of the stars in the heavens, whenever there are striking constellations of planets or eclipses of the sun and moon. For the gods have also written coming destiny in the sky, in the cuneiform script of the stars, just as they have in the 'cuneiform script' of a lamb's entrails. In order not simply to lock people into the cage of an inescapably appointed fate, the *baru* often added the description of a possible prophylactic ritual. It is by means of a magic ritual that an evil fate can be turned away and directed to other objects or persons; moral action is seldom required.

It was the Babylonians who, in pre-Christian times, elaborated inductive divination in a way unheard of in other cultures. No wonder that the Babylonian examination of entrails and, later, Babylonian astrology exercised such a fascination on the surrounding civilizations, even on the otherwise sceptical Greeks. Even today, the horoscopes we find in popular magazines go back to Babylonian principles.

2.3 The future is revealed in a different way when the diviner perceives future events *intuitively*. Here, too, the basis is general experience. At some time or other all of us have woken up suddenly during the night knowing that this or that is the solution to the problem we had tried in vain to solve the previous day. Or we may even be certain that something or other is going to happen tomorrow and we must brace ourselves for it. It is understandable that at moments like these some people believe that they are perceiving an inner voice, or even a voice from outside, which presses mysteriously in on them. There are people who have dreams or second sight about things which are far away in space or time, whose premonitions have a high 'percentage of success', often to their own consternation. In non-European civilizations, attempts are often made to increase by training this capacity for hearing mysterious voices or this pursuit of second sight. The origin of the phenomenon is then sought for in some supernatural person, a spirit or a god. Contacts with this being can be strengthened and the inspirations multiplied, either through interior withdrawal and fasting, or through ecstasy and intoxication.

This form of divination was especially cultivated in pre-Israelite Syria (although inductive divination was not unknown there either).

We already have evidence for the *nābī'* – the kind of prophet most common in Israel at a later stage – in Ebla in North Syria, in the twenty-third century BC. In the city of Mari, which lay on the Euphrates, on what is now the frontier between Syria and Iraq, archaeologists have excavated a royal archive dating from the eighteenth century BC. Over twenty official letters report the visions and spoken messages received by prophetic figures, which were passed on to the head of the state, who was away from his capital at the time.

The recipient of the divinely inspired secret information was either someone appointed to the sanctuary for the purpose of discovering the future, the *muḫḫum* or *apilum*, or a private person who, perhaps during a visit to the temple, was suddenly surprised by a divine voice. We find the same juxtaposition of cultically appointed, official prophets and charismatically endowed private persons a thousand years later in Israel.

The way in which the Mari prophets talk also points forward to the prophecies of the Israelite prophets. As in Israelite prophecy, first the historical situation, with the essential trends which are of decisive importance for the deity, is analysed, or depicted in pictorial terms. This is followed by an announcement of impending events – either that the god will pursue the present trend of things, or that there will be some necessary counter-reaction. For example, when King Zimri-lim of Mari is at war with the nomadic Jaminites, without being able to force a decision, the god Dagan has a prophetic message passed on to him. He rebukes the king for the lack of contact with him: 'Why are the ambassadors of Zimri-lim not continually before me?' He then commands: 'Send your ambassadors to me', and gives a promise for the future: 'Then I will make the sheikhs of the Jaminites wriggle in a fish basket and will place them before thee.'[2]

The promise is therefore not simply a clairvoyant announcement about some future event which will break in without any relation to anything else. It is the continuation of a history which is already taking place, even if this history is now given a new direction. Human behaviour is not eliminated here, any more than it is in the inductive divination of the Babylonian type. On the contrary; it is even more emphatically called for. The prophetic saying is sometimes sharply directed against kingly measures or omissions. Zimri-lim has not given the god Adad the necessary 'site' for his cult, for example, although at one time, after Zimri-lim had fled the country, Adad (as a corresponding saying makes clear) had helped him to regain his throne, in a kind of salvation history. If the king does not give the god his due, Adad will take away everything he has already given him. If, on the other hand, the king complies with the god's wishes, he will receive world-wide dominion.[3] This shows that even the intuitive enquiry into the future which was carried on in the north-western Semitic area took place in a world-wide context and with a far-reaching claim. It breaks through the wall dividing the visible world from its generally invisible divine background. One of the prophets of Mari sees how the great God Ea mixes earth from Mari into a drink, gives it to other gods, and makes them swear by it to guarantee the continuing existence of the kingdom.[4] But there is also erroneous prophecy – for example, a prophetic declaration that Hammurabi of

Babylon would be defeated in the war against Mari.[5] Exactly the opposite happened; Hammurabi destroyed Mari for ever! All these are features which can also be demonstrated among the prophets of the Old Testament.

Mari can probably serve as an example of conditions at Syrian courts of the time. A good 700 years later, the Egyptian Wen-Amun tells of a frenzied prophet at the court of Byblos, through whom a god commanded the king to deliver the wood required for the god's ceremonial barge.[6] In prophecy of this kind, Syrian society permitted itself an astonishingly critical court of appeal which is independent of particular instructions and can take even the rulers themselves to task.

2.4 The religion of the Bible is not something on its own. It grew up out of the extraordinarily complex religious history of the ancient East. But then it took a highly individual turn, which carried it further and further away from the rest of the ancient world. Its roots in the religious history of the Fertile Crescent are particularly evident in a phenomenon such as prophecy, even if for 800 years we are lacking in detailed information about possible intermediate stages of intuitive divination between Mari and Israel.

Surprisingly enough, however, at the time of the literary prophets in Israel, some indications do appear for neighbouring civilizations, too, which not only report the occasional appearance of prophetic figures, but also indicate their essential importance. For the ninth century BC, the story about the ordeal on Carmel (I Kings 18) is evidence that Jezebel was surrounded by 450 prophets belonging to Baal of Tyre. Even if tradition puts the number too high, the indication that prophets played a part in the Phoenician Baal worship of the time will hardly be pure invention. We have an inscription of King Zakir of Hamath in Aramaean Syria dating from about 800[7] which praises the god Baal Shamain because, in a critical situation during a war, he had seers and men versed in knowledge of the future pass the following message on to him: 'Fear not, for I have made thee king. I will save thee' – a promise which was then fulfilled. An inscription dating from *c.* 700 BC was found in Der-Alla in Transjordan a short time ago which reports sayings about the future made by a seer called Balaam, who is also mentioned in the Old Testament as a foreign seer (Num. 22–24). Oracles of the goddess Ishtar of Arbela revealed to the Assyrian king Esarhaddon date from the following century.[8] They also begin 'Fear not!', and not only proclaim the annihilation of the enemy but also add, 'I have established thy throne beneath the mighty heavens for eternal years' (cf. II Sam. 7). The Esarhaddon oracles derive from an important instance of intuitive divination in Mesopotamia, where, as we have already said, inductive divination is otherwise to the fore. Does this represent the penetration of North-west Semitic cultic forms into the Assyrian area? At all events, from the ninth to the seventh century we are told of prophets in ancient oriental religions in which we no longer hear of any such figures in the centuries that follow. And this is precisely the period in which Israel's prophecy reached its zenith. Afterwards prophecy disappears from history in Israel, too. We cannot therefore exclude the possibility that Israel's famous prophets represent the contribution of the religion of Yahweh to *an international movement* belonging to those particular centuries of world history, full of unrest as they were. However, no definitive judgment can be made here in the present state of research.

Be that as it may, it is not by chance that Israel's prophets are the only ones belonging to those remote centuries of ancient times who have remained known down to the present day. For they tower far above all comparable intuitive diviners or soothsayers of their environment in the acuteness of their thinking and the precision of their language, as well as in their concentration on the one God and the unity of human responsibility. It is true that in the Hellenistic period, from 200 BC onwards, a mantic movement arose in the form of apocalyptic, and this had its parallels in Syria and the rest of the East too. But its erudite language, pregnant with symbols, is much more difficult to understand. Consequently apocalyptic has not had nearly as enduring an effect as the prophecy which had come to an end centuries earlier.

A word may be added about ancient Greece which, as far as our subject is concerned, represents as it were the most modern province of the ancient Near Eastern world. In the Homeric period we have no evidence for the existence of intuitive divination; but it entered Greece soon afterwards (from Asia Minor?) with the god Apollo. It was associated with the Pythian oracle at Delphi, where it became a determining factor in Greek history, a factor which Plato in his *Laws* and his *Republic* still sees as being irrelinquishable. Although it reached its zenith before and during the Persian wars, Greek divination did not lose its importance after 500 BC to the same degree as its eastern counterparts. The *prophētēs* in Delphi, who put into official and comprehensible form the words ejaculated in excitement by the Pythia[9], actually provides the name which the Greek translation of the Old Testament later used as the term for the Israelite mantics – the name which has also given the present book its title.

2.5 Late nineteenth-century biblical scholars viewed the prophets who were active between 750 and 500 BC as the great reformers of

Israelite religion, and they reduced their find to the concept of 'ethical monotheism'. This term has come into increasing disrepute in recent decades, but it has not been replaced by anything better. Now, the prophets were indisputably not the first to introduce the worship of a single God into Israel; and on the other hand, none of the prophets drew the conclusion that the numinous beings worshipped by other nations did not exist at all. Moreover, as far as the ethical determination of religion is concerned, this stress is not merely from the very beginning characteristic of Israel; to a considerable degree it belonged to Egyptian and Babylonian religion too. Yet it remains true that the fundamental principle of what was in practice monotheism – 'I am Yahweh and there is no other god beside me' – was formulated by Deutero-Isaiah for the first time. He thinks through to the end what his prophetic predecessors had suggested. And an undivided moral responsibility of men and women, especially the Israelites, for their historical destiny – a responsibility allowing no escape into any cultic abrogation in the case of failure – can also be found among the critical prophets for the first time. If we remember these qualifications, and if we avoid the notion of a metaphysical argumentation, the expression 'ethical monotheism' is not ill-chosen. At the same time, one objection to it is that it suppresses the mantic element. The supporters of the theory of ethical monotheism (pre-eminently Wellhausen and Duhm) also saw the prophets as 'men of the eternally new'; but they failed to link this with the concept of God. As we shall see, this link is an essential one. If the connection is made, if we talk about an *ethical, futuristic monotheism*, this covers a complex of ideas in which Israelite prophecy goes far beyond all comparable ancient oriental divination. (Here the word 'futurism' is used in a wider sense than it is in certain stylistic trends of our own century.)

It would be a gross misunderstanding of the prophets if we were to assume that they were concerned with a doctrine of God in his essential nature – God as he is in himself. Whatever they proclaim about God emerges from their strenuous attempt to fathom the destiny of their people, the men and women belonging to their own environment. In the measure in which they imperceptibly change the view of God, the interpretation of man alters too. The concept of monotheism (in its closer definition) can only be used to describe the prophetic achievement if a corresponding understanding of human existence is set parallel to it. I would here suggest talking about *concentric monanthropology*. In using this term I am anticipating the results of the following account. I have chosen the word monanthropology because people seem to be the focal point of both being and creation, all life is seen as deriving from human life, and the course of nature largely appears as a function of human acts. Yet monanthropology is not merely presupposed where non-human reality is concerned. It also applies within human existence, too, since for critical prophecy, ultimately and before God, there is only a single, unified human race with a common responsibility for this world, a human race linked together through its common doom of guilt and death, but also through a common peace and salvation. Neither differences of race nor differences of class are important. For the prophets, monanthropology is the essential reverse side of their monotheism. Human beings are certainly not viewed as a homogeneous unity, but in concentric spheres. Israel forms an inner circle, since it is Israel alone who has conscious dealings with the one God. Consequently it is more directly touched by salvation and sanctity than other nations, but also by guilt and repentance. Within Israel there are other, still narrower spheres – Israel's capital and, in the capital, the king. What takes place at the centre is a model for the surrounding area. As the head of the body of the people, to put it in Isaiah's terms, the general destiny is included in what the king does and what happens to him. In the same way the day of Yahweh which Israel calls down on itself will be a day of calamity for all peoples, while the temple, which belongs to Jerusalem's era of salvation, is to be the centre of blessing in the peace of the nations. Anthropology is therefore thought of concentrically.

As prophecy developed, there were shifts of emphasis. From the time of Jeremiah, great foreign kings appear as the centre of all mankind which, in terms of political power, is also concentric; and from Ezekiel onwards this political sphere was confronted with the second, cultic sphere of the Israelite priesthood, centred on the temple on Zion. But this was only a further development of concentric anthropology. It is significant that the human individual is never left to himself. Pronounced personalities – and therefore individuals – though the prophets themselves were, this does not show up in their view of people and human nature as a whole. (Even Ezekiel 18 – see Volume II – must not be torn out of the book's context. Individual destiny becomes a theme only from apocalyptic onwards.)

Thus concentric anthropology forms the one pole and ethical futuristic monotheism the other, in a field of force which is described in categories which are knit together into a metahistory. Almost every one of the elements can be traced back to pre-prophetic Israel, and very much of it to ancient oriental divination. Yet out of these bricks the critical prophets built a thought structure which was all their own.

3. Seers, Men of God, Nabis. Pre-literary Prophecy from the Early Period of the Monarchy

3.1 The term prophet

In the following account we shall be looking at the critical or 'literary' prophets; that is to say, the men whose books we possess, in which their prophetic sayings are collected. The Hebrew canon of the Old Testament contains fifteen prophetic writings. Surprisingly enough, the period when the men to whom these writings have been traced back were active is confined to a relatively short part of the history of pre-Christian Israel: c. 750–500 BC. In order to understand how the writings came into being, we have to look at what prophecy means in Israel at an earlier time. For literary prophecy shows itself to be part of a very much more comprehensive movement. The 250 years during which prophetic figures of this kind can be shown to have existed are preceded by an equally long period of pre-literary prophecy – what can in many ways be called pre-critical prophecy. Yet even these earlier prophets cannot be shown to have existed from the very beginning in Israel. In addition, it may well be asked how far the concept of prophecy is an appropriate one for the multiplicity of highly varying figures of whom we are told in the early period.

Intuitive divination does not always mean one and the same thing. In ancient times impending events could be explored in many different ways – in dreams, visions, auditions, and in other ways too. Premonitions could overtake people unexpectedly, evoked by music, dance and ecstasy. The presage of what was to come might fall upon an isolated individual or be the shared experience of a group. In one case the message was of importance only for the recipient. In another case it had nothing to do with him individually, but only affected the people round him. Soothsaying and prophecy could be carried on professionally; they were skills that could be trained by the appropriate techniques, such as incubation – sleep in a sacred place for the purpose of inducing an oracle. They could also be experienced by ordinary people without any preparation at all.

These differences make it understandable why there is no single name for divination and the mantic in Hebrew. Expressions like *'īš hā*ᵉ*lōhīm* (man of God – who holds a deity in his possession? – also found in pre-Israelite Ugaritic), *rō'eh* (seer), *qōsem* (fortune-teller, soothsayer), *ḥōzeh* (also seer – found elsewhere in Syria-Palestine as well), *nābī'* (prophet – in the narrower sense of the word) are all found (none of them precisely represented by the English translation). But they are not variant descriptions for an essentially identical phenomenon. They all undoubtedly have to do with intuitive divination, but in each case they have their individual meaning and may perhaps have to do with a different social position. To apply the terms 'prophet' and 'prophecy' (which come from the Greek *prophētēs*) to people named in the Old Testament involves certain difficulties for historical investigation. For the content of these words is associated with the notion of a spokesman clearly authorized by God (or even with the author of a biblical book) who – left to his own resources, in duty bound to his conscience and no one else – preaches the law of God, harshly condemns violations of it, and prophesies future events which God is going to bring about for the salvation of men and women, or for their doom. For Jews and Christians alike, Moses counts as being the prototype of a prophet. Yet this very Moses, who belongs to the beginnings of Yahwistic religion, is never described in the early narratives by any one of the terms we have named (except perhaps 'man of God'). Theological tradition is largely accustomed to equate 'prophet' with *nābī'*, the most widespread of the descriptions we have mentioned in Hebrew. *Nābī'*, which probably means literally 'entrusted with a message', is already found in Syrian Ebla in the twenty-third century BC, but in Israel it turns up relatively late – only at the beginning of the period of the monarchy. The term was then probably taken over from the pre-Israelite inhabitants of Palestine, the Canaanites; and with the term doubtless went the corresponding religious phenomenon, which had long been widespread in the Canaanite area. The figures who are then called *nābī'* in Israel in the period of the monarchy all seem to have been institutionally connected with a sanctuary or with the court, and therefore to have had a number of different duties. They are by no means as charismatically independent as the word 'prophet' inevitably suggests to us.

The problem of terminology and the differences between representatives of divination has a particular importance because the 'literary' prophets, whose activity we are going to discuss here, never call themselves *nābī'* in the initial, early-Assyrian phase; on the contrary, they attack contemporary *nᵉbī'īm*. This would seem to indicate that they represent a different type.

When I use the word 'prophet' I shall mean first of all the prophets whose books we possess. In addition I shall be using the term for all mantics who appear in a similar way and with the same kind of language in the context of the religion of Yahweh – that is to say I shall apply the word, largely speaking, to the *nābī'* too. I shall therefore be using the term 'prophet' in a very much wider sense than is covered by any one of the Hebrew terms in question.

3.2 The pre-prophetic age

Even figures such as seers or men of God only turn up sporadically before the time of the monarchy and do not seem to have played any decisive part in Israel's cult and life. It is clear from the stories in Genesis that there is no evidence at all for any mantics in the pre-Mosaic period. The 'patriarchs', Abraham, Isaac and Jacob, have no need of a prophet. When God reveals something special to them, he does so in a dream (Gen. 28), or perhaps through the rustling of a tree, which can be interpreted as an augury (Gen. 18.1); or, in especially important cases, Yahweh appears as *mal'āk*, 'angel' – that is to say, takes human form. In this form he encounters the patriarch incognito. Or it may be a woman, or perhaps a slave, whom he meets (Gen. 16; 22.11). He talks to the person, revealing new vistas of what is to come.

In the first centuries after the immigration into the cultivated lands of Palestine, the priesthood which was then developing took over the task of discovering the future through technical oracles. For public affairs, this enquiry of God was of decisive importance. In addition, in early times there was a tent 'of meeting', where an authorized person enquired into the will of God in a way no longer clear to us. Frequently mentioned is a sacred garment, an ephod, which could be hung round an image of God and could also be worn by a priest. In the latter case the priest was thereby enabled, with the help of two stones used for casting lots, *'ūrīm* and *tummīm*, to obtain oracles which declared the divine 'yes' or 'no' in response to the enquiry. Of course the question had to be formulated in such a way that a 'yes' or 'no' decision was possible. For example, before David goes into battle, he calls the priest Abiathar to him. When the Philistines, with a numerically far superior army, besiege the city of Keilah, God is appealed to in the following way (I Sam. 23): 'Shall I go and attack these Philistines?' Abiathar goes into action, and a 'yes' stone appears. Abiathar interprets this as follows: 'Go and attack the Philistines and save Keilah.' Because David's men are still nervous, the question is put again. And again Yahweh answers through the sacred stones: 'Arise, go down to Keilah; for I will give the Philistines into your hand.' After this David dares to attack and is victorious. Yahweh has apparently helped him and fulfilled what he prophesied. The answer here was technical in kind and was translated by the priest into a statement which was simply replying to a question transposed in an appropriate way. But in the second case an individual formulation is added, as a divine word: 'I, Yahweh, will give the Philistines into your hand.' We have evidence that this deliverance formula was used in ancient oriental oracles long before the emergence of Israel. (It will play a role again in Israel later in prophecy.)

Besides these technical, priestly methods of discovering the future, in the period before the founding of the nation particular persons were marked out by their capacity for having premonitions and their second sight. This is true especially of the heroes of the Book of Judges, the *šōpᵉṭīm*, for whom the translation 'judges' is a misleading term. They were really charismatic leaders of the army – farmers who, seized by the wind of Yahweh's spirit (*rūᵃḥ*), put themselves at the head of the army in times when the people were in danger. As soon as the *šōpēṭ* became aware of God's voice proclaiming to him the deliverance formula 'I will give them into your hand', he ventured the decisive battle.

In addition there were people who went about the country offering their skill as soothsayers. They were called 'seer' (*rō'eh*), although we have actual evidence for the title only in the case of Samuel. We read rather more often about a man of God, *'īš hā'ᵉlōhīm* (Judg. 13; I Sam. 2.27; I Kings 13). Samuel can also appear in the ranks of these men of God. He apparently played a decisive role in the transition from the pre-national stage to the monarchy, and he is an equivocal figure, with his many different institutional ties. I Samuel 9 describes in graphic terms how a peasant farmer turned to a man of God of this kind because his asses had run away. By virtue of his second sight, a seer, a man of God, was able to tell where the animals were wandering.

It is surprising to note that, with the rise of the monarchy and the setting up of the great sanctuaries, we are no longer told that the priests sought for oracles by technical means, even though the priesthood now assumed a much firmer position than before in the life of the people. Similarly, no general is vouchsafed divine inspiration any more (with the exception of the king of Judah, I Kings 3). Even seers are no longer mentioned. (The title 'man of God' is to some extent an exception. This is later probably used to describe someone who is set above a group of nabis. We shall be discussing it in due course.) The capacity of any Israelite at all for hearing the voice of his God directly disappears even more completely. Under the kings, the nabis have almost a monopoly when it is a matter of asking the deity about the future. This asking is essential for the Israelites from now on, whenever fundamental decisions are in question – for example, discovering who is to be king, or how a war should be conducted. The more the nabis become accepted – only a few other figures, such as the seer (*ḥōzeh*, see below), were also recognized – the more other kinds of soothsaying are pushed into the background and suppressed. This is true of calling up the spirits of the dead, which was a favourite practice elsewhere. It was an act for which Saul, in his zeal for Yahweh, first imposed the death penalty, though he himself took to it again towards the end of his life, in a desperate situation (I Sam. 28). It also applies to other kinds of soothsaying or fortune-telling the precise character of which we are no longer able to discover.

Qōsem was apparently the name given to a man who linked inductive and intuitive divination by means of little idols or lots. These practices were condemned very early on in the North (I Sam. 15.23), but in Judah they were still recognized in Isaiah's day (Isa. 3.2; Micah 3.6f.), whereas a kind of calling up of the future, called *'ōnen*, is condemned by Isaiah, too (3.7). Compared with the broad spectrum of divinatory practices in the rest of the ancient East, Israel, because of its special view of God, shows an increasing concentration on the communication of the future through the nabi and the divine word he passes on.

3.3 The rise of the nabis. Prophecy as a literary genre

Nabis are first mentioned in Israel round about the end of the eleventh and the beginning of the tenth century BC, at the same time as the rise of the monarchy. (For the sake of simplicity I am coining a plural adapted to English usage. The correct Hebrew plural form is *n^ebī'īm*.) Both institutions – the nabi and the monarchy – emerged after Yahwistic religion had long become established in the agricultural areas of Palestine. We hear of the first ecstatic nabi groups in connection with the first king, Saul; they came down from the cultic high places making music, dancing and singing (I Sam. 10). At the court of the second king, the famous David, Nathan is the first nabi of whose name we have adequate historical evidence. (I am leaving on one side here the doubtful evidence in Judg. 4.4. for a *n^ebī'ā*, Deborah.) What distinguishes the nabi from the seer and man of God of earlier generations? The answer is a simple one: his language. Nathan was concerned about cultic matters: whether or not a temple should be built in Jerusalem; the enthronement of a king; and the duration of a dynasty (II Sam. 7; I Kings 1). But something similar had already been seen to be the task of the seer Samuel (according to I Sam. 3; 9f.; 13; 15; 30). Nathan appears as the king's conscience and, when the king offends, dooms him to death (see below). In this way Nathan becomes a kind of supreme moral guardian, who spies out secret wickedness and heralds retribution, without himself playing any active part in that retribution. Here, too, tradition gives Nathan a forerunner in Samuel (I Sam. 30). But in these cases Nathan uses the genre of prophecy. And this is a novelty, though we find it again in almost all the later nabis.

The particular kind of language used can be seen in an especially vivid way in the Bathsheba episode. According to II Sam. 11f., from the heights of his palace David sees the beautiful woman bathing. He has her brought to him and sleeps with her. But Bathsheba is married to Uriah, an officer who is at the front fighting against the Ammonites. By sending the appropriate letter, David gets Uriah seconded to a suicide squad, and he is soon killed. David then has Bathsheba brought to his harem, and she bears him a son. The king imagines that the story behind this is unknown to anyone. But, as a nabi, Nathan has second sight and perceives by supernatural means what has happened. One day he appears before the king and tells him a parable about a rich farmer who seizes the only sheep belonging to a poor fellow-countryman and slaughters it for his own purposes. The parable is Nathan's own invention. We are not intended to see it as being in itself divinely inspired. When the king reacts with indignation against the rich evil-doer and threatens him with death, Nathan comes into the open and becomes the direct mouthpiece of his God:

I You are the man!
Thus says Yahweh, the God of Israel:
A 'I anointed you king over Israel, [. . .]/delivered you out of the hand of Saul.
Why [. . .] have you smitten Uriah the Hittite/with the *sword*?
B From now on therefore:
the *sword* shall never depart/from your house for immeasurable time.'

The present composition has intertwined with this saying a second pronouncement which can easily be detached from the first:

II A I gave you your master's *house*/and your master's *wives* into your bosom.
And you have taken [Uriah's] *wife*/to be your *wife*.
Thus says Yahweh:
B 'Behold, I will raise up against you/evil out of your own *house*;
and I will take your *wives* before your eyes,/and give them to your neighbour,
and he shall lie with your *wives*/in the sight of this sun.
C For you did it secretly;/but I will do it [. . .] before all Israel.'

Before I go into the rest of the story, let me point out the special textual form of these sayings. At the very beginning we have an *indication of situation*, which analyses the moral quality of past and present human activity, perhaps contrasting it with God's activity in the past. Here this section is marked A. A *prediction* follows. This generally begins with some divine counter-action to the present state of affairs; but it is a counter-action which points to human forces for its implementation. This section is marked B here. It is followed, thirdly – but only sometimes – by a concluding characterization, C, which picks out one particular element of the action and behaviour of one party, or of both.

The genre illuminates the whole way in which nabi thinking was built up and developed. Although the saying is based on divine inspiration, its construction is none the less subject to the rules of art. Probably we are intended to think of the nabi as hearing certain sounds which he had then to translate for himself into comprehensible language. Down to the period of the exile, all prophecies are couched in poetic terms, and follow the principles on which Hebrew poetry was built up. This poetry depends on *parallelismus membrorum*, a 'thought-rhyme', in which a statement in the first half-line is further developed by a similar statement in the second; the two statements correspond in length but are not identical in their wording. What is especially noticeable in prophecy as a genre is the sharp dividing line between present and future, between A and B, or, to be more precise, between what has been hitherto and what is to come. For the indication of situation does not merely describe what is actually present; it sometimes covers events belonging to the remote past. And the prediction B begins in Hebrew (II) with a participial noun clause which indicates the simultaneity of the divine 'reaction' and the human behaviour prompting it. Where there is human wickedness, God is always already at work bringing some answering evil to pass. Another possibility is to begin B with a negative clause which, as it were, establishes negative facts about the future (I): David has used the sword and from now on his family will never be free of it. After a divine intervention of this kind (which is marked in every case by the proclamation of the corresponding announcement, and in the second case by an additional resolve), the divine intention is then transmitted and implemented by earthly agents. There is a significant use of keywords, like sword, house, wife (in italics above), which build the logical bridge from A to B. (In other cases terms are used which vary between A and B, but which belong to the same semantic field.) It is the keywords especially which show that a nabi is not just anyone who prophesies; he is a person who lays stress on a logical connection with previous history.

Either the whole saying, or the part of it that relates to the future, is introduced by the phrase: 'Thus says Yahweh' (*kō' āmar yhwh*), a phrase which is taken up later by almost all the literary prophets. Scholars usually talk about a 'messenger formula' here, and see its function as a legitimizing one: the nabi is the authorized mouthpiece of the deity. But one could equally well talk about a 'proclamation formula', since it not only stresses the content of the following statement as coming from God, but also declares it to be valid for the future and avoidable only to a limited degree. It is noticeable that in giving form to their prophecy, the nabis do not borrow cultic types of text; they adopt the language of diplomats. 'Thus says so-and-so' is the phrase with which ancient oriental kings or dignitaries legitimate themselves when sending verbal messages, or in their letters (I Kings 20.3). But royal messages do not have a poetic form, and do not as a rule lay any stress on the distinction between what has been and what is going to be. To this degree the prophecy of nabis is something other than the imitation of a herald's message. Men like Samuel had perhaps already used the *kō' āmar yhwh* formula (I Sam. 15. 1–3), but they did not frame the Yahweh saying that followed it in the strict form of prophecy. Preliminary stages of this genre can already be found – without messenger or proclamation formulas – in the letters about the prophets in Mari. Yet among other forms of divination there are no parallels to the carefully constructed sayings of the nabis, which aim at a close connection between the indication of situation and the prophecy by means of keywords or other points of reference. Even the linguistic form points to the ruthless determination with which the Yahwistic order of nabis, as they had become, soon championed the worship of Yahweh in Israel, demanding that public life should be moulded so as to be in accordance with the dependence of country and people on this particular God. More than the priests and infinitely more than the kings, the nabis became the prime advocates of the watchword that Israel's existence rested solely on its indissoluble bond with Yahweh.

After these comments on the literary genre, let us return to the Bathsheba episode. The narrator (who doubtless came from Nathan's circle) tells of the king's deep repentance, which makes him answer Nathan's accusation: 'I have violated (sinned against) Yahweh.' Nathan has so intimate a contact with his God that he is able to respond immediately:

> Therefore Yahweh has let the sphere of your sin (*ḥaṭṭā't*) pass you by. You shall not die . . .
> Nevertheless, the child that is born to you shall surely die.

The modern reader finds it appalling that the guilty father should escape scot free and an innocent baby should die in his stead. But the Hebrews thought in the framework of a collective family community, where all the members of the family feel that they belong together as a 'total self which finds its particular embodiment only in the head of the household, the father and breadwinner. It is therefore better for a single member to die than for the head. The same viewpoint may explain why Bathsheba is not called to account; as a woman she has no independent responsibility in this case. To this degree that really is forgiveness in the sense in which forgiveness was conceivable for pre-exilic Israel. In contrast to our modern view, where sin is a matter of values only, ancient Israel saw sin as an inner-worldly reality. Every morally qualified act, whether good or evil, produced a kind of invisible sphere or aura round the head of the person responsible, which in the course of time brought about his corresponding destiny. This means that the deed of an evil-doer could only end in, and disappear with, death. It would not have helped if God had simply forgiven David. God can only exculpate a person if the sin encircling him can be transferred to another specific member of the group who goes to his death vicariously for the whole community. The sword that Yahweh evokes so that it may fall on the house of David works in secret, killing the baby without any human assistance (but see II Sam. 13.28f.; 18.14.; I Kings 2.13ff.).

In this context the nabi appears as the person who does not merely 'establish' future events by way of the divine pronouncement transmitted to him, but even has the authority subsequently to divert or deflect such an event. This Nathan does only in the case of the first saying, about the sword. He does not touch on the second, about the women. According to the sequel to the story, it will one day be fulfilled completely (II Sam. 16.21f.).

3.4 Orders of nabis

It is almost exclusively the books of Samuel and Kings which give us information about the nabis and the pre-literary prophets in general. These books are part of the Deuteronomic History, which comprises the books of Joshua, Judges, Samuel and Kings (with perhaps Deuteronomy as introduction), all of which have separate titles in our editions of the Bible. This history came into existence in the sixth century BC. Its aim is to give an account of the history of Israel from the settlement in the promised land until the collapse of the Jewish state, presenting it as the continuing alienation of Israel from the God of its initial salvation history. In showing this, nabis play a substantial role. For they try to bring kings and people back to the right path by preaching repentance and by threats of doom. They therefore represent a retarding element in the story of decline. But what they proclaim has no effect on their contemporaries; so the history becomes a history of the fulfilment of Yahweh's doom-laden words which, expressed by prophets, are all sadly fulfilled in the course of time.

Under the sway of this conception, certain prophetic figures – Nathan and Elijah, for example – are given prominence while others are not mentioned at all. All the literary prophets except Isaiah are missing, although their influence – which was also political – must have been known to the historians. Silence about the prophecy collected in the prophetic books of the Bible is one of the riddles of the Deuteronomic History. The kings proved to be failures; and the intention was to contrast them as often as possible with a nabi as true leader of the people. This means that individual nabis are mentioned and seem to act as lonely and independent figures.

This prominence given to particular nabis, combined with the impression which the prophetic books give of their authors as lonely individuals, has led to a widespread conception of the prophet as a great religious champion who has given up every institutional security for the sake of his inner call, and who utters his message whether anyone listens or not. The sociologist Max Weber has seen Old Testament prophecy, characterized in this way, as a typical example of his distinction between charisma and office, which seems to him to be basic to human society in general. 'Office' means institution, permanence, consolidation, being closed to anything new. Priest and king stand for all these things in Israel. Charisma, on the other hand, means the creative outsider who dispenses with every kind of security. For a society it signifies the power of innovation – see the prophets.

Ever since the publication of the third volume of Sigmund Mowinckel's *Psalmenstudien* (Studies in the Psalms, 1923), with the title *Kultpropheten* (Cultic Prophets), the views of scholars have changed increasingly. For Mowinckel showed that the picture of the individual prophet is hardly ever appropriate, at least for the nabis. Whenever they protest against nabis, the 'literary' prophets are attacking what were apparently self-contained groups, who were generally associated with a sanctuary (e.g., Isa. 28. 7–13). In addition, individual psalms and the prophetic liturgies (several of which find a place in the Old Testament) presuppose that the nabis were also active in cultic affairs; for example, after an official hymn of lament, they proclaim an oracle of assurance, expressing confidence that Yahweh has heard. This oracle was spontaneous, but was expressed within the framework laid down for it. Or the nabi interceded for the people during some religious ceremony, since a private person did not have sufficient authority for this. The Chronicler's History still puts the nabis among the Levites and Temple singers; and, on closer examination, even the Deuteronomic History indicates that nabis generally lived together in groups. The nabis mentioned in the period of Saul already enter the scene as a group. They come down from some sacred hill, for example, or live in Rama, which was evidently valued as a sanctuary in those days (I Sam. 10; 19). There are supposed to have been 400 prophets (and at another time even 450) at the North Israelite court, and they appeared together in order to prophesy, or for public religious ceremonies (I Kings 18; 22). The disciples whom Elisha gathered round himself belonged to cultic sites like Bethel or Gilgal; there they sat and listened to the instructive discourses of their master (II Kings 2–6). They probably also practised meditation and trained themselves in ecstasy and inspiration.

All this means that we have to assume that in pre-exilic times the expression 'nabi' is the term used for a cultic prophet who, like a priest, performed particular tasks laid down for him at the sanctuary, though he certainly also had the explicit function of spontaneously proclaiming God's intentions for the future. Although they were outsiders with a charismatic vocation, the nabis organized themselves into an order just like the Islamic dervishes at a later period. They took their meals together, practising a kind of communism, with a 'father' over them, like Elisha. In this case, therefore, there is no contradiction between charisma and institution. On the contrary, in these orders established at the sanctuaries the Israelite cultic community permitted itself a critical institution in which spontaneity of expression and act was an explicit charge.

What was a nabi's life like? We have no biographical account, but we can reconstruct a certain amount. A nabi was cut off from normal civil life. This was the result of his vocation, for one thing. For example, a master prophet comes over the fields to Elisha as he is ploughing, throws the nabi's mantle over him – and Elisha immediately leaves his fields and his oxen, and goes off with his master (I Kings 19.19ff.). Or a horde of prophets passes by, intoxicated with music and wild dancing. The sober peasant farmer's son is fascinated by the spirit that moves them; and so Saul finds himself among the nabis (I Sam. 10). Social origin played no part. From then on, anyone who had once been a nabi could wander through the countryside with only a tenuous connection with an order. He might turn up here or there and cry out a divine message. Elijah, the greatest of the pre-literary prophets, lived a life of this kind, and so did Micaiah ben Imlah (I Kings 22). But most of the nabis seem to have lived round about the king's court or the main sanctuaries.

The great moments, the climaxes towards which a nabi's life was directed, came about when Yahweh's *rūaḥ* seized hold of the people. The word is generally translated 'the spirit of the Lord', but what the Hebrew expression means is a gusty, stormy wind, a squall. It also means the breath in the living being, and everything else that bursts out dynamically in intermittent starts. Since Israel presupposes only one God, all *rūaḥ* is ultimately traced back to Yahweh. Martin Buber translated the word into German as 'Geistbraus' – the rushing of the spirit – a good translation. So in pre-exilic times *rūaḥ* does not mean a particular mental capacity. It is a power which seizes on the self, transporting it into ecstasy, enthusiasm, frenzy, making a person capable of psychological and physical acts which would seem inconceivable in a normal state. If a nabi is seized by the *rūaḥ*, he may be swept away by it, so that no one can follow him (I Kings 18.12; II Kings 2.16). But it can also lay hold on a whole collection of prophets. Then they shout and dance until they tear the clothes from their bodies and lie naked all night under the stars (I Sam. 19.23ff.). At the same time, the *rūaḥ* does not act in blind rage. The wind sings its song, and the person who is seized by the *rūaḥ* breaks into words, into singing, shouting and yet poetical words. For at the same time the *rūaḥ* has opened his eyes and given him second sight. He has seen what may be taking place hundreds of miles away, or over a hundred years later; or he has listened to what the king of Aram said in his bedroom (II Kings 6.12). Out of the ecstasy (*nb'*, hitpael) there finally emerges the prophecy (*nb'*, niphal), which is directed to the people, bringing them a *dābār*, a saying of Yahweh.

But to the ordinary Israelite, possession by this rushing of the spirit meant nothing. So how did he react to the nabi? The people wavered between shy reverence and mocking contempt. On the one hand, because he was concerned about his future, the Israelite needed the nabi. On the other hand, he found him; unpleasant and uncomfortable, because of his fanatical zeal for Yahweh and because he ignored the ordinary rules of polite behaviour. Where common sense was not enough, the nabi was approached in an attempt to find out what God had to say, for example, if a child fell mysteriously ill, or if a well gave bad water. This information was even more urgently required in nationally vital events – in military expeditions, or famine (II Kings 3; 19; 22). The nabi could also make intercessions better than anyone else – intercessions which God would hear. When he had performed a service of this kind, he was given a gift of money, and from this he and his group lived. Nabis were also regarded as fabulous miracle workers, who could heal the sick and even call the dead to life again (II Kings 5; I Kings 17.17ff.).

On the other hand, these eccentric, down-at-heel figures were despised. The literary prophet Hosea complains that the people mock him: 'The man of the rushing spirit is mad' (*mᵉšuggaʿ*, Yiddish 'meschugge'). Even in Jeremiah's time there was still a priest at the temple in Jerusalem as overseer to the 'mad' nabis. He could arrest them when they behaved too wildly and lock them up overnight in the stocks (Jer. 20), as a kind of sobering-up cell. Nabis were sometimes imprisoned at the royal court, too (I Kings 22). It can well be imagined that poor-spirited civil servants did not deal any too gently with a frenzied prophet.

Curiously enough, the literary prophets of the earlier period, beginning with Amos, never appeal to the *rûaḥ*. It is a matter of dispute whether they rejected the ecstatic manner of receiving revelation and arrived at their inspiration in a different way, or whether they did not stress the power that inspired them to the public, because the content of what they said was more important to them than the circumstances in which they received the message. Or didn't the earlier literary prophets not belong to the ranks of the nabis at all?

3.5 The contribution of the nabi to a military campaign

An Israelite king never waged war without having a nabi beside him. The part played by this nabi is made clear in I Kings 20, a dramatic episode belonging to the almost hundred years' war between the northern Israelites and the Aramaeans of Damascus. The aggressive Ben-hadad has besieged Samaria and boasts to his North Israelite opponents that the rubble of Samaria will not be sufficient 'to fill the hollow hands of all the people (*'am*) who follow me'. The situation seems hopeless. The numerical superiority of the Aramaeans is indisputable. Then, surprisingly, a nabi comes to the help of the king of Israel:

Thus says Yahweh:
A Have you seen all this great noisy pack?
B Behold I will give it into your hand this day, / and you shall know that I am Yahweh.

The nabi describes the situation as it is. But he evaluates it in a new way. What the Aramaean king proudly describes as *'am*, a well disciplined army, becomes for the nabi what he contemptuously describes as a great noisy pack. Facts which are clearly obvious at the time are therefore certainly evident to the nabi, too, but they have to be judged differently from the way everyday understanding would judge them. That is why he can use the deliverance formula: Yahweh gives them into your hand!

After this unexpectedly favourable message, the Israelite king asks about the strategy to be employed: which division of troops is to attack the enemy? Here, too, the nabi knows God's answer: the henchmen of the district governors. The king enquires further who is to open the attack. God has him told: 'You yourself'. The battle is opened. The Israelite army, though it is inferior in numbers, inflicts a severe defeat on the Aramaeans.

The following year the Aramaeans come back in order to repair their mistake. They have rearmed. Like all ancient peoples, they too assume that numinous powers contribute to victory and defeat. 'Their god [i.e., the Israelites' god] is a god of the hills.' So now they plan to fight a battle in the plains. But by relativizing Yahweh as a god of the hills, the arrogance of the Aramaean king goes beyond all bounds. The following year the Aramaeans again fall upon Israel with superior numbers, and the Israelites lie opposite them at Aphek 'like two little flocks of goats'. Shortly before the battle begins, the man of God himself – *'îš hā^elōhîm* (the master of the nabis in North Israel?) comes to the royal commander:

Thus says Yahweh:
A Aram has said:
A god of the mountains is Yahweh / and not a god of the plains.
B (Therefore) will I give the whole noisy pack, / great as it is, into your hand.

Again the Israelites achieve a glorious victory. The North Israelite king and his hand therefore constitute as it were the extended hand of Yahweh himself. The God, invisible though he is, plays so giant a part in the war that he has both armies in his hand and disposes of them as he likes. But the war continues. The man of God has disappeared again. The royal commander has to make his own decisions, and he makes grave mistakes. He agrees too hurriedly to an armistice and to a peace treaty.

Now a lesser nabi has to act. He peremptorily commands another nabi to strike him (or does he tell him expressly that this is Yahweh's *dābār?*) The other refuses. He is unwilling to hurt his fellow nabi. Then the first nabi announces to the other that he will be killed by a lion because he has not obeyed Yahweh's (lion-like) voice. For us this is an extremely strange decision. For a nabi of the time it was a 'professional risk' which was taken as a matter of course. Another nabi is then found who is prepared to beat the first speaker until he bleeds. The wounded nabi stands at the side of the road as the king returns from the battlefield and, by means of a fictitious case, makes the king pronounce judgment on himself (as in II Sam. 12). This judgment is summed up in the words:

A The matter is thus: You have let go out of your hand the man whom I had condemned.
B Therefore the strength of your life (*nepeš*) shall stand for the strength of his; / your people for his people.

Now the Israelite king has also violated his God. For anyone who, by way of God's word spoken through the nabi, is delivered up by

Yahweh's hand (in this case the Aramaeans) becomes Yahweh's property. Now becoming Yahweh's property means being put to the ban, a primitive custom of dedication through execution in a holy war. The king has barred the way to this by letting his opponent go.

To people living in the Western world, the course of these events seems appalling and brutal. The men who give their names to the prophetic books apply other, more refined ethical standards, as we shall see. But they share with the nabis the conviction that Yahweh is a god of battle, and shows in battle whom he gives into whose hand, though not without previously having proclaimed his decision through his *dābār,* his word. The war appears as something taking place on different levels. On the level of superficial military strategy, it is the affair of the king and his officers; but it belongs just as much on the level of moral warfare, and this the nabis disclose. Even the authors of the prophetic books, like Isaiah in the Assyrian campaign, and Jeremiah during Nebuchadnezzar's attack on Jerusalem, are active in this sense (cf. I Kings 22 and the Elisha legends; I Sam. 15 already shows Samuel in the same conflict with the king because of the command to destroy the enemy). This gives master prophets like Elisha self-confidence, for they are really the decisive factors in the war – 'the chariot of Israel and its horsemen' (II Kings 2.12; 13.14).

However, the prophetic word did not always prevail. During a campaign against Moab, no less a man than Elisha promised that Yahweh would give the enemy into the hands of the king of Israel and Judah (II Kings 3). But the Moabite king sacrificed his eldest son to his chief god and moved this god so greatly that Israel was beaten back into its own country. Elisha's prophecy was therefore not fulfilled. This was the result of the superior power of an alien god in an alien land. The thinking of the nabis still did not reach as far as monotheism.

3.6 Divinely willed revolutions

According to the Deuteronomic History, the prophets were even more concerned with the appointment and deposition of kings than they were with war. In Yahweh's name they designated candidates for the throne and saw to it that they were deposed again if necessary – and deposed by the sword. Because of an infringement of the ritual of the holy war, the same Samuel who nominated the peasant farmer's son Saul to be king with the words, 'Yahweh has anointed you to be chief (*nāgīd*) over his heritage,' declares to him a few years later, 'Yahweh has torn the kingdom of Israel from you this day, and has given it to one who is better than you'; and this implies the death penalty for the king (I Sam. 10.1; 15.28). The next king, David, is fortunate because after the Bathsheba episode the same Nathan who, after the conquest of Jerusalem, had promised him that his dynasty would be eternally established on the throne, only threatened him: 'The sword shall never depart from your house' (II Sam. 7; 12.10). For David's sake, his son Solomon was also fortunate, in spite of his many wives and the idolatry they necessitated, because the nabi Ahijah of Shiloh only declared, 'Thus says Yahweh. Behold I am about to tear the kingdom from the hand of Solomon', and did not add the death sentence that was really due. Indeed he even left Solomon's successor the limited rule of a *nāsī* ('prince', I Kings 11.31–37).

Samuel, Nathan and Ahijah were the prophets who arose at the time of what was in the Deuteronomic view the triple constellation of Saul, David and Solomon. The three prophets did not merely help to put their respective rulers on the throne, and threaten them later with the end of their government, but saw to it (at least, Samuel and Ahijah did) that an active opposition, bent on revolution, soon appeared on the scene. Samuel anointed David immediately after the dispute with his king. Ahijah encouraged Jeroboam to rebel. Even Nathan's speech attacking David indirectly promoted Absalom's insurrection. That, at least, is the way the books of Samuel see things.

According to the account in the books of Kings, after the division of the kingdom in 926 it was almost exclusively in the Northern kingdom that there were prophets whose names were worth recording. And for what reason? Because they instigated revolt! The aging Ahijah, indignant about the cultic policy of Jeroboam I, whom he had once designated king, hurls at him the terrible words (I Kings 14.7–11):

B Behold . . . I will cut off from Jeroboam every one that pisseth against the wall.
Any one belonging to Jeroboam who dies in the city / the dogs shall eat;
and any one who dies [of Jeroboam] in the open country / the birds of the air shall eat.

The destiny he pronounces falls upon Jeroboam's son. 'Baasha conspired against him.' He succeeded to the throne and rooted out the male members of the royal house that had been deposed, 'according to the word of Yahweh which he spoke by his servant Ahijah of Shiloh' (15.25–29).

But fifty years later the new royal line from Issachar again aroused prophetic protest. Only one saying has been passed down to us from Jehu ben Hanani, the next prophet of the Northern kingdom: 'Behold, I will utterly sweep away Baasha and his house!' An echo on the political plane is not lacking. 'But his servant Zimri, commander of half his chariots, conspired against him', i.e. against Baasha's son. He leaves none of the dynasty alive, 'not one that pisseth against the wall, according to the word of Yahweh which he spake by Jehu the prophet' (16.1–13).

The second generation of the third dynasty, Omri, comes up against the opposition of one of the mightiest of the prophets, Elijah. After the judicial murder of Naboth, the sentence of doom on Ahab is due: 'In the place where dogs licked up the blood of Naboth shall dogs lick your own blood' (I Kings 21.20f.). It is true that Ahab is granted a period of grace, but disaster strikes his son Jehoram with full force. The prophet Elisha then instigates Jehu's revolt, one of the bloodiest episodes in the history of the Northern kingdom. Again all the male members of the dynasty are killed, so that people may see 'that there has fallen to the earth nothing of the word of Yahweh which Yahweh spake concerning the house of Ahab' (II Kings 10.10).

According to the books of Kings, Jehu's rebellion against the Omrids is the end of opposition prophecy for a while, and at the same time the end of revolutions in the Northern kingdom for a hundred years. (Amos and Hosea then, under new auspices, announce the end of the house of Jehu.) Down to the middle of the ninth century BC, the nabis seem to have been the strongest driving force behind the political opposition. They not only fought for new men on the throne but also for the renewal of the state. Unfortunately the Deuteronomic editors hardly indicate the motives which impelled the prophets to go over to political resistance against the reigning king of the particular period; and their ideas about the correct constitution of Israel as Yahweh's people are less clear still. But with men like Elijah and Elisha, the call for the sword is hardly conceivable without firm conceptions about the way Yahweh's people and Yahweh's land ought ultimately to be constituted.

Still one other aspect ought to be mentioned. In the prophecies Yahweh is always the subject: 'I will cut off; I will sweep away.' But these prophecies are always fulfilled through the medium of a particular human person, who becomes the leader of a conspiracy aimed at murdering the king. No tension is felt between the announcement of a *divine* act and its implementation by means of a purely *human* one. The assassins are Yahweh's extended arm. Western distinctions between a miraculous divine salvation history and an everyday earthly secular history have no place here. For this period, the unity of prophetic theory and political practice is obvious. After a few years, what the prophets proclaim turns into political action – bloody action, as a rule. Since prophetic theory was only partially developed, and was concerned with individual cultic-political or social grievances, the direct way to action was simple – all too simple, as it subsequently appears to the Christian observer; and this was the way it already seemed even to some of the later literary prophets. This form of political activity on the part of the prophets weakened Northern Israel in particular and turned its history into what Alt has called 'a history of divinely willed revolutions'. The country's relatively early collapse was due in part to the prophets.

The nabis chafed against human – all too human – conditions. Gripped by the God who possessed their inmost being, on whom their thoughts were unceasingly concentrated, they came up against the indifference of the masses, the tepidity of the kings, and the contradiction between everyday Israelite life and the religiously inspired ideal of the people of God. For 200 years they made continually new beginnings, in an attempt to bring the utopia of a people of God into harmony with political and military reality. A revolution every fifty years seems to have been a last resort. In the long run it failed to fulfil its purpose every time. Within a short period, the dynasty which had been raised to the throne for the first time displayed the same signs of wear and tear as the old dynasties that had been rooted out. Can the notion of a people of God, at one with that God, filled every hour with the forces of divine activity, be realized at all in political terms? At this point the authors of the prophetic books take a step further, prophesying the total downfall of this state and people; they then reckon with world-wide changes, perhaps introducing an outlook which can already be termed eschatological. The expectation of fundamental future transformations after a long period of waiting did not suit the impatient nabis of the earlier period of the monarchy. They wanted the kingdom of God here and now. They wanted it in Israel. That is their greatness, but also their tragedy. It is shown in a particularly striking way by the greatest representative of the era: Elijah.

3.7 Elijah

According to I Kings 17.1, Elijah not only came from the remote area of Gilead, east of Jordan, but also belonged to the class of small tenant farmers (*tōšab*) who owned no land of their own. He shows how people of lowly origin could, through their prophetic activity, come to play a decisive role for the whole of society. The Israelite order of society, which took its character from Yahwistic religion, was fundamentally always open to a charismatic element in its leadership; and this prevented the class barriers from becoming rigid. Elijah can issue commands even to his king, making him call the whole of Israel together. At the public sacrifice which Elijah celebrates, priests are superfluous (I Kings 18; 19.21). We cannot be quite certain whether Elijah saw himself as belonging to the ranks of the nabis. He is occasionally called nabi, but perhaps only later on (18.22, 36; 19.16). His classification as man of God (17.18, 24) – that is to say, as a person who has a specific permanent relationship to God, not merely at the moment of inspiration (17.18) – sounds more archaic and is better adapted to his wandering existence, which shows no traces of any tie with holy places or with the court. Perhaps we may assume that as a man of God, Elijah – like the slightly younger Elisha – was at the same time the recognized master of a guild of nabis (cf. Num. 12; I Sam. 19.18ff.).

The few stories about Elijah that have been preserved for us admittedly begin only when there are no longer any nabis and when Elijah has gone underground, because he is the only one left. This is put down to the first persecution of Yahwistic nabis in Israel by the notorious Jezebel, a Phoenician princess who, with missionary zeal, spread the cult of the Baal of Tyre (the god of her native country) and whose efforts met with great success in the country. She appointed some of her own nabis to serve Baal (their number – 450 according to I Kings 22 – is probably exaggerated). This is only explicable if her god was thought to be capable of shaping future events through prophetic words in the same way as the Israelite God Yahweh. At that time Tyre was enjoying an economic heyday. Its merchants dominated the shipping trade in the Mediterranean. Phoenician colonization spread as far as Spain. The deity who was at work in all this could be no minor god! At the royal court of Samaria, people no doubt put the Tyrian Baal on the same level as Yahweh and therefore simply used the title of dignity 'Lord and Master' (*baʿal*), and not the proper name Melkart, under which the God was worshipped in Tyre.

But Elijah expressed the conscience of the old Yahwistic religion. On Israel's soil there can only be the one worship: the worship of Yahweh. Every alien god who exerts his influence from outside makes people and country tabu (*ʿākār*, I Kings 18.17) and destroys the healthful condition of its life. The author of the Deuteronomic history drops the designation of Jezebel's god as *Tyrian* Baal, and presents things as though Elijah had struggled against any worship of a deity called Baal. But this is the viewpoint of a later period. It was not until a century later that Hosea questioned whether even Yahweh himself should be called Baal, and hunted down baalized elements in Yahweh worship. As yet Elijah has no suspicions of this kind. He has no misgivings when, in what had once been Canaanite sanctuaries – in the plain of Jezreel, for example – the name of Baal is used in the Israelite cult, or when the image of a bull plays a part in the cultic ceremonies at Bethel and Dan, in connection with fertility rites. What he is continually concerned with is 'divinity in Israel' (18.36; II Kings

1.3, 6, 16), the self-contained unity of Yahweh and the powers bound up with him. For Elijah, the sole worship of Yahweh, the land, and the community of the people form a unity that is indispensable for living, a unity into which no foreign element must intrude. It is this which explains why the Elijah stories show the prophet engaged in dispute, not merely about cultic sites and rites (I Kings 18; II Kings 1), but also about the right of the individual Israelite to the land which is his ancestral heritage.

According to an attractive supposition of Alt's, the background of the famous story about the divine judgment on Carmel is that Mount Carmel, which had formerly belonged to Israel, was ceded by the Tyrians on the occasion of Ahab's marriage to Jezebel. It then became a matter of dispute whether the ruined sanctuary on the mountain top should be newly consecrated according to Tyrian rites, or according to the ancient rites of Yahweh. There is a gripping description of the way Elijah persuades the people to choose the latter by way of an ordeal by fire. The rival prophets of the Tyrian Baal are defeated and are slaughtered at the brook Kishon. For the modern reader this is a cruel act, but for that time it was an absolutely necessary undertaking. The person who was defeated in a divine ordeal was doomed to die. If Elijah had not been victorious, he would have been killed. Moreover, Elijah had maintained that the country was being defiled by foreign cults and that its vital power was being sapped. Because the deity declares that Elijah is right, it is essential that the pollution should be eradicated by means of some impressive act. It corresponds to the elimination of the aura of sin which appears in the country in the case of an unexpiated murder (Deut. 21.1–9).

Another of Elijah's famous appearances is made on the occasion of the dispute about Naboth's vineyard (I Kings 21). Ahab wants to buy a piece of land from his Israelite neighbour. But Naboth is horrified at the thought of giving up a part of the land he has inherited (*naḥ^{a}lā*), passed down to him from his fathers – that is to say, ultimately assigned by Yahweh in the salvation history. Ahab nonetheless succeeds in acquiring the land through a mean judicial murder – unnoticed by the public, as he imagines. But thanks to his prophetic vision, Elijah sees what Ahab has done. He confronts the king:

A You have murdered, / you have taken possession of the land
. . .
Thus says Yahweh:
B In the place where dogs licked up / the blood of Naboth
shall dogs lick your blood / even yours!

The prophecy is then fulfilled, not on Ahab but on his successor. In the framework of the Hebrew view of 'the extended self' – a view which takes it for granted that there is a cohesion of life and liability between the generations – this was in no way disturbing or disconcerting. The narrator further explains that because of the king's repentance (as in II Sam. 12), the implementation of the divine sentence has been postponed.

Whenever Elijah appears, his proclamation is determined by his zeal for the integrity of the land given by Yahweh. He sees it as divided in a hierarchical way. What Israel possesses as a whole is divided between twelve tribes (for the symbol twelve see also I Kings 18.31; 19.19). What is owned by the tribe is apportioned as a particular share to the individual clan. This is the background that explains the unity of what Elijah says; he never insists on a divine commandment (such as 'you shall worship no other gods but me') but argues solely from the indissoluble connection between Israel's life and the God who guides her.

Wherever Elijah appears, there is an eruption like the outbreak of a volcano. No other prophet of the early period of the monarchy approaches him in effectiveness, or in his readiness for complete involvement in Yahweh's cause. According to a later story, even Yahweh did not feel quite at ease with his ruthless temperament and his uncompromising zeal. He orders Elijah to Mount Sinai and there lets a mighty storm of wind (*rū*^{a}*ḥ*) pass over him; then an earthquake; then some great fiery apparition; and finally a 'still small voice'. It is only in the last of these events that Yahweh can be perceived. Catastrophes are not the real media of the divine self-revelation (I Kings 19).

III

Unconditional Prophecy of Doom at the Beginning of the Assyrian Period

4. Amos

4.1 A seer and his offensive speeches

The first prophet whose sayings have been gathered together in a book of their own is Amos.[10] The only passage which tells us anything about the circumstances of his public activity is a third-party report included in the book (7.10–17), which is otherwise written in the first person. About 760 BC, the chief priest Amaziah reports to his royal master Jeroboam II from Bethel:

> Amos conspires (*qāšar*) against you / at the centre of the house of Israel!
> The land cannot comprehend / all his words.
> For thus Amos has said:
> Through the sword shall Jeroboam die / and Israel shall surely be deported from its land.

So what Amos proclaims at the very heart of the nation, i.e. at the central sanctuary, is seemingly provocative and subversive. The chief priest sums up the proclamation quite accurately in two sentences of his own. He does not exaggerate. Like the North Israelite nabis of earlier times, Amos proclaims the death of the king, according to divine decree. Amaziah does not suggest that Amos is directly preparing the insurrection himself. But he knows from the history of his country how often a nabi's proclamation that Yahweh had resolved on the deposition of a certain king or dynasty had made ambitious officers feel that they were a suitable instrument for a violent dethronement; and the immediate consequence was *qešer* – conspiracy.

As a servant of the state, in duty bound to make his report, the priest seems on the other hand to have been slightly nervous of the charismatic Amos. Otherwise he would not have summoned him. He tells Amos about the report he has made, and advises him to escape over the frontier if he values his life: '*Ḥōzeh* (seer), flee into the land of Judah!' From this time on, Amos is forbidden to prophesy in Bethel: 'for it is a house of the king's / indeed the house of the kingdom itself.' It is not enough for Amaziah merely to fulfil his professional duty. He defends his faith and the faith of his people. Israel's bond with its *ʾadāmā*, its homeland, the actual ground on which it lives as the foundation of its life, has been for centuries the subject of a covenant between Yahweh and his people; it has been the goal of a divinely guided salvation history ever since the days of the patriarchs (Gen. 15.18). Bethel especially is the place where the possession of the land promised to Jacob, and later occupied for ever through the deliverance from Egypt, is ritually celebrated (Gen. 28.10ff.; I Kings 12.28f.). The dynasty of Jehu, to which the reigning Jeroboam II belonged, evidently understood how to fit itself into this cultic view of history. Bethel, the place where God promised and gave the land, is at the same time *bēt-mamlākā*, the house of the kingdom. It is therefore Yahweh's will that the possession of the land shall be ensured and guaranteed by the monarchy, which is thereby given a religious justification. When Amos now prophesies that Israel will disappear from its land, he is denying the very foundation of religion and state, which had till then been inviolable. He is going far beyond what any nabi before him had ever dared to say. Amaziah must have felt not merely that Amos' speeches were rebellious; he must have found them blasphemous. But even so, he does not want an open scandal. Is he sorry for the man in front of him? Or is he not completely certain of his own position? Instead of being grateful for the advice, Amos swells with indignation. He hears within himself an inexorable word of Yahweh, which he flings at Amaziah:

I no nabi, / I no prophet's disciple,
but I, a herdsman, / also a cultivator of mulberry trees,
away from the herd did Yahweh tear me, / he told me, Yahweh,
Go, prophesy / to my people Israel!

A But now hear the word of Yahweh, / you that say:
'You shall not prophesy over Israel, / nor spit venom against the house of Isaac.'
For this, so has Yahweh said,

B Your wife will have to go a-whoring in the city, / your sons, your daughters through the sword shall fall.
Your land, by the yardstick shall it be parcelled out, / you yourself shall die on unclean ground.
But Israel shall surely be deported (torn away) / from its land.

Scholars dispute whether Amos was setting himself apart from contemporary nabis as a whole, and was demanding another status for himself; or whether the opening should be understood as referring to the past – once I was not a nabi, but now I am one, because I prophesy (Heb. *nibbā'*, which has the same root as *nābī'*). The differing interpretation goes together with contradictory views about the institutional background of Amos. Was he a charismatic, independent peasant farmer, or had he through his call become an office-holder, bound to the cult? The dispute hardly deserves the attention that it has been given. Even a thousand years before, in Mari, we find charismatic and cultic prophets side by side, with the same aim. According to the context, Amaziah is addressing Amos as a seer, and this was probably exactly what he was regarded as being. Amos was a *ḥōzeh*, not a *nābī'*, which apparently meant an (ecstatic?) cultic prophet. If he had been a nabi, he would have belonged to the official personnel associated with the cult. Amaziah might then perhaps have locked him up, but he would certainly not have driven him away. But although he had no official position and was not an ecstatic, Amos commanded the same respect. Like the nabis, he had been marked out because Yahweh had made himself directly perceptible to him and had entrusted him with a commission.

At the same time, here as elsewhere in Amos, the carefully structured poetical sentences and the use of the common *nābī'* genre of prophecy show that Amos had undergone training. He did not run straight from his pastures to Bethel, to say what he had to say there quite spontaneously. The call made him practise the prophetic way of listening to the 'inner' voice, as well as visionary withdrawal and inwardness. This meditation strengthened his awareness of his mission, his sense of being the voice of the deity and of knowing what God desired and planned, better than all the priests who claimed to be experts. To this degree the scene is an exemplary reflection of a conflict between charisma and office. Amos does not doubt for a moment that he is right and that the person who denies him the opportunity for proclamation is resisting the fundamental power of God in history. Amaziah wants to prevent his king from dying by the sword, and Israel from being torn from its homeland, in which case the priest's own children too would be drawn into the orbit of the destructive sword, and Amaziah himself would lose his land for ever. The reversals are intentional. The doom approaches inexorably. The only question is, who will be drawn into it and who will not? But Amaziah will undoubtedly be one of the victims.

Unfortunately we are not told what happened next in this dramatic encounter. Most scholars suppose that, in spite of his protest, Amos withdrew to Judah, but that there he set down in writing what he had prophesied in Bethel; and that this was the foundation of his prophetic book. It is an acceptable hypothesis (see also Section IV.9 below). No doubt Amaziah really was deported by the Assyrians thirty years later, together with Israel's upper classes; otherwise Amos' saying would not have been preserved in such detail. The upper classes who were torn from their homeland at that time never returned. So what Amos proclaimed came true. Admittedly, Jeroboam was not killed; it was only his son Zechariah who was put to the sword (II Kings 14.29; 15.10). But since the Hebrew view of the 'total self' of a family saw the fate of the son as inherent in that of the father, the Israelite will have seen this, too, as a complete fulfilment of the prophet's prediction.

4.2 Oppressive visions of downfall

1. Amos counters the chief priest in no uncertain terms. He is not plagued by any doubts about his mission. But in the written records he left behind him the seer shows another facet of himself. In *the visionary accounts* which are now included at the end of the book (chs. 7 to 9), another person comes to light, an introspective one, with another side to his character. 'Thus the Lord Yahweh showed me' are the words which introduce every vision, and which are followed by mysterious voices. The voices count for more than the vision. What they say is fixed for the future. 'Then the Lord said.' During the mysterious visions, which go far beyond what can normally be seen, all his assurance falls away from Amos. 'O almighty Lord Yahweh, forgive!', he interpolates at the beginning when scenes of horror are shown him. Later, his awe of the One who send the visions grows. He no longer dares to interrupt. In the editing process the account of the dramatic outward events accompanying Amos' appearance in Bethel have been coupled with the visionary accounts about dramatic 'inward' events in chs. 7f., so that as we read them, the two contrasting sides of the man Amos appear vividly before our eyes.

What is the content of the visions?

First of all, a supernatural figure is visible in the distance, who is ceaselessly forming locusts (grasshoppers), which then fly away to eat up all the green growth on earth. Anyone who knows the fearful danger posed to the harvest in Asia by swarms of insects like this, even today, can understand the seer's horror, and why he ejaculates the cry 'forgive!' And indeed the divine voice relents: 'It shall not be' (7.1–3). The second vision takes a similar course. This time Amos stands before a terrible fire which threatens to lick up, not merely the primordial waters (and thereby the water reserves of the earth), but the cultivated land too. Again a cry, and again God gives way (7.4–6).

The third vision is different. This time God himself appears standing on a wall, with an object made of metal – lead or pewter – in his hand, which he turns against Israel's central point, so that sanctuaries and palace disappear (7.7–9). In the fourth vision Amos sees a sheaf of ripe grain. Perhaps he actually sees it physically, for prophetic visions do not take place in a different world from this one; they extend the potentialities of real perception into what lies behind this present world (in Hebrew both are called *rā'ā*). God as it were widens the prophet's range of vision. To that degree the concept 'inner vision' is insufficient. It is impossible to exclude the possibility that in the first three visions, too, grasshoppers, fire and metal object were visibly present to everyone, although in the case of the prophet they provided the stimulus for profounder vision. The sheaf of ripe grain (or basket with ripe fruit) is given a symbolic interpretation by the divine voice:

> The harvest (hardly 'the end', as in most translations) is coming for my people Israel / I will never again pass by them;
> The songs of the temple must become laments. / Many the dead bodies at every (cultic) place (8.1f.).

This, then, is the sequence of the four visions. Scholars assume that in them Amos is clinging to the beginning of his prophetic experience, because in the first two he is granted a withdrawal of the doom threatening the earth; and none of Amos' other sayings ever allow us to expect this. So ever since the divine voice tore him away from his herds (as he put it to Amaziah) visions have forced themselves upon him. Probably we are given only a selection. In those we have, we can find the world-picture of the eighth century BC. Locusts are formed and given life by a supernatural hand. They do not simply develop out of larvae. Primordial waters surround the earth or lie beneath it, providing the source for all moisture. Israel has a centre (probably associated with the sanctuary at Bethel) on which its existence depends. There Yahweh, in bodily form, can either pass by mercifully, or can strike down men and women. In the second case only dead bodies remain. Here Amos' mind is grappling with the foundations of the universe. The God in whom he believes is not tied down – not partially confined – to any particular place. The descriptions follow a certain trend from the outside inwards, from nature as a whole to Israel, and finally to the Temple where Amos makes his appearance. The angle narrows down, but the prospects become more and more sombre.

In the final chapter we have a further vision. Now the Almighty stands above (or beside) 'the altar', apparently in Bethel, and commands that the *kaphtōr* (pillars?) should be smitten until the threshhold shakes:

> Their [unjust profit] on the heads of them all!
> and what are left of them I will slay with the sword.

The perspective widens out to take in the universe. Whether the guilty (who are no more closely identified than that) flee into the underworld, or the depths of the sea, or the heavens, Yahweh will seize them and his sword will slay them (9.1–4 [5a?]).

No one in Israel had ever prophesied so terrible a doom before. Amos does so at the command of a God who had hitherto been worshipped as the guarantor of the existence and preservation of Israel's society. It is not surprising that Amaziah, who was the appointed servant of his religion, should have intervened. At the same time, revolutionary though the demands were, the ideas in their general framework were not in themselves new. Amos took them from a cultically-based world-picture. The linguistic forms have been taken over too. As a genre, the vision is found among other prophets of the same period (I Kings 22; Isa. 6). The visions show colourfully, mythologically, and in terms of a world-wide perspective, what Amos expressed in his own speeches soberly, in everyday terms that are related to the real conditions of the nation and its religion.

2. Before we turn to the sayings themselves, however, we must look at some of the theories which have grown up round the Amos visions in recent years, and which are also important for the evaluation of prophecy as a whole.

(i) Do we have to reckon with one basic *experience of vocation*? In exegetical literature the visions are largely viewed as a single, unified experience and as a reflection of the prophet's call. For Amos as for Isaiah (ch. 6), Jeremiah (ch. 1) and Ezekiel (chs. 1–3), a single, non-rational experience of being called by God is supposed to have provided the starting point for all later prophetic utterances. These utterances are only a development of that first, unique, divine call. The psychological or dogmatic category of 'call' – which is never actually mentioned by this particular prophet – does away with awkward questions about the cause of astonishing prophetic clairvoyance or disconcerting errors. In short, it provides a sufficient explanation for the unshakable sense of mission with regard to certain aspects of the future which the prophets display in public. When a call of this kind is even equated with the appeal of the divine word which every Christian experiences today, suggestions based on depth-psychology or parapsychology have the wind taken out of their sails.

But here certain doubts must be registered. The visionary descriptions are not felt by either Amos or his editor to be fundamental; if they were, they would have been put at the beginning of the book. Nor is it certain that the visions – especially the fifth – were experienced by the seer at one single point in time. A sense of mission is certainly one of Amos' most profound characteristics; but he says nothing about any all-decisive moment of call. (And the same may be said of the other contemporary prophets.) It is easier to agree with the scholars who see the clear break between the second and third visions – i.e., from a vision of revocable to a vision of irrevocable doom – as representing a biographical or psychological turning point in Amos' life. The prophet of salvation who, like his people, believes in Yahweh's readiness to forgive ('Yahweh, a merciful and gracious El', Ex. 34.6), turns into a nonconformist prophet of disaster. Only we do not necessarily have to understand a prophet of salvation as being a cultic nabi, as the supporters of this theory often assume. It is certainly true that, in spite of early premonitions of disaster, the prophet arrives only gradually at the conviction that Israel is drawing inexorably to its end. Amos' visions are the beginning of an unconditional prophecy of doom which is soon shared by other literary prophets of the time, and which was something unique, not merely for Israel but for the whole of the ancient East.

(ii) At the beginning was there really only a *premonition of disaster*? The 'call' theory is often linked with a second one, according to which the certainty about a disastrous *future* in Amos (and other prophets, too) was the primary experience, whereas insight into the intolerable situation of *the present* came later and was of secondary importance. This seems to emerge from the visionary accounts. The seer is overcome by one nightmare after the other – locusts, fire, annihilating metal and (lastly) the fruits of harvest. What looms up is only a future full of terror; nothing is said about present conditions. This has made German scholars, in particular, ascribe a kind of Cassandra experience to Amos. They view the social criticism which emerges from his sayings as secondary expedients which the prophet thinks out for himself, without special divine inspiration, to help to make his terrible visions of the future more understandable for his listeners. Weiser stressed this approach for the first time: 'Amos went about among his people, whose death sentence had already been pronounced . . . In the visions, Amos has learnt only that Yahweh was no longer prepared to forgive. But Yahweh left it to his prophet to perceive and name *what* he was no longer able to forgive.'[11]

But if we have to presuppose a fundamental premonition which is as undeducible and irrational as this – a premonition that the future will bring only disaster – it means denying to Amos' God, the author of this premonition, any kind of continuity with the previous Israelite understanding of what God was like. What kind of God is this, who one day radically revokes the readiness to forgive men and women which had hitherto been taken for granted in all Israel's traditions? A God who suddenly abrogates all his fellowship with men and women without giving any adequate reason for it? Even a nonconformist like Amos remains in some way tied to his language and the thinking which it conveys. He never claims that he is discovering a new God. Is it therefore permissible to raise the status of the visionary accounts in such a way that they become the centre of Amos' thinking? Could not the nature of the genre be the reason why the present is not described? Not to mention the fact that by using key words like forgive, judgment, not pass by, harvest, unjust profit (7.2, 4, 8; 9.1) in each of his visions, Amos does in fact point to human behaviour as the factor evoking God's reaction. In most of Amos' prophecies, it is impossible to detect any predominant stress on statements about the future. Pointers to the present situation always come first, and generally take up more space than the prophecies that follow. Moreover, if the series of visionary accounts were intended to be understood as being of such fundamental significance, would they not have been put at the beginning of the book?

Of course this does not mean that Amos built up his criticism of the present empirically and analytically, and that he simply pinned a number of visionary panoramas to it at some later stage. But his statements about the present *and* about the future are probably equally inspired, and equally prompted by a divine voice. For both he looks into himself for subsequent insight, and demands the same from his listeners.

(iii) It would seem that the unconditional prophecy of doom begins with the third vision. Yet there are some interpreters who see Amos, like all the other prophets, as a *preacher of repentance*. According to this view, Amos saw and proclaimed the coming disaster only conditionally – on the presupposition, that is to say, that Israel would not repent, as the prophet in his heart of hearts hoped it would. It was simply for didactic reasons that Amos did not expressly preach 'Repent, for the kingdom of God is at hand', as Jesus did (Mark 1.15). Instead, he stressed only the single, negative possibility.

Is a hypothesis of this kind not reading too much between the lines? Is it not giving too relative an importance to the content of the visions? The only thing which Amos has to say otherwise about a possible relenting on God's part is formulated in a single passage, with a highly significant qualification – 'it may be'; and it is explicitly restricted to a remnant: 'It may be that Yahweh will then be gracious to the remnant of Joseph' (5.5). The genre itself tells in favour of the irreversibility of the doom Amos foresees; it is a genre for which we have no evidence in the earlier proclamation of the nabis, and which Amos was probably the first to take up: the funeral lament. They have been taken from burial rites and bewail the people whom the prophet sees as being guilty as though they are already dead. Here, then, the future judgment is already anticipated (5.18ff.; 6.1ff.).

(iv) It must, however, be conceded that Amos never talks as if the Israelites are going to be completely blotted out, although almost all the textbooks interpret him as saying this. When 'the harvest' for Israel comes, it will bring ruin for the people who are responsible for the present grievances, though hardly for 'the righteous' who suffer under them (2.6; 5.12). Even the deportation of Israel which Amos fears does not mean that afterwards laments will not still be sung in the temple (8.3), and that there will not be people to raise the song of mourning in the cities and vineyards (5.16f.). Nothing will be left of the ruling classes in Samaria except two ear lobes (as if they were a sheep or cow savaged by a lion), which is to say, practically nothing at all. But this only applies to the inhabitants of Samaria, who lounge about on their cushions (3.12). A foreign nation will occupy the country and will oppress it. So there must be someone left to oppress (6.14). The unconditional doom destroys the foundations of religion and state, but it is not total in a quantitative sense. A miserable remnant is left, even though it no longer deserves the name of Israel.

4.3 The exploitation of the dallīm. *Amos' social criticism*

4.3.1. In his prophecies Amos develops what the visions only suggest: the guilt of Israel's leaders as the reason for the downfall. The very first saying against Israel in the book is the most detailed (2.6–16):

Thus says Yahweh:
A [Hear, you] who sell the *ṣaddīq* ('the righteous') for silver, / the needy for a pair of sandals,
trampling (?) [to] *earth* the head of the *dallīm* ('the poor') / the way (*derek*) of the godly is bowed.
A man and his father sleep with the (same?) girl / so as to defile [my sanctuary].
Whereby they lay themselves down on garments taken in pledge / beside (every) altar
and drink wine that has been taken as a fine / in the house of their God.
Yet I had destroyed / the Amorite for their sakes.

High as the cedars were they, / mighty [as oak trees],
I wiped out his fruit above / and his roots beneath.
I had brought you up / from the *earth* of Egypt,
led you in the desert / forty years long,
so that you might inherit the *earth* of the Amorites . . .
Then I raised up nabis from your sons, / consecrated men from your youth.
Was it not indeed so, / sons of Israel? So Yahweh's murmur.

B Behold I will cauterize (?) / beneath you [the *earth*].
The refuge of the lightly armed shall perish, / and the heavily armed shall not stand . . .

The sale of men and women is condemned – a gross inhumanity for modern readers. Amos immediately has our assent when he inveighs against it. But probably what disturbs the prophet is not primarily that people are being turned into goods for sale. The sale of men and women was permitted according to ancient oriental and Israelite law, if debts could not otherwise be paid. For Hebrews, slavery for debt was restricted to six years (Ex. 21.1). Yet it can only have been in exceptional cases that a person who had once been enslaved was able to rebuild his livelihood again afterwards. In ancient Israel only the man who was independent – the person who possessed his own land, inherited from his fathers – could enjoy legal status, undertake military service or play an active part in the cult; and it was only a person like this who counted as a member of the *'am*, the civil and religious community. The person who was enslaved because of debt was excluded from playing an independent part among the 'people' of Israel, and he was also shut off from direct contact with its God. Amos does not oppose the existing law in principle, but he is enraged at the irresponsible and devastating spread of the sale of human beings. Like other exploitative practices, such as the unreasonable seizure of clothing as security, or of wine from a debtor, it was the sign of a fatal tendency in contemporary society. Under the pretext of justice, the *derek* of a particular class of people is being 'turned aside'. The Hebrew word *derek*, which is translated in the English Bible as 'way', really means the unity of a person's conduct and the course of his life. It can be found only among people who have the chance of a successful, harmonious life and a healthful existence. If the *derek* is 'turned aside', broken, it can no longer continue to run straight. Meaningful living is made impossible. The previous sentence is saying the same thing when it sees the *dallīm* as trampled into the earth. (The translation is uncertain, but the word 'earth' is certainly used.) Amos is making an accusation. He is concerned, not with individual events, but with their background and consequences. For his *derek* anthropology (and this is true of pre-exilic Israel as a whole), the ties between human beings and the God who confers salvation are inextricably linked with the economic freedom given by possession of one's own land. *Derek* on one's own land, given to the patriarchs by God, counts as the precondition which makes a successful and harmonious life possible. A person has to be able to stand up straight on his own inherited ground. If he is bent down to the earth, then his vital hope is extinguished. He is, for all practical purposes, dead.

The fruitful earth itself is affected by the ejection of the *ṣaddīq* from his inherited land. Since it is a bequest to his people by the God who is victorious in salvation history, the land remains in contact with this God. God can easily make the earth quake. Then the whole Israelite army, with all its different branches, will fall down like a house of cards. There will be no need for any external military enemy. This is the prediction (B), which arises out of unbearable conditions.

It is not clear where the saying in 2.6ff. was delivered, or who its addressees were. A second prophecy is generally localized in Samaria, because the ladies of the court are the target (4.1–3).

A Listen [. . .] you cows of Bashan / on the mountain of Samaria,
exploiting the *dallīm* (the poor), / crushing the needy,
saying to your masters: / 'Bring that we may drink!'

B Sworn has Yahweh in his *qōdeš* (holy place? holiness?) . . .
They (he) will drag you away with ropes through your noses, / your back parts (your children?) with fish hooks.
You will be drawn out through the breaches . . . / [you will be cast forth] towards [Hermon].

A heedless, luxurious life led by an exploitative ruling class: this is the picture which Amos paints of the capital. He calls the elegant ladies 'cows' – cows of Bashan, which were a much valued breed of cattle at that time. Like replete cattle, they wilfully trample down their pastures, the lower classes of the people, on whom their existence in fact depends. Their fate will meet them on the same level. Foreign cattle-drivers, coarse butcher-boys, will drag them away with ropes through their noses and if necessary with hooks in their hindquarters. Perhaps the comparison is not the work of Amos' own outraged imagination. He may be mockingly picking up a cultic name the women gave themselves, since they imagined themselves to be the worshippers of the mighty bull of Samaria (Hos. 8.5f.), a North Israelite manifestation of Yahweh. Again Amos puts the relation between people and land in the foreground. The women will not be raped or killed, but they will be driven out of the land that nourishes them. (The Hermon lies to the north of the Israelite frontier.)

The liberty Amos takes here goes far beyond the bounds of what was usual prophetic behaviour at that time. If we want to make clear to ourselves how shocking it was, we have to imagine someone in London or Washington declaring at the top of his voice that the wives of the Prime Minister and the President and their Ministers are fat cows, wallowing in luxury at the cost of the taxpayer. God has solemnly sworn – and the speaker has heard this personally – that a foreign power will very soon carry off the cows in some degrading way, having first of all destroyed the city. Israelite society evidently put up with talk like this for a considerable time.

The husbands of the women attacked do not come off any better. In a 'woe' song (6.1–7), Amos lashes out at their revels at the banquet in which they celebrate Israel's status as the firstborn among the nations. Here he takes up a genre which was otherwise only used in a lament over the dead. Amos, that is to say, publishes the people's obituary in advance. Here, too, the inner logic points to deportation from the country, with the people as the first of others to be deported. In the very elaborately constructed 'stronghold' saying in 3.9–11, attention is concentrated on the splendid palaces of the rich in Samaria. Amos looks through the splendid façades into houses full of two sinister forces – violence and destruction. The shelter of home is part of the Hebrew view of the ties between a person and his land. The Israelite builds his own home on his own inherited land. There he lives with his family, or even his clan. In this criticism, too, Amos remains true to his *hā-'āreṣ* conception. Consequently it is logically consistent for him that the enemy should already have surrounded *hā-'āreṣ* and that the palaces should soon be easy prey because their power of resistance has been eroded from within.

The officially sanctioned injustice that takes place in the capital is continued in the provinces. According to the Israelite constitution, every enclosed township has communal autonomy. In the gateway of a township of this kind – i.e., in the portico behind the one gateway in the town walls – the free, adult men of the community assembled. They alone had legal status and were empowered to take part in cultic ceremonies and to bear arms. The communal village democracy had legal and administrative competence. It decided on questions of inheritance, and even pronounced judgment in the case of capital crimes. It probably also had the task of allotting to individual members of the community the taxes or compulsory labour which the state imposed on the local community. In case of war it called up its section for the army. It looked after the local hilltop sanctuary, which its members visited. In spite of this democratic constitution, influential families gained the upper hand, since it was they who were able to provide most members for the local council. It was a great temptation to use a majority vote to distribute taxes in such a way that families which were small and economically weak bore an undue burden. This led to Amos' rebuke in 5.11f.:

A This is the way things are: your plundering from the *dal* (poor man) / that you exact from him taxes in wheat.
You have built houses of stone blocks, /
B but you shall not dwell in them!
You have planted fruitful vineyards, /
you shall not drink their wine!
C For I have seen:
Many are your transgressions, / mighty your sins.
You who afflict the *ṣaddīq* ('the righteous') / accept wergeld, / turn aside the needy in the gate.

In the gate, too, there are particular taxation practices which have certain consequences. Wergeld means the payment of money as a compensation for murder or manslaughter – a practice which was rejected in Israel. Here Amos uses the term in a transferred sense. The ruthless sale of human beings into slavery for debts amounts to murder; the profit made out of it is as dirty as wergeld. What is gained in taxes from poverty-stricken fellow countrymen through extortion of this kind is invested in well-build houses and vineyards. Again, the affiliation between a person and the fruitful earth is also expressed in the house he lives in. What has been unjustly acquired will drive out its owners in the long run. The way the *dallīm* are ground down is also to the fore in the saying about the fraudulent weights, 8.4–8. The level of the reaction is clearly evident:

Shall not the earth tremble on this account, so that all have to wither who dwell on it?

4.3.2 What Amos says against the court, therefore, is true in a modified form of every township. A certain group, the *dallīm* or the needy (*'ebyōnīm*), are bent down (*hiṭṭā*, 2.7; 5.12; cf. 8.4) until they are ground into the earth. They are loyal to the community (*ṣaddīq*), and are devout or resigned to God's will (*'anaw*); but they are completely at the mercy of the greed of the mighty. Being bowed down means *losing their independent livelihood*. The injustice to which this group is subjected is at the heart of Amos' social criticism. What group is being humiliated in this way? Since taxes in grain, wine and other natural resources are exacted from them, these cannot be serfs – people without property. *Dallīm* means, rather, a socially distinct class of peasant farmers (II Kings 24.14). Amos is not lashing out at any specific crime, and he does not name any of the guilty. But what he says is not a general taking-to-task which bewails the lack of moral behaviour existing at every period. Amos is looking at critical social developments which were taking place in the Northern Kingdom in those particular years and which were compelling smallholders first of all to sell their little piece of ground with the house on it, and then perhaps even to fall into slavery for debt. Unfortunately we do not know any details about the economic circumstances of the time. The underlying reason for them will have lain in the Aramaean wars, which went on for over a hundred years, and which will have forced the state to enlist mercenaries and to compensate them with land. This will have led to an increase of large estates, whereas the smallholder class must have increasingly sunk into serfdom because of the growing burden of taxation.

Why is the prophet's God so indignant about these shifts in the social structure, presenting them as a great sin? Does this not presuppose that Amos belonged to the class affected? Old Testament scholars have in fact often drawn a romantic picture of the poverty-stricken Amos, to whom God gave a voice so that he could maintain the justifiable interests of his fellow-sufferers, in the face of a merciless upper class. But the explanation is hardly a tenable one. What speaks against it is not only the 'professional' description of Amos as *nōqēd* (1.1: possessor of herds?), which is otherwise only used for a foreign king (II Kings 3.4), but Amos' familiarity with the world-picture of the time (which emerges from the visions) and his precise knowledge of the constitutions and political conditions in all the surrounding nations, presupposes that he had studied the wisdom of the time. This would have required an education which would certainly not have been available to a poor shepherd or peasant farmer. The same factors also tell against another common explanation, according to which Amos was an unspoilt country child who had been stunned by the capital and appalled at the dissipated luxury there. However, it was not luxury as such that shocked the prophet, but the way it was financed.

But what then *was* the offence that makes comprehensible a criticism of ruling circles so radical that their downfall was inescapably imminent? Why was the class of peasant farmers to be kept independent at all costs? Among all the possibilities that have been discussed, Alt's suggestion is the most convincing – that Amos had in mind a particular *constitutional ideal*: that equal rights of participation in the actual soil of the promised land belonged to Israel, with all its members, as the people of Yahweh. This view was an old one. In the Yahwistic history it was already the starting point from which the promise to the patriarchs about the growth of the nation and the gift of the land (Gen. 12.1–3; 15) became positively the driving force of salvation history. In the case of the Northern prophet Elijah, it probably played a part in making the theft of Naboth's vineyard of such momentous importance that the royal house was brought down because of it (I Kings 21). Where – as was widespread in Amos' time – numerous countrymen lost the land they had inherited, the 'ruin' of Joseph (6.6f.) was already in progress, and deportation was an inescapable result.

Perhaps we may even go a step further. Was the land issue connected with fixed ideas about the significance of cultic places? The fruitful earth had its 'centre' in the temple at Bethel; this emerges from the visionary descriptions which are connected with this (7.7–9; 8.1–3; 9.1–4). What took place there spread out like ripples over the whole area. It is therefore hardly by chance that the social criticism often culminates in the accusation that holy places and seasons are being violated in the course of these outrages. The indication of the situation in 2.6ff. ends by bewailing three times the fact that sanctuary, altar and house of God are touched by the aura of sin. In the prophecy against the fine ladies of the court, Yahweh swears by his *qōdeš* (4.1–3; this is followed immediately by a saying about the pilgrimage to the place of worship, (4.4f.): i.e., it presupposes a religious, ceremonial context). The lament about the spendthrift behaviour of the firstborn of the peoples was probably sung at a cultic ceremony (6.1–7). In the saying about the fraudulent scales, it is stressed that the sacred seasons, the new moon and the sabbath, are touched by the outrage. It therefore seems as if the offence is never so grave as when it touches the sphere of the holy, and that it is therefore there, at the house of God, that the doom also begins, then spreading out to cover secular spheres of life.

However, in supposing that Amos' social criticism is connected with a religious attitude to the land, I am at variance with most of my fellow scholars, who set Amos firmly apart from any kind of piety connected with the cult. They appeal here to the criticism of the cult which he himself made. What is the substance of this criticism?

4.4 Criticism of the cult and the search for God

1. In three or four sayings the prophet condemns the religious places and ceremonies of his people (to the delight of certain Protestant commentators and to the embarrassment of Catholics). But criticism

of religious practices and criticism of social conditions are not on the same level. Whereas Amos uses the genre of prophecy for the latter, religious criticism is expressed more seldom, and then through texts that are priestly in character.

When a sacrifice was offered at an Israelite sanctuary, the priest usually provided a declamatory formula. This generally declared the act to be 'well pleasing to God' and only exceptionally as 'Yahweh's abhorrence'. Amos dares to express a wholesale rejection of cultic offerings in Yahweh's name (5.21ff.):

> I hate, I despise your feasts . . .
> I have no pleasure in your food offerings, / I will not look upon the saving offering (?) of your fatted beasts.

Where social criticism is in question, the divine displeasure is never as emphatic as this. Attending divine worship seems to be worse than questionable practices in dealings with the peasant farmers! If we remember that Israel's pre-exilic religion was a cultic one, and knew no stronger assurance of divine existence and activity on behalf of men and women than the celebration of religious feasts; and if we remember, too, that the earliest commandments of Yahwistic religion categorically require participation in these festivals (Ex. 34.18ff.), then it is easy to imagine that when Amos' listeners heard these words a cold shudder ran down their spines. At the beginning of a festival, a priest called upon the pilgrims to perform sacred actions. He did this by means of a *tōrāh* – an instruction about sacred matters – using words such as: 'Go into Bethel, / bring your sacrificial offerings in the morning.' Amos imitates sentences like this (though probably not in the context of an actual cultic occasion); but he adds sarcastically: 'in order (through which) to perform *peša*ʿ' (sacrilegious rebellion, 4.4f.), meaning the worst of all possible misdemeanours. The imitation must have seemed pure mockery, as blasphemous as if we were to use a parody of a verse in the Bible in order to criticize religion. Another *tōrāh* which ran, 'Seek Yahweh and ye shall live, / seek Bethel' was remodelled by Amos no less provocatively (5.4–6):

> Verily, so had Yahweh spoken to the house of Israel:
> Seek me that you may live, / but Bethel you shall not seek.
> Do not enter Gilgal / or cross over to Beer-sheba.
> Verily, Gilgal shall surely become *gōlā* ('exiled'), / Bethel *'āwen* ('naught').
> Seek Yahweh, that you may live, / lest he break out like fire,
> [It will have to devour] the house of Joseph, / none shall quench Bethel,

since there they turn *mišpāṭ* ('justice') to wormwood / and cast down *ṣᵉdāqā* ('righteousness') to the earth.

Again the sanctuaries of Bethel and Gilgal are named in horrifying terms, and Beersheba – which lay beyond the frontier – is added. Amos' listeners believe that they will find Yahweh and life there. In Bethel Jacob once heard a divine voice: 'The land on which you lie I will give to you and to your descendants' (Gen. 28.13). At that very place Jeroboam I set up a cult for the God who 'led up Israel out of the land of Egypt' (I Kings 12.28). 'Leading up' is a word indicating possession of the land of other people, as Amos himself stresses in 2.10. Gilgal was the first stage in the promised land, the beginning of the consummation of salvation history in the early period. It was there that Joshua gave the word of Yahweh to his people: 'A living God is among you, he will without fail drive out the Canaanites for your sake', and other nations as well (Josh. 3.10). Traditions like these, passed down from the primal period – traditions which helped to found the nation – were probably recollected, brought home to the people and given new force in the ceremonies which enraged Amos. Because of this link with salvation history, the places Bethel and Gilgal were more important than Samaria and Dan. There was nowhere in the Northern Kingdom where time-hallowed Yahweh worship could be better experienced. Here it was possible to obey the apodictic commandments of the ancient divine law, to appear three times a year before the face of God (Ex. 34.23). Yet it is precisely these places which Amos declared were the breeding places of sacrilege. A perverted sense of religion is to be found at the very places where the occupation of the promised land and the exodus are celebrated. What Amos attacks are not idolatrous cultic practices, or the number of altars everywhere in the country – as his contemporary Hosea does. The objects of his polemic are practices which, in the opinion of his listeners, were absolutely enjoined by Yahweh on every Israelite, like services in a cathedral, or mass in St Peter's! His listeners sought Bethel that they might live, expecting their physical existence (*ḥayīm*) to be revitalized there, probably especially through the sacrament of the sacrificial feast (*zebaḥ*, 4.4; *šelem*, 5.22). Added to this was the strengthening of their faith – the faith that Israel would never again lose this land into which Yahweh had once led them. 'Yahweh is with us' (5.14) was the formula coined for this. Amos turns this assurance upside down. Gilgal, once the pivot-point of the occupation of the promised land, becomes the beginning of *gōlā*, the stripping of the country through deportation. Bethel which – as its name suggests – was a house filled with El, with divine 'atmosphere', becomes the place which is the source of suppurating disaster (*'āwen*). Anyone who continues to go there not only acts falsely but will be affected by the forces of doom which are rampant there.

What forces Amos to bring down the pillars of traditional religion? His religious criticism is less easy to explain than his criticism of social conditions. Because of what he says about the exploitation of the peasant farmers, one would like to conclude that Amos attacked the sacrificial meals and the sanctuaries especially because there the indulgent luxury of the rich was at the expense of the poor man (cf. 6.1–7, where an extravagant cultic celebration in Samaria is probably being castigated). But if this were the decisive point, then it is not clear why the genre of prophecy is not used here too, and why no reference is made to the different treatment accorded to the *dallīm*, or the exploitation of the weak (as in 4.2).

2. In addition Amos hints at an alternative: a sincere search for Yahweh. What does this mean?

(i) Another saying of Amos' is often drawn upon for an explanation (5.14f.):

Seek good (a good person?) and not evil (an evil person?) / that you
may live and permanence (?) may come about.
Yahweh will (then) be with you – / as you like to say.
Hate evil (an evil person), love good (a good person), / so that you
set up *mišpāṭ* ('justice') in the gate.
It may be that Yahweh Sabaoth / will have mercy on a remnant of
Joseph.

If we compare both *tōrāh* sayings, can the search for Yahweh mean anything other than living as an upright person in society? Many scholars therefore see Amos and his prophetic followers as mighty reformers, who reject outward worship and religion in its cultic form. According to this view, God can be truly found only in social action, without hymns, sacrifice and incense. Amos seems to reject, not merely false religion, but organized religion in general. He sets himself apart from the God of Israel whom the people worship in the cult, calling him 'your' God (2.8; 5.26; 8.14). Amos seems already to guess that, as modern theologians suppose, God is only a cipher for co-humanity.

In recent years, however, our increased knowledge about the way Hebrew thinking is embedded in the context of ancient oriental civilizations has made a growing number of scholars doubt whether a person belonging to the ancient world in the era before Christ could have thought in terms of a purely moral relation to God, or could have conceived of a purely inward fellowship with him, without cult and sanctuary. Is it permissible to interpret the first saying (5.4–6) solely in the light of the second (5.14f.)? Moreover, the phrase 'seek Yahweh' is otherwise used for the pilgrimage to the sanctuary (in the Psalms 'those who seek him' are fellow-worshippers); or it may be used for the question a prophet puts to God.

(ii) Consequently some commentators suppose that Amos is pointing to himself as the source of information about appropriate behaviour towards God. This would of course also mean that Amos was assigning himself the role of exclusive mediator in dealing with Yahweh. Does he really mean to go as far as this?

(iii) In the light of the other meaning of the phrase (pilgrimage to the sanctuary), some commentators imagine that Amos thinks that another sanctuary is the only legitimate one, and not those he names. With things as they were this could only have been Jerusalem; for it is noticeable that Jerusalem is not condemned like Beersheba, which lies much further to the south, and was probably less frequented. (Later, under the Deuteronomic reform, Jerusalem was made the only legitimate cultic centre for Yahwistic religion.) But how was a North Israelite listener supposed to associate the call 'seek Yahweh' with Jerusalem, without any further explanation?

(iv) Amos probably did not see things as simply as his interpreters.

(*a*) His attacks were concentrated on Gilgal and Bethel (the attack on the cult in 5.21ff. was probably directed towards Gilgal and Bethel, too, in view of the procession to the cultic 'house of the kingdom' mentioned in v. 26; cf. 7.12). Ritual practices in Samaria (6.1–7), Beersheba (also 8.14) and Dan (8.14) are rejected with less acrimony, and clearly come after the others in importance.

(*b*) What Amos condemned were almost exclusively sacrificial feasts and the acts associated with them (tithes, songs of jubilation), but not general intrigues by the priests there (though these practices are attacked in the case of the upper classes in Samaria) or a degenerate idea of God (even though the God of Bethel shows himself accompanied by the image of a bull).

(*c*) Above all, for Amos Yahweh's actions have a decisive connection with these particular places. We must look at this more closely. When Bethel becomes *'āwen* and a source of doom, it represents more than one place among others in the country. When it is described as the centre of the land (7.8, 10), this is not merely a conventional phrase; more is probably behind it than that. For in Bethel Yahweh stands beside the altar and unleashes fearful billows of disaster over the land (9.1ff.; cf. 3.14). When Yahweh swears by his *qōdeš* (4.2), we may presume that the reference is to a holiness that dwells on earth, given the parallel with the pride (*gā'ōn*) of Jacob, by which Yahweh also swears yet which he is nonetheless prepared to condemn to a horrible fate (8.7; 6.8). In his petition in the very first vision, Amos knows only one way out: to pray for *sālaḥ* (7.2). In the Old Testament this means cultic atonement. So it is quite improbable that Amos views the cultic places as being anywhere at all on earth, just as it is equally improbable that he should deny the force and efficacy of every form of cultic activity.

Could it be – though this is a theory to be propounded with great caution – that the search for Yahweh which Amos demands is meant in an entirely cultic sense? In that case it is not a feast of jubilation but a rite of repentance, which could be carried out anywhere and which did not require the splendour of the ceremonies in Bethel and Gilgal. A rite of repentance (*ṣōm*) was an unusual ceremony. The people appeared before God with gestures of self-humiliation – torn clothes, ashes in their hair, general hymns of lament – in order to hear (if possible from a prophet's lips) an oracle showing that their prayers had been heard, or that some collective doom had – or had not – been averted. The prayer 'restore us' (Ps. 80.19) belongs to this context. In Amos the search for God is bound up with the same aim. And his contemporary, Isaiah, puts the search for Yahweh parallel to 'turning to him' (*šūb 'ad*, 9.12; about the Northern Kingdom). A pre-exilic Israelite was probably unable to conceive of repentance like this without some external rite. Here Amos admittedly avoids the lofty word 'repentance'. Where he uses it in another passage (4.6ff.), it indicates a possibility that had once existed but has now been thrown away. Of course such a search for Yahweh, if it was to be sincere, was linked with a new attitude to social behaviour in relations between people. Consequently part of it, but not all, was to seek the good within the community relationships established by Yahweh.

Admittedly, an interpretation of this kind is hypothetical. We lack the historical and semantic knowledge which would be required for a complete understanding of the background to Amos' criticism of religious practices. According to the context, 5.4–6.14f. could also point to alternatives which had once been valid but were now superseded.

3. But how is the vehement attack on the sacrificial feasts in Bethel and Gilgal connected with Amos' social criticism? The squandering of extorted goods is only intended to be one point among many; for when all is said and done, the *dallīm* also made pilgrimages to these sanctuaries. The essential point is rather that it is precisely these cultic places which, in the Israelite view, were connected with the gift of the land which Yahweh promised to the patriarchs in days of old, implementing his promise through the events of salvation history.

But, as we have seen, the inherited land is central to the remarks about the situation of the *dallīm*; it is the condition that makes a free life possible. To this degree Amos has an especial interest in attacking the festivals connected with the settlement. And it was logical for him that the all-embracing doom should take its course from these places. For his assertion of the total reversal of *mišpāṭ* and *ṣᵉdāqā* (which is the sum of his reproaches against his contemporaries) is ultimately anchored in cultic criticism. This passage shows more clearly than any other how, despite all his attacks on institutional worship, Amos remains, and intends to remain, within the context of a cultic view of the world. In saying this, however, I am adopting a different opinion from most other scholars, who usually draw quite different conclusions from the exhortation to seek Yahweh.

4.5 Mišpāṭ *and* ṣᵉdāqā. *Their reversal, and* pešaʿ

4.5.1 The saying about the true and false search for Yahweh in 5.4–7 ends with the reproach that the house of Joseph and Bethel are together transforming *mišpāṭ* into bitterness (wormwood) and have cast *ṣᵉdāqā* down to the earth. Two factors are named here which are apparently of the highest importance for both Amos and his hearers. And in fact they provided him with *the link between social criticism and criticism of the cult.* The background is a Hebrew ontology which he assumed to exist among his hearers and which he also shared himself. The paired concepts turn up in another prophecy which is also probably motivated by criticism of the cult (6.12–14):

A Do horses trot over rocks? / Or does anyone plough [the sea with oxen]?
That you should turn *mišpaṭ* into poison / and the fruit of *ṣᵉdāqā* into wormwood?
You who rejoice over Lo-Dabar? . . .
You, who say: Have we not by our own strength / conquered Karnaim?
B Behold, I will raise up against you / a foreign people . . .

They are celebrating victories over the Aramaeans, the Syrian enemy who had been feared for decades. Israelite territory had been extended far north-east of Lake Gennesaret. The triumph of the politically and economically successful years of Jeroboam II echoes from the words which Amos puts into his opponents' mouth. The cultic festival of victory (*śmḥ*) probably took place in Bethel, 'the house of the kingdom'. But Amos is not impressed by the conquest. He states bitterly that in this campaign *mišpāṭ* and *ṣᵉdāqā* have been reversed

– i.e. destroyed. He does not say why. Had special taxes been levied for the campaign, which had fallen particularly heavily on the *dallīm*? Or had the peasant farmers been press-ganged into military service and forced to pay a high toll in blood?

The paired concepts turn up a third time (5.23–27) in the continuation of the negative divine response to cultic offerings in 5.21f.:

A Take away from me the noise of your (festal) songs! / To the melody of your lutes I will not listen.
Then *mišpāṭ* ('justice') would flood down like water / and *ṣᵉdāqā* ('righteousness') like an ever-flowing stream.
Did you have to bring me common sacrifices and food offerings / the forty years in the wilderness?
B So you must (in the future?) carry (away?) the [festal booths] of your king / and [Kewan] the star of your God.
I have to deport you from here to Damascus . . .

Only when the extravagant and now meaningless feasts have been ended can the people expect *mišpāṭ* and *ṣᵉdāqā* again. All the same, Amos can conceive that such a new event might be possible, as a positive alternative to the present, in line with what is to be expected from the search for Yahweh (5.6).

The paired concepts therefore represent the highest values of human behaviour and the human condition; and Amos can only declare that they are totally lacking at the present time. Because these values have been lost, Yahweh is incensed against Bethel and Joseph, and sends an occupying power into the country. So great is Yahweh's displeasure that he gives over to destruction the only people whom he had ever recognized in history – the people who then in its turn knew Yahweh. For a religion of the ancient world this was an inconceivable procedure. Which God did not have an elemental interest in preserving the group of his worshippers? Amos' God emancipates himself from men and women and from their ritual worship.

4.5.2 Up to now when I have translated the two terms *mišpāṭ* and *ṣᵉdāqā* I have used the most usual meanings.

A. The words are always translated as 'justice' and 'righteousness'. Nineteenth-century scholars therefore saw the stress on justice and righteousness as now representing the highest values for man and for God, as a mighty religious revolution: Amos and the prophets who succeeded him broke through the barriers of what Israel had hitherto accepted as a national religion, a religion of election. God now became the strict custodian of a non-party, supra-national righteousness. We may quote the great Wellhausen:

> This is the so-called ethical monotheism of the prophets. They believe in the moral order of the world; they believe in the validity of righteousness as being without exception the supreme law for the whole world. From this point of view Israel's prerogative now seems to become null and void.[12]

But although the evidence for this view makes such a consistent and well-founded impression, there is a difficulty about it. It stands or falls by the accuracy of the translation, and involves giving the concepts of justice and righteousness a content deriving from the theological and philosophical tradition of the West.

B. The context and the meaning of the words themselves point in another direction. Research into these two concepts (which are central not only to Amos' anthropology and ontology, but to the anthropology and ontology of the whole of the Old Testament) is still in a state of flux. But in my view certain points about the pre-exilic view have already crystallized out, making it possible for us to understand Amos' dispute with his listeners.

1. It is already noticeable that the phrase is used in the context of *the cult*, and not in connection with social criticism (cf. the way in which Amos' contemporary Hosea uses it in connection with the cult, 2.20f.; 10.12f.).

2. Both *mišpāṭ* and *ṣ*ᵉ*dāqā* appear as spheres of power which already exist in advance of human actions. In 6.12 they are compared with draught animals, productive powers which a person needs in order to live. They are destroyed through misuse and turn into their opposites – poisons with a sinister effect (cf. also Hos. 10.4).

3. When we look at them more closely they resemble a *fluid*. They pour out healingly like a river over the people (5.24) when the objectionable religious practices end; otherwise they turn into a bitter liquid. The river comes from above. It is Yahweh who makes it 'rain' *ṣ*ᵉ*dāqā* (Hos. 10.12; Joel 2.23).

4. Amos' listeners expect their participation in the sacred festival to give them strength for living, in the form of *mišpāṭ* and *ṣ*ᵉ*dāqā*. How? In the pre-exilic period the sacrificial offerings and communal offerings (*zebaḥ*) eaten at the sacrificial meal were probably understood as a sacrament which allowed the power for *ṣ*ᵉ*dāqā* to flow over from God to men (Deut. 33.19; Ps. 4.6; 51.21; cf. 24.5). The two powers did not enter into men and women like a scholastic *gratia infusa* but became the invisible auras which accompanied participants in the ritual into everyday life. The Israelite did not *possess* righteousness; he was *in ṣ*ᵉ*dāqā*. It is still not clear to us how far other observances brought about a transference of this kind. According to 5.26 we have to assume

that even a procession with the picture of Saturn belonged within this context; for in Babylonian its name, Kewan, means the 'steadfast' star, which serves as the guarantee of righteousness on earth and as the star of kings, through whose power they communicated righteousness to ordinary men and women.

5. Of course the precious gift had to be employed in inter-personal relations. It communicated the capacity for moral action: the capacity to use the *mišpāṭ* and *ṣᵉdāqā* received at the feast in order to act in faithfulness to the community, as the wife still does even towards her dead husband (Gen. 38.26) or the officer towards his king and vice versa (I Sam. 24.18). *Mišpāṭ* must continually be established anew in the gate of the city, says Amos (5.15). *Mišpāṭ* means, rather, the institutional order, the intact but dynamic form of community, its specific characteristics and actions, the positive order of existence *per se*. *Ṣᵉdāqā* means the spontaneous act in favour of an ordinance of *mišpāṭ* – in the individual case it may be in favour of a neighbouring clan or place or a fellow-countryman. A person has to 'plough under' the *ṣᵉdāqā* given to him through what he does (6.12; cf. Hos. 10.12). He will then reap the harvest of a successful and harmonious life in the framework of the very society which he upholds. What the cult gives therefore makes moral 'causality' possible. For Amos, of course, the *ṣaddīq* who lives in conformity with the order of the community is now to be found only in the lower strata of society (2.6; 5.12). But he is prevented from reaping the harvest of what he does, which is why *mišpāṭ* no longer exists in the land.

6. The efficacious auras of *mišpāṭ* and *ṣᵉdāqā* not only surround the individual agent but also radiate out to the whole land, creating harmony between *society and nature* (Ps. 72.1–3; Joel 2.21–23). The reversal which turns *mišpāṭ* into the bitterness of wormwood destroys the environment, making fields unfruitful (Hos. 10.4).

7. When the two spheres of activity are bound up with the place of worship (with Bethel, cf. also Hos. 10.4f., or with Gilgal, Micah 6.5), we have to suppose (in accordance with the ideological thinking of the Israelite cult) that this is legitimated through a 'founding' tradition, which anchors them firmly in salvation history. And there are in fact indications outside the Book of Amos that *mišpāṭ* and *ṣᵉdāqā* were first transferred to the people in the context of the goal of salvation history – the giving of the land to Israel (Hos. 12.5, 7; cf. 2.21ff.). For example, after the first of the tribes, the tribe of Gad, had taken possession of its inheritance, it began to create Yahweh's *ṣᵉdāqā* and *mišpāṭ* for other people (Deut. 33.21). That is to say, it received these things at the same time as it received its share in the land. So the gift of the land included more than the bestowal of fruitful agricultural

country for productive purposes. It also meant the transference of powers which then made possible truly moral action in the community.

8. Since in the period of the monarchy the social order depended on the king, *mišpāṭ* and *ṣ*ᵉ*dāqā* were especially associated with him (cf. I Kings 10.9; Jer. 23.5). *The king* became the intermediary between God's *ṣ*ᵉ*dāqā* and *mišpāṭ* on the one hand, and the *ṣ*ᵉ*dāqā* and *mišpāṭ* of the people on the other; and this viewpoint makes it clear why the monarchy and the court play so central a role in Amos.

9. *Mišpāṭ* and *ṣ*ᵉ*dāqā* were therefore spheres of activity and not abstract concepts like their English equivalents, justice and righteousness. This can be supported by historical linguistic and religious parallels. In Canaanite religion, *ṣedeq* and *mišōr* (also used for *mišpāṭ* in Isa. 11.4) were gods. But they were not self-contained, individual figures. They were active forces which a person adopted and made his own, and in which he realized himself. When Israel took over the language of Canaan, it rejected the ritual veneration of forces of this kind and gave them a new function as Yahweh's active powers. But since Israel went on using Canaanite words which carried this significance, it was unable to turn living deities into mere abstract concepts simply from one day to the next.

To view moral forces as powers which transcend individual experience seems strange to the modern reader. The notion generally accepted with us assumes that by nature every individual has the opportunity to act well and rightly if only he follows the innate call of his conscience. But is a presupposition of this kind any more open to proof than continual mediation through the cult? For the Hebrew, what was moral was not self-evident. It required the right 'atmosphere', from which alone correct action issued and prospered. In the enthusiasm of the feast, sharers in the ritual experienced the presence of God and recognized one another as brothers. This aroused a sense of the solidarity between all Israelites, a consciousness of community, not only between God and man but between man and nature. It was an awareness that probably cannot be achieved today by even the most careful teaching. It is entirely understandable that an experience of this kind was enormously effective. Those who shared in the ritual took home with them a conviction of being endowed anew with faithfulness to the community. If they thought about it afterwards it must almost inevitably have been along the lines I have described, in view of the structures of meaning underlying ancient Hebrew as a language.

4.5.3. So much for Israelite thought in general. Let us return to Amos. It is no less understandable that the rapture of enthusiasm at the sacrificial feast was not always sufficient to do away with exploitation and fraud in everyday life afterwards. Amos makes this his starting point and brings out the deficiency with a clarity which leaves nothing to be desired. The religion of these people does not achieve what it claims to do. Amos' conclusion is paradoxical. It is only after the sacrificial feasts have been abolished that God will let the stream of his *mišpāṭ* and *ṣᵉdāqā* flow once more. This is corroborated by salvation history. In the early period, there were forty years in the wilderness without any sacrificial feasts; yet the people felt bound closely together, with one another and with God. Is Amos denying sacramental power? Unfortunately the way in which he conceives of this new flow of active forces is not clear. Does he associate it with the search for Yahweh through fasting and lamentation (5.4ff.; cf. Hos. 10.12)? That is to say, with a different kind of encounter with God and with different religious practices? From now on is it perhaps the force of the prophetic word alone which is capable of promising, and therefore, evoking, *mišpāṭ* and *ṣᵉdāqā*?

One observation may serve as a warning against separating Amos totally from his ties with the cult. In the 'palace' saying in 3.10 he reduces his description of exploitation and oppression to the single, common denominator: 'They do not know how to do *nᵉkōnā* (the right)'. The Hebrew means 'what has been permanently founded or established'. Where did this foundation take place? In its various forms and derivations the word is frequently associated with *mišpāṭ* and *ṣᵉdāqā*. Yahweh establishes (*kūn*) the power to act uprightly through his theophany at the feast; this is what Psalm 99.4 praises. Both God's throne and the king's are 'steadfastly founded' on these two forces (Ps. 97.2 and frequently elsewhere). The same root underlies the name of the constellation Kewan, which the Israelites carried round in order to fortify the steadfast power of their king's *ṣᵉdāqā* (5.26). According to this, Amos certainly assumes that what he is attacking has a religious foundation in the cult. However, these things are not realizing their potential, not turning their possibilities into realities. They are sufficiently surrounded by the forces of *mišpāṭ* and *ṣᵉdāqā*, but they are simply not using them.

Instead, what Israel is producing is *pešaʿ*, which is the term Amos uses to sum up the people's transgressions. This is not a term for sin. It is rather an expression deriving from the political sphere, where it is used to describe revolt against legitimate rulers (I Kings 12.19; II Kings 8.20). *Pešaʿ*, too, is not an abstract term; it is a negative sphere arising from an unjust rebellion. In Amos' view, the rebellion against God is taking place at precisely the point where the people allegedly pay homage to their God and recognize his rule – at the cultic sanctuary. Like the reversal of *mišpāṭ* and *ṣ'dāqā*, the rebellion is bound up with Bethel and Gilgal (4.4f.), thence to spread to the gates of the local community (5.12). At the very altar where the smell of the burnt offerings is supposed to rise to Yahweh as a pleasant fragrance, the aura of continued rebellion against God, now objective, is found in concentrated form. The people is as it were bringing its stinking, poisonous cloud to the sanctuary, and so the abomination accumulates there, because this is the place where the whole of Israel is gathered together. *Pesa'*, the content of the main charge, belongs to the sector of 'constitutional law'; but underlying it is the ontological trinity of God, country and people. Through his history of salvation, God has acquired the land for Israel; but in such a way that he continues to be bound up with the forces of the land itself. Every Israelite peasant who makes a living for himself and his family from his ties with the soil, so acquiring freedom of action, will only retain that freedom as long as he respects the fact that this soil is his thanks to God and salvation history. But this also means respecting his fellow-countryman on the land which God has granted to *his* particular kindred. Attacking the laws of the land, dispossessing the *dallīm*, means rising against the Almighty and the order he has created through salvation history; and it is this order alone which provides the conditions and possibilities for a successful and harmonious life. *Pesa'* therefore does not only mean rebellion against the Almighty. It is at the same time a stupid demolition of the foundation of one's own life.

4.6 The downfall of state and religion. Visitation on the day of Yahweh

4.6.1 The thinking of the literary prophets is like an ellipse. The intolerable present situation provides one focus; the other is the future event that surpasses everything that has existed hitherto. The elliptical way of thinking is in line with the genre of prophecy, since it cleanly divides the indication of situation (the upbraiding or exhortation, A) from the prediction or foretelling of the future (B). In Amos, as we have seen, the section about the present – i.e., the first focus – circles round social and cultic criticism as well as round *mišpāṭ* and *ṣ'dāqā*, as active powers which cover both sectors. How does Amos express himself in his statements about the future? What connecting lines does he see between A and B?

What he says about the future is concentrated on a point which he calls *the day of Yahweh* (*yōm yahweh*). The song of lament in 5.18ff. begins:

> Woe to you who desire / the day of Yahweh!
> What shall this be to you [. . .]? / It is darkness and not light.

The prophet is picking up an idea which is important for his listeners. They can hardly wait for the special day of Yahweh to dawn. They are hoping for light, salvation, victory over the neighbouring peoples – in short, a turn of events which will far surpass the present peaceful conditions under Jeroboam II. The origin of the phrase 'the day of Yahweh' is disputed. Von Rad would like to derive it from an ancient term for the holy wars of the time before Israel became a nation, concluding from this that Yahweh will come with a holy war. Mowinckel sees it as a name for the great New Year festival in the autumn, and interprets Amos as meaning that a New Year Festival of vast dimensions is imminent. Whatever the origin of the term, by Amos' time it had become the important expression of a popular eschatology which hoped for a better future for Israel through a visible victory by Yahweh on that particular day in history. Amos agrees that a day is imminent when God will appear in power. But he reverses the obvious conclusions: on that day Yahweh will not bring salvation to the people who are so specially bound to him, but utter disaster, darkness and death. It is only in this one passage that Amos talks about the day of Yahweh. But we shall not be far wrong if we see his announcements of doom as all converging on this decisive point in time. We are not, of course, supposed to understand the day of Yahweh in the sense of a day lasting twenty-four hours. Amos means a certain period of concentrated divine activity, in which God will emerge from the inscrutability of his work.

4.6.2 What is impending involves the movement of history on at least four levels. Present and future are linked on each of them. The ***highest, divine*** level must be mentioned first of all. For this, Amos employs personal, anthropopathic categories. His prophecies almost all begin with a sentence about a direct resolve or an action on God's part (cf. already 'I will not revoke it', 1.3ff.). On this personal divine level word is given that a 'visitation' is being prepared (3.2; 3.13f.). In English, 'visitation' is a cloudy word, but its Hebrew equivalent, *pāqad*, has a quite precise meaning. *Pāqad* describes the personal inspection by a superior, of his subordinates, with all the consequences arising from it. Yahweh appears as the eternal, primal ground of life for men and women. But when he approaches, spheres of operation in the earthly partner involved are activated. When Yahweh visits the faithful Sarah, the barren woman becomes a mother (Gen. 21.1). But if, when he approaches, Yahweh comes up against a people burdened with *pešaʿ*, he is lit up by a consuming fire (5.6). He can then no longer pass by indulgently (7.8; 8.2). In an encounter of this kind, Yahweh reacts against the auras of wickedness he perceives in his counterpart (9.4, 8).

> Therefore thus will I do to you, O Israel / because you yourself have done it [to yourself] before (4.12).

So this is what visitation on the day of Yahweh means: God's activity prevails over all superficial, inner-worldly causality. Amos' prophecies almost always begin with a statement about a direct divine action or resolve of this kind (e.g., 'I will not revoke it', 1.3ff.).

4.6.3 But God does not strike men and women directly. He does not encounter even Israel in merely personal terms. Every prophecy of Amos', after pointing to God as first cause, discusses the instrument that implements his will. For his visitation, God uses underlying forces which form *a second level*, a level of *efficacious powers*. The earth, the soil, is one of these: 'Shall not *hā-āreṣ* (the land) rise up on this account (the Israelite transgression), like an arm of the Nile?' asks 8.8. The defeat of the troops will be preceded by a shaking 'beneath you' (2.13; for the passage cf. pp. 44f.). Opposing armies are not named at all. When the book was put together, the statements about the reaction of the earth were taken literally and thought to be fulfilled in an earthquake which took place two years later (1.1). But perhaps Amos was only thinking of the earth as being active in a deeper sense. This is at least true, in other passages, of the independently raging sword (7.9, 11; 9.1, 4, 10; cf. 4.10) or the blazing fire (7.4ff.; 1.3ff.). So for Amos, a second level of mythologically efficacious powers seems to underlie the first level, which is directly assigned to God. This second level, too, will be set in motion on the day of Yahweh.

4.6.4 But on a third level events take place which affect the human subject himself. *Human spheres of activity*, which still veil the agents concerned, are full of importance for the future; for on the day of Yahweh they will be transformed into visible destiny. Then the harvest will come for the *'am*, the deeds of the people who act irresponsibly will come to fruition within those people themselves, and will mean death for them (8.2f.). Their shameful striving for gain will then descend on their own heads and destroy them (9.1). The palaces, which are impregnated with acts of violence, will become the easy prey of violent attacks (3.11; cf. 5.11). The Israelites will be bowed down to the ground through the weight of their own acts which, the Hebrew imagined, cast invisible auras round the head of the agent. Because they lack the auras conferred by good deeds, they cannot get up again – that is to say, they cannot find their way back to life and activity (8.14; 5.2; 7.2, 5). It is this *level of moral causality* given through the connection between action and outcome – between what one does and what happens to one in life – which more than anything else links together the first focus of Amos' thinking – criticism of the present – with the second focus – statements about the future.

4.6.5 Finally, there is an *evident, realistic* level. Here Amos sees military operations taking place. The Israelite army, with all its different branches, will be defeated (2.3ff.; 5.2). Samaria will be captured. Breaches will be made in the walls. The palaces will be plundered. Hardly anyone will be left alive (3.11; 4.3; 6.8f.). Outside in the country, too, there will be bodies and laments for the dead everywhere (5.16f.). The upper classes will be deported in the direction of Hermon and Damascus (4.3; 5.27; 6.7). Afterwards the country will be occupied and oppressed from north to south by a foreign nation (6.14). In each saying, one particular point in these events is spotlighted. Yet it all dovetails perfectly. The chief priest therefore puts together everything that Amos says about the future on the political and military levels, and reports that he has announced the king's death and the deportation of the people.

4.6.6 The doom that is to descend on the people is therefore being prepared on four levels – one above the other, or one behind the other. Unfortunately the aphoristic sayings do not show exactly how the levels interlock for Amos. Consequently some things may seem contradictory to us which were not so for the prophet himself. Locality is a case in point. Seen from the first level, the deadly stroke on the day of Yahweh falls on the centre of the country, Bethel, the place of Yahweh's visitation, where he will appear in bodily form (3.14; 5.6; 9.1). From here the disaster spreads out in ripples, affecting first kings and court and palaces; then the other sanctuaries in the country; and only finally the mass of the people, the *'am*, to the point when they are actually deported. On the military and political level, on the other hand, the starting point is outside the country. Amos probably sees the enemy as approaching from the north – the enemy which destroys the Israelite state with military force. When the perspective shifts, differences about the extent of the catastrophe emerge too. Seen from the divine and personal level, Israel will disappear as an independent power. On the lowest level, this by no means signifies that everybody in the country will be exterminated.

The prophet does not therefore proclaim a wholesale divine judgment, taking more or less fortuitous images to make his point. What he has in mind when he painstakingly formulates his prophecies is the complex structure of a 'universal moral order'. Although the extent of the catastrophe has actually been revealed to him in a kind of second sight, he is none the less able, in a process of subsequent insight, to grasp what is imminent, why, and what its effect will be. How far any nabi before Amos thought in this differentiated way, we do not know. But at all events Amos is distinguished from his forerunners, if only because for him the damage can no longer be undone by replacing one dynasty with another. This is ruin which can no longer be dealt with in terms of domestic politics, either through reform or revolution. So a fearful day of Yahweh has to come upon Israel.

4.7 The downfall of neighbouring nations and the historical fulfilment of the prophecies

4.7.1 When Yahweh wants to bring to an end the wickedness of Israel, which has meanwhile developed into dense spheres of disaster over the country, his prophet does not think of the most obvious tool, the dangerous Syrian enemy, the Aramaeans, though this was the conclusion drawn by many a nabi before him, Elijah included. The wide scope of Amos' thinking is shown by the series of oracles about the nations at the beginning of his book. It is impossible to prove conclusively that they derive from Amos himself, but it is probable, because their main reproach is *peša*ʿ. In 1.3–5 he already hurls a prophecy of doom at the Aramaeans:

> Thus has Yahweh spoken / over the three rebellions of Damascus / and the four:
> B I will no more revoke the punishment
> A because he has threshed / Gilead with threshing brooms of iron.
> B I have fire to send upon the dynasty of Hasael, / that it may devour the palaces of Benhadad.
> I have to break the bolt (?) of Damascus, I have to root out the rulers of Biqat-Awen, / and him that holds the sceptre of Bit-Adini.
> Deported will the *ʿam* of Aram be to Kir, / says Yahweh.

Amos takes up all the neighbouring peoples one after another – the Philistines, the Phoenicians, the Edomites, the Ammonites, Moab (even Judah, if the stanza is genuine). A burden of *peša*ʿ has gathered on them in the course of history, which Yahweh is no longer prepared to ignore. He will send a cleansing, destroying fire on them. The oracle series now closes effectively with the stanza on Israel (2.6–16) which I have already quoted. Earlier interpreters therefore thought in terms of a single, dramatic appearance by the prophet before the people. On this occasion Amos – so it was thought – cleverly picked up the popular hope that Yahweh would bring ruin on the neighbouring states through some tremendous stroke (the day of Yahweh). By playing rhetorically on this hope, Amos roused his listeners, increasing enthusiasm from stanza to stanza, only to confront them abruptly at the end with the terror of their own downfall. There are even scholars who seriously consider whether Amos might not really have meant what he said about the nations, but only included it in order to bluff his listeners! But a saying introduced by the proclamation 'Thus says Yahweh' was deadly serious for any prophet. Moreover, the different style indicates that the stanza on Israel probably did not originally belong to this context. So when we come to detail, what does this doom threatening the foreign nations look like?

It is surprising to discover how, in spite of a basic linguistic pattern, the situation of particular states is individually picked out. Precise historical facts are taken up, the constitution of the state in question is outlined and the doom measured out accordingly. Amos must have had an astonishing knowledge of the conditions of his day. For him, Aram and Philistia are associations of states with their chief kings in Damascus or Gaza, each supported in other royal cities by subordinate kings in the form of a ruler and a sceptre bearer. Among the Ammonites, on the other hand, the government consists of a king and his ministers; and in Moab there was a *šōpeṭ*, with his ministers.

What makes the *peša*ʿ of these neighbouring countries overflow is always inhuman cruelty in war. This cruelty harms Israel, but on one occasion its brother-people Edom as well. It is only for Edom, as Israel's brother, that the waging of war as such is a severe crime. Among the other nations *peša*ʿ results only from war crimes: the extermination of the population of a conquered territory, the sale of prisoners of war into slavery, the slitting of the bellies of pregnant women, or the burning of the dead body of a foreign king. The prophet does not expect *mišpāṭ* and *ṣ*ᵉ*dāqā* from Israel's neighbours – Yahweh applies stricter standards to his own people – but he does assume knowledge of the simplest feelings of humanity, and reverence for the divine existence that lies behind every man or woman. It is only from Edom that more than this is expected. Edom ought to have a sense of solidarity (*r*ᵃ*ḥāmim*), for it is Jacob's brother.

The promised doom will be gradated in accordance with the political organization. All over Syria-Palestine the main cities and their palaces will be destroyed by fire. Where the crimes of the people responsible are within bounds, comparatively speaking – as in the case of Tyre or Edom (Judah) – no more than this will happen. In the case of the Ammonites, the government will also be deported. In Moab both army and government will be exterminated. The Aramaean rulers will be exterminated, whereas the *ʿam* will be deported.

The Philistines, Israel's old enemy, are to have the hardest fate. There the remnant of the people will be destroyed as well.

4.7.2 Anyone who reads the oracles about the nations soon notices that Amos is thinking of a great military power who will sweep through Syria-Palestine, waging an appalling war. According to things as they were, he can only have meant the Assyrians. It is in line with this that the Israelites should be carried away into exile towards the north (4.3; 5.27); it was from the north that the Assyrians came. If all the Aramaeans were deported to Kir, which lies in Mesopotamia, the foreign power must also have had control of this area too. However, to think of the Assyrians as the coming great military power round about 760, as Amos did, was anything but obvious. It is true that Assyrian armies had already reached Damascus forty years earlier; but the state declined increasingly during the following decades. The stable conditions at the time of Jeroboam II will hardly have made anyone else in Israel arrive at the conclusion that the Assyrians – who lived far beyond the Syrian-Arabian desert – could endanger their own state. It was only a good ten years later, in 746/5, that the energetic Tiglath-pileser seized power in Assyria and soon set his armies on the march in the direction of the Mediterranean. Damascus fell in 734, North Israel in 722/1, after Samaria had been besieged for several years. All the states threatened by Amos fell, one after the other, and there were huge deportations. What Amos had prophesied was fulfilled in an astonishing way, thirty to forty years later. The fulfilment exceeds anything comparable which we were able to discover about earlier prophecy by nabis in Israel. For a nabi at that time to announce the extermination of a dynasty and bring this about through the agency of a compliant officer (II Kings 9) can still be considered as self-fulfilling prophecy. But for a peasant farmer from Tekoa, in peaceful times, to prophesy years in advance the approach and the complete success of the Assyrian army borders on the unfathomable. Did Amos run a kind of institute for strategic studies all on his own? Since this seems unlikely, the accuracy of his prophecies remains a riddle. This prophet possessed unbelievable clairvoyance, which he himself put down to a voice which forced itself compellingly on him (3.8). Are there any explanations except parapsychological ones?

4.7.3 One striking fact is that the nations threatened by doom are limited to the minor states of Syria-Palestine. Why did Amos not include Egypt, which after all was Israel's neighbour and had inflicted severe damage on her, and not just at the beginning of her national history? Why was Assyria not mentioned, although seventy years before Jehu had had to pay a heavy tribute to her? Why does Amos call the evil acts of the states attacked *peša'*, rebellion, revolt against their legitimate rulers? It seems to me that there is only one satisfying answer. Amos is listing the nations that had once belonged to the Davidic empire and which, through David, had been subjected to the lordship of the God of Israel. Is the seer the representative of an idea of Greater Israel which – in the face of continual disappointments with the North Israelite kings – pinned its hopes to the dynasty of the Southern Kingdom?

4.8 The restoration of the Davidic kingdom and the problem of the prophet's origin

4.8.1 Can anyone like Amos, who ceaselessly sees horrors, war and destruction in his mind's eye, still believe that the future has anything positive to offer? There are occasional gleams of a vague alternative when the people are urged to seek Yahweh (5.6), or when there is a hint that *mišpāṭ* and *ṣ'dāqā* will yet flow down upon them (5.24): 'It may be that Yahweh will then be gracious to the remnant of Joseph' (5.15). Amos 9.11f. goes far beyond these cautious comments:

> In that day
> I will raise up the fallen booths of David / and repair [their] breaches.
> I will raise up their ruins / and rebuild them as in days of old;
> That they may inherit the remnant of Edom / and all the nations over whom my name was once proclaimed.

This is unmistakably a reference back to the oracles about the nations. The Davidic kingdom which is there in the background – the kingdom in which and with which Yahweh's name is named – will rise again after the great catastrophe. Not only will North and South Israel be united – that does not have to be stated expressly (cf. the contrast between the booths here and those of the North Israelite king in 5.26) – but the remnant of Edom (it deserves special rank as a brother nation, 1.11) and the other nations over whom Yahweh's name was once proclaimed (which means in the days of David) will all belong to it.

Wellhausen, who has been followed by many other scholars, questioned Amos' prophecies of salvation, with the argument that the prophet must have forgotten himself, suddenly to deal out 'roses and lavender instead of blood and iron'. Impressive though this sounds, the argument puts Amos too hastily on the same level as a Christian theologian, ruled by dogmatic principles. Does this fit in with the prophet's own differentiated world of ideas which has a foundation beyond politics? Amos certainly proclaims unconditional disaster, but he does not proclaim it wholesale. He imagines precisely what is in preparation between present and future, on the different levels of God-guided history. As *šᵉʾerīt*, the remnant plays a part in what he says, not only for Israel but for the neighbouring peoples as well (1.8; 5.15).

One objection to the authenticity arises from the linguistic form. The structure of the 'on that day' oracles (8.9f., 13f.) differs from the usual prophecies, and we still know very little about their origin. In view of this, there is some uncertainty over the saying about the booths of David. But the tendency to envisage the kingdom of David as the divinely willed form of government after the impending end of the North Israelite monarchy is entirely in accordance with Amos' other discourses.

4.8.2 A 'Greater Israel' approach would be a matter of course if Amos had been Judaean in origin, and not from North Israel. And this is how Old Testament scholars today almost unanimously interpret the remark that Amos came from Tekoa (1.1). This is thought to be a reference to a little place south of Bethlehem, in the Judaean desert. A difficulty is that Amos would then have been unable to cultivate mulberry trees (7.14), because they do not grow there. Moreover, we then have to assume that Amos proclaims unconditional disaster to Northern Israel from an onlooker's standpoint, and is able to exclude himself, his family and his own country. Is this conceivable with so committed a prophet? It would therefore seem more obvious to think of a Galilean Tekoa, which is attested in post-biblical times. It is no argument against this that after his expulsion from Bethel, Amos actually did cross over to Judah (7.12).

4.9 God and metahistory

Anyone who wants to understand Amos must investigate his interpretation of Yahweh. No saying is without a reference to this God. Here as elsewhere in the Bible we easily tend to assume an idea of God drawn from Western theology. But Amos as yet knows nothing about a Christian God. What he does know is that Yahweh has taken possession of him. He senses this insistent power everywhere, round him and his people. He cannot even endure the word which we translate as 'God'. He occasionally uses 'Almighty Lord', but generally the subject of his sentences is 'Yahweh', without any honorific title, but with verbs pulsating with supreme activity.

4.9.1 Yahweh's initiative is expressed in the messenger or proclamation formula, 'Thus says Yahweh', which Amos uses fifteen times. He feels himself to be God's mouthpiece. As soon as he utters the formula, he proclaims God's own word which has been given to him, in Hebrew and poetically. But what God makes known, shapes the future. What I may perhaps call, for short, an *anticipatory speech event* moulds history. Amos is not concerned with God's claim or promise to individual people. He is concerned with the announcement – more, with the preparation – of historical developments. Yahweh's word, which Amos passes on, is an efficacious word. It realizes itself, even materializes, in the imminent future. In order that it may reach its goal, it has to be heard at the central place, for example in Bethel. The person who hears it has to pass it on to other people (3.8), and the person who resists it does so at the risk of his life (7.10–17).

4.9.2 God also acts outside his word. When Amos sees him, he is standing high above the centre of the earth, reaching from there, it may be, to heaven and the underworld (7.7f.; 9.1–4). Yahweh does not always stand there, any more than he continually speaks. Amos shares the view of pre-exilic Israel that Yahweh is certainly present everywhere in history and nature, but that for men and women he is experienced only where divinity appears as it were in concentrated form – at sacred places and at sacred seasons, where there is a theophany. Amos does not think of seeking his God in heaven. The mark of God is his earthly multivolipresence, to use a theological term – in other words, his presence whenever and wherever he wills it. That is why Amos stresses the visitation, a physical appearance on the Day of Yahweh at the cultic centre of the earth.

4.9.3 Multivolipresence and anticipatory speech events are not the only things that determine Amos' view of God. Yahweh operates through active *forces*. Apart from divine utterances in the sense of 'speaking', 'not forgetting' or 'visiting', Amos likes to talk about divine actions using the causative verbal form known in Hebrew as the *hiph'īl*. Yahweh will not cause to turn away (1.3), to cut off (1.5–8), to kindle (1.14) – forms which already in the oracles about the nations indicate a mediated activity. I have already mentioned the sinister sword hanging over the earth, the blazing fire and the earth itself as being powers which Yahweh occasionally uses. The forces of *mišpāt* and *ṣ^edāqā*, which I discussed above, belong on the same level. Other active forces are Yahweh's holiness (*qōdeš*), which for Amos is connected with the pride of Jacob's *gā'ōn* (the mountain of Samaria as the centre of blessing? 4.2; cf. 8.7; 6.8). For Amos visible natural forces such as rain, stars, locusts, belong on the same level. God uses a wealth of these active forces as instruments through which he guides the world and history. To the Westerner, this seems like mythological fantasy. But it must be remembered that the dividing line between abstract and concrete ideas, which we draw as a matter of course, takes a different course for the Semitic peoples of the ancient world from that taken in Greek tradition and philosophy. This made possible a vivid grasp of the trans-subjective aspects of social tendencies and powers, and indeed it enabled people to find an orderly cohesion in reality, in the direction of which man could mould his own destiny and purposes.

4.9.4 People too, as Amos sees them, are accompanied by some kind of active forces through the spheres of their activity – even though these have only a limited efficacy. *Mišpāṭ* and *ṣ*ᵉ*dāqā* already make this clear. These forces are to be taken over by people and put into action in the form of faithfulness to fundamental institutions. Amos' contemporaries, however, were inclined to reverse (*hāpak*) the constructive trend of these forces, so that they became highly damaging to themselves and their environment. In addition they let *peša*ʿ grow up round them – sheer rejection of the foundation and Lord of life, spheres of sacrilege which were actually concentrated at the main sanctuaries. The Western observer may shake his head over a mystical ontology of this kind. But it must be remembered that an anthropology is being expressed in these categories in which man is not a finished being, by nature or creation. On the contrary, everyone is called, either to find himself through what he does – divine gifts are given him – or to lose himself through acts of wickedness. A conception like this etches moral causality into what happens in the world – even if it is absorbed collectively and seen in elastic temporal terms – and gives supreme dignity to human life, as life in history. For Amos, the auras created by what a person does are more than anthropological determinations. They do not just include the earthly surroundings of the agent. They touch God himself too, as soon as they begin to spread in an injurious way. They cling to the sanctuary, to the *gā'ōn* (the pride) of Jacob, touching a sphere which God for his part uses as the centre of his life (*nepeš*) as an essential witness to his oath (4.2 cf. 6.8). The capacity to come into being and to exist historically as a people and a state is the result of a divine enabling act, an act which permits existence (*qūm*, qal and hiphil forms, 5.2; 7.2, 5; 8.14; 9.11) and in which divine active powers and human 'deed-auras' work together. Where *pesa*ʿ spreads out wave after wave, Yahweh will no longer hold back. He will visit his people with affliction. Amos sees this visitation as imminent. But it is also for the world's sake that Yahweh is going to act – the world that is tormented, divided and destroyed by spheres of wickedness.

4.9.5 Amos therefore presupposes an ontological structure which I should like to call *metahistory*. What is meant is not a timelessness beyond history, but a theory about the cohesion of all reality as a single, all-embracing though complex process, in which Israel and Yahweh form the two essential poles. The prophet always talks about Yahweh under the aspect of movements, processes which get under way slowly. In this sense his God is historical by nature, and man is certainly so. What is also historical is the conviction of a purposefulness and irreversibility of events, which points to the *yōm yahweh* (the Day of Yahweh), both for Israel and her neighbours. At the same time, this concept is alien to the modern notion of history, which sees only the link between cause and effect in 'visible' processes in the world. Amos is certainly aware of these too – the exploitation of the *dallīm* by royal officials and by local assemblies at the gates; the war crimes of Aram, Gaza, etc.; and the approach of a numerically superior enemy army. But beyond economic, legal and military causes, there is a more profound interaction. For Amos, behind the outward face of a brutal reality, which is all that modern times can see as history, is the inner aspect of reciprocal effects on a level where people find or lose themselves – the level, too, of Yahweh's activity, which interpenetrates all reality, and his potency, which creates time, retarding it or hastening it.

Yahweh spans – as it were in a fourth sphere – three other sectors which build up the suprahistory of which metahistory renders an account:

the reality of economic, cultic and military causation;

the moral causation of spheres of fate brought into being by the acts of human beings;

active powers accompanying nature and society which come from God and are directed towards the community of men and women.

Yahweh does not span these sectors in any deterministic way. It is true that doom strikes Syria-Palestine; and what he proclaims comes unconditionally true. Seen historically and suprahistorically, however, this need not have happened. Nations and states, if not individuals, were certainly the masters of their decisions and had freedom of choice. Some interpreters have ascribed to Amos the conviction of a divine omni-causality, usually appealing to 3.6: 'Does evil (*rāʿā*) befall a city, unless Yahweh has done it?' But this sentence should not be torn from its context. According to the parallel statement, which adduces the summons of a trumpet to a military campaign, Amos is talking about war. But in 'omni-causality' Yahweh does not unleash a war against his own people. At most he does so in order to 'finish off' an aura of wickedness which has become excessive. *Rāʿā* does not mean a first, original cause. It signifies the absorption and implementation of the results of human wickedness. But as soon as Yahweh promises in an anticipatory word to enter upon a cohesion of events where action and destiny are related to one another, coming events are determined and the doom is unconditional. The only question still open must be, 'Who will be affected, and who will be spared?'

4.9.6 Apart from his ties with present and future, has Amos' God ties with the past as well? Or, to be more precise: does Amos stress an inseparable link between *Yahweh and salvation history*? He presupposes that there are valid traditions which provide the basis of understanding between himself and his listeners. Do these traditions include a common belief that Yahweh has revealed himself in a chronologically remote history of salvation, extending from the exodus to the settlement in the promised land, or to the Davidic period? Von Rad emphatically maintained this, both for Amos and for the other prophets. Others have vehemently denied it. Even H. W. Wolff, a scholar otherwise sympathetic to von Rad's views, believes that Amos was hardly affected at all by notions of salvation history. What is often in question in this controversy is not, ultimately, the interpretation of Amos: the underlying point at issue is the dispute between contemporary theologians as to whether God reveals himself in history, or whether history above all signalizes the absence of God as does nothing else. But when we are considering Amos' views we must free our minds of modern judgments about the possible presence of God in history, and look at the text as we have it.

The exodus from Egypt and the wanderings in the desert are only mentioned twice (2.10; 5.25–3.1f. is probably a later interpolation). This is very little. But can we expect a historical digression at all in the genre of prophecy, which has to deal succinctly, and with poetic emphasis, with the present situation and the prospects of the future? It must be said that the two passages cited have a considerable importance for the argument in the context. In addition, it is noticeable that Amos, more than the other prophets, calls his people by the names of the patriarchs – Jacob six times, Isaac twice and Joseph three times. In accordance with the idea of corporate personality, contemporary Israel is equated, beyond time, with figures who are linked with the promise of the land and the anticipatory utterances of God in an epoch belonging to salvation history. Finally, every saying of Amos' returns explicitly or implicitly to *hā-āreṣ*, the fruitful land given by Yahweh (the centre of which is the sanctuary). How can this be explained if the land is not seen as the achievement of salvation history? If the oracles about the nations (chs. 1f.) and the prophecy of salvation in 9.11f. are Amos' own, then for him the great period of divine appointment culminates and ends with David. (Only one thing is never mentioned: the convenant on Sinai, or any divine law.)

The saying about the wanderings of the nation in 9.7 is frequently cited as evidence against a link between God and Israel's history of salvation. But surely this can only be interpreted as an ironic termination of Israel's special character and its salvation history?

A Are you not like the Cushites / to me, O Israelites? . . .
 Have I not brought up Israel / from the land of Egypt, the Philistines from Caphtor / and Aram from Kir?
B Behold, the eyes of Yahweh / are upon the sinful kingdom.
 He will utterly destroy it / from the surface of the fruitful earth (except that I will not utterly / destroy the house of Israel).

(The last line is probably a later interpolation.)

The saying is undoubtedly intended to shake Israel's sense of being an élite. Even the traditional enemies, the Philistines and the Aramaeans, look back to a history of guidance which allowed them to take possession of their land. Although the uncircumcised Philistines are certainly not aware of it, their history, too, was Yahweh's work. Like Aram, they presumably belong to the peoples over whom Yahweh's name was proclaimed in the time of David (9.11f.). According to this, David's subjugation of the neighbouring peoples was not, seen metapolitically, wilful and wicked annexation, but the implementation of the historical motive power which ruled the Philistines, for example, from the time of their emigration from Crete. Perhaps Amos still supposes that his listeners are familiar with ideas of this kind. But he then extends his viewpoint – which certainly no one in Israel before him had thought of doing – to the ends of what was then the known world: Yahweh concerns himself even with the Cushites in the African Sudan. In the framework of world politics, Yahweh lets kingdoms rise and fall again as soon as they trespass and sin (*ḥaṭṭā'*; it is impossible to talk about *peša'*, conscious rejection, where Yahweh's name is unknown.) The particularist Israelite dogma of salvation history as the way to Israel's own land is therefore universalized. Is it abolished in the process? Inasmuch as Amos' view of things is linked with the emergence and disappearance of kingdoms, with the migration of peoples, and with shares in the fertile earth, it obviously remains within the framework of divinely guided historical processes. Universalization does not mean a levelling process. According to the view of the people of Samaria, Israel is the first-born of the peoples. Amos confirms this in his own way by declaring that she will take first place in the future deportation (6.1–6).

Consequently it is more than rash to deny the fundamental historical – or, to be more precise, metahistorical – element in Amos' thinking. The prophet finds himself in a world in which everything is in a state of flux: Israel in her moral decline; the neighbours who were subjected to the Davidic kingdom, with their increasing *peša'*; nature, too, which is becoming increasingly closed to man (4.6ff.). Even God, who is preparing everything for his Day and who anticipates it in his word. Only someone who ignores all this can see Amos as nothing more than a preacher of divine 'judgment', though this is the view that has been passed down from one Old Testament scholar to another. Yet there is not a single word in Amos that says anything about a divine judgment. So can one say that, for Amos, God reveals himself in history? If we understand revelation in the modern sense, as the self-communication of God, which makes his existence and nature plain to men and women, and is far more than any partial manifestation of divine power, then it must be said that we find no information about this in Amos. God rules in the historical processes which he proclaims; but does he reveal himself in them? In this sense, however, he does not reveal himself any more in what Amos says! Nor does the book consider the question whether Yahweh's revelation is made at a place of worship or in the salvation history which was celebrated so much. Amos does not see it as his function to talk about where and when and how God reveals himself, in the full meaning of the term. Among later prophets – Ezekiel perhaps – this may be different. What Amos sees himself as being compelled to utter is not the expression of a closed system – not a doctrine, nor even a faith. It is the experience of an ultimately positive ground of reality, which speaks to him in the midst of an explosive world situation. He knows that it is for this historical moment and the elucidation of its meaning that he is competent, not for salvation history, and not for metaphysics either.

5. Hosea

5.1 Hosea's Relationship to Amos

During the peaceful period under Jeroboam II, shortly after Amos – indeed perhaps with some overlap – a second prophet appeared in the Northern Kingdom. He too committed his discourses to writing (see Section 9 below). His name was Hosea ben Beeri. In his proclamation he points to the same unconditional catastrophe as Amos. Hosea, too, foresees the downfall of state and people, the advance of Assyrian power, military defeat and deportation. Behind political and military events there is a divine impulse. Yahweh afflicts his people and cuts himself loose from those who had been intimately linked with him for centuries.

And yet how different the language of the two men is! Amos was a *hōzeh*, a seer, and not a nabi, yet we can see the structure of nabi prophecy and the demands of oral delivery – short and emphatic sentences, easy to learn off by heart. In Hosea, on the other hand, there is not a single prophecy (much less a vision) which can be shown to be a pure example of its genre. Instead there are extensive sections in which Hosea switches backwards and forwards between sayings about the present and sayings about the future. In language, Hosea is even more remote from the nabis than Amos. Or did he undertake a radical revision when committing what he said to writing, transforming oral forms of speech into literary ones? Perhaps these are bordering on dramatic sketches in which his listeners' interpolations and reactions are worked into his own sayings.

The picture of God communicated by the two eighth-century prophets differs, too. Amos is inexorable and utterly matter-of-fact. And his God is equally implacable, planning, as it were strategically, the downfall not only of Israel but – in degrees – that of all her neighbouring states. Hosea's God, on the other hand, is infinitely compassionate, torn this way and that by a situation which is no longer bearable. 'What shall I do with you, O Ephraim?' (6.4) – a loving God who loves with a love no other prophet so lovingly proclaims. From the very beginning a new future salvation shines through beyond the catastrophe.

The two men also diverge from one another in their criticism of the present. With Amos, social injustice is in the foreground – the alienation between Israelite and Israelite. His criticism of the cult derives from this. In Hosea we also come upon notes of lamentation about a *mišpāṭ* which has been perverted into a poisonous weed (10.4). But criticism of the cult is at the centre. It goes far further than it does in Amos, not merely exposing the religion of the present generation as ineffective, but revealing behind the service of Yahweh the service of Baal, with rites which for Hosea could only be branded as degenerate. Social criticism, where it occurs at all, springs from this.

The two prophets do not seem to take any note of one another at all. They were probably active in different places. Perhaps they did not even know each other's names. Of the two, Hosea has had incomparably more influence on posterity. His understanding of God later helped to form the attitude of Jeremiah and Ezekiel, and his view about the danger of ascribing religious significance to sexual experience and sexual practices still colours Christian individual and social ethics today, even if in a very different way from what Hosea had in mind.

5.2 Hosea's marriage and family drama as a symbol

With Hosea too it is worthwhile beginning from the few external facts we are told about his life. This makes it easier to understand the heart of his proclamation. Nearly all we are told about him relates solely to his unhappy experience of love and marriage. Sometimes people have seen a cry of despair, uttered in intolerable conditions, as coming from the prophet himself: 'The nabi is (will become!) a fool, mad the *ruᵃḥ* man, because of masses of iniquity' (9.7). This would put Hosea in the ranks of the nabis. But the passage can just as well be related to other spokesmen of Yahweh's *dābār*. So we remain uncertain about the status Hosea gave himself. Nor do we know where he came from, his social background, or the place where he proclaimed his message. (It was probably not Bethel, since he refers to conditions there far less than Amos does.) He resembles a *ḥōzeh* or *nābī* in that he proclaims his message in the first person, of God himself, and performs symbolic actions. The only surprising thing is the sector of life he chooses. His own marriage and family life are made the living symbol of his people's situation in the present and the future – and so much so that he even makes public the secrets of his bedroom. The book begins with a private oracle addressed to Hosea himself:

> Go, take to yourself a wife of harlotry / and children of harlotry.
> For the land is committing great harlotry, / forsaking Yahweh.

Obedient to his inspiration, Hosea marries a woman called Gomer. She bears him three children, one after the other, to whom he gives names which suggest that their paternity was, at the very least, a matter of doubt: Jezreel (see below), No-family-solidarity and Not-my-people. A personal account in ch. 3 supplements the third-person report here, telling us about the family drama. A private oracle tells Hosea:

> Go, love a woman / loved by another and adulterous!
> Even so is Yahweh's love affair / with the Israelites.
> For they turn to other gods / and love cakes of raisins.

Without letting us know how he felt about it, Hosea tells how, in response, he took the woman to be his wife. This time his dealings with his wife after their marriage take a strange and symbolic form:

I said to her: you must stay quiet for many days; you will not be able to play the whore. You will not belong to any other man, and I will [not go in] to you either.
For the Israelites shall remain many days without kings and ministers, without sacrifice or pillar, without ephod and teraphim.
Afterwards the Israelites shall return and seek Yahweh, their God . . .

For centuries Christian and Jewish interpreters thought that it was absurd to suppose that this reflected actual events. It seemed impossible that God should force any man to marry someone, least of all a woman of bad reputation. Accordingly, it was assumed that this was an allegory, a fictitious narrative. But ancient Israel did not as yet pursue the respectable paths of middle-class morality. Rather, it reckoned with the fact that God himself can disregard individual human happiness for the sake of the common good. Nothing in the story permits us to doubt that it was sheer fact. So for months and years Hosea experienced his family misery as a symbolic happening, pregnant with significance, which ran its course for the sake of the people. He did not permit himself to consider his personal happiness. Having been appointed Yahweh's messenger – destined, indeed, for a gesture anticipating future history – he no longer had a private life of his own. Not only was his own existence and that of his wife robbed of its privacy; his children were drawn in too. He claims that they are bastards, giving them names with a sinister meaning.

Anything without significance remains unspoken. This means that the account of Hosea's marriage is full of riddles. Does the first-person account refer to a different woman from the one in the third-person narrative, or are they one and the same? If two women are involved, did the first one die or run away before the marriage with the second? Did Hosea marry the second woman at all, or was she only hired, as a prostitute? If the two accounts refer to the same woman, is Hosea describing two different experiences? Is chapter 3 describing a remarriage, perhaps, after a temporary separation? Or is the divine charge bound up with the first and only marriage, merely being repeated later in different words in chapter 3? The measure of agreement in the course of events and the themes make me incline to the last view. In considering chapter 3 we then have to presuppose that abstinence from marital relations ended after a certain time, since the couple later had children.

What exactly is meant by the woman's whorish past? Does it mean that she was a public prostitute, or a ritual one – a priestess *(qedešet)?* The 'professional' description, 'prostitute', is never actually used. The verb 'to play the harlot' or 'go whoring' and the abstract noun 'harlotry' can have a wider range of meaning. So is Gomer perhaps being accused of only one sexual lapse ('loved by another')? An interpretation of Wolff's has found wide acceptance. He points to ancient near Eastern rites for opening the womb, in which the defloration of a girl of marriageable age was undertaken by a priest or associate in the cult, as representative of the god, at the sacred place (a kind of *ius primae noctis*). The other sexual rites of which Hosea accuses his contemporaries (see below) make it reasonable to suppose that a rite of this kind existed in Northern Israel, too. In Wolff's opinion, most contemporaries saw this act as absolutely necessary for their daughters. So Gomer represents no more and no less than an average Israelite girl. (Though how many or how few girls participated in this practice is ultimately unimportant.) Although – or indeed just because – this rite takes place in Yahweh's name, Hosea abominates it profoundly. He sees it as shameful harlotry, not as a sacred act. Rudolph has disputed this assumption that there were 'prepared virgins', and has shown that some of the ancient Near Eastern parallels cited are untenable; but since his own solution draws heavily on questionable literary-critical procedures and aims all too clearly at letting Hosea be married to a perfectly respectable woman, in order to exonerate his God, Wolff's interpretation is to be preferred. (Unless what is meant is in fact a notorious whore, which would fit in best with the application of the image.)

But this does not bring us to the end of the questions involved. Is God really supposed to have commanded his prophet to go into an unhappy marriage with his eyes open? Since we can hardly assume that divine inspiration made itself known to the prophet in well-formulated Hebrew, we may perhaps suppose that Hosea married in good faith, only subsequently discovering that he had made a mistake in supposing his wife to be a virgin. Did he then trace back this experience to God's will and guidance, in a process of subsequent reflection? However, questions like these stretch the framework of historical verification and reconstruction too far. We do not know, either, whether Hosea had been secretly drawn to Gomer before the divine call, and whether the word of God came to him as the fulfilment of an unacknowledged desire; or whether, filled with horror at Israel's prostitution, he sought an especially drastic way of expressing his views. Since we are told nothing about his own feelings, psycho-analytical interpretations are also bound to miscarry. Where they are attempted they become fictional embroidery rather than historically authentic, proven facts.

5.3 Yahweh's 'family drama' as the content of the symbolism. Religion and monarchy

What takes place between Hosea and Gomer is outward reality, but in its truest sense. It is only a game, a reflection of a profounder reality in which this couple, too, is ensnared. For the prophet, Yahweh is the foundation of all reality in the nation. But in the personal sense he is also the husband of the promised land, acquired in the process of salvation history. The land is Yahweh's wife. The Israelites are seen as children of the invisible but real marriage between Yahweh and *hā'āreṣ*. But the marriage is spoilt by the unfaithfulness of wife and children, whereas the divine husband still continues, even in the present, to cling to his paradoxical love. The land is involved in harlotry, and the Israelites, sons of the land, do not love the head of the family, their Father, but are running to other gods, preferring raisin cake – the ritual food of the Canaanite goddess of love. Hosea uses the root *zēnā*, 'to whore', with its various derivatives, nineteen times, always at central points in the dispute. In so doing, he is not simply taking an arbitrary, random image for spiritual unfaithfulness, godlessness, religious apostasy. *Zānā* is the spearhead of his attacks on the cult; and criticism of official religion is the centre of his assertion that for Israel things as they are have become untenable. He believes that in Israelite religion harlotry is rife – in both the literal and the transferred sense.

Between the third-person and the autobiographical account of conditions in Hosea's family, there is a fairly long passage which probably welds several oral sayings into a literary whole. At the beginning the reader is uncertain whether the prophet is talking to his own children when he announces a divorce, or whether Yahweh is addressing the children of the country (2.2ff.):

> Quarrel with your mother, quarrel, / for she is no longer my wife / nor I her husband.
> Let her put away the signs of harlotry from her face, / the marks of adultery between her breasts.
> Lest I strip her naked / and lay her down as in the day she was born, make her like the wilderness, / cause her to be like parched ground, / slay her with thirst . . .
> A For she said, 'I will go after my lovers, they give me my bread and my water, / my wool and my flax, / my oil and my drink . . .'
> But she does not understand / that it was I, I who gave her / the grain and the wine and the oil . . .

The patience of the divine husband is now at an end:

B Therefore will I take (from her) again / my grain in its time, / my wine in its festal season.
Now I will uncover her pubic parts / before the eyes of her lovers . . .
I have to end all her pleasure, / her feasts, new moon and sabbath / and all her feast days . . .
I have to afflict her for the days of the Baals . . . whom she followed as her lovers, / while me she forgot.

It emerges from the end of the passage that the sons who are addressed are the Israelites. This means that the mother represents the land from which they spring. Hosea sees the products of the land as Yahweh's gifts, but they are gifts in the framework of conjugal concern and commitment. What distinguishes the cultivated lands of Palestine from the desert has been brought about by a divine husband, to cover the nakedness of his wife, the earth, and to supply her with nourishment and enjoyment. Fatal misunderstandings have crept in. The mother and her Israelite children attribute the grain, wine and silver to other givers, to lovers – the Baals. With this word, a name for God crops up which already played a large part in the pre-Israelite, Canaanite religions of Syria-Palestine (cf. Elijah). Yet Hosea never points to the religions and gods of foreign peoples. It is the religion of his fellow-countrymen, celebrated in all splendour in Yahweh's name, which he sees as a pernicious religion, under foreign influence. Even the sabbaths are being celebrated in a way that distorts their significance. Like Amos, Hosea continually attacks the animal and communal sacrifices, *zebaḥ* (already in 3.4), though his perspective differs from that of his predecessor. It is remarkable that he sees the king as being entangled in the toils of the religion which has become estranged from Yahweh. The first result of the divorce which Yahweh now envisages will be the disappearance of king and ministers (3.4). Just as Amos sees the house of the monarchy as founded on the sanctuary of Bethel, so Hosea identifies the kingdom with Jezreel, by giving that name to his first child (1.3). Jezreel – 'El inseminates' – was at that time the winter residence of the Israelite kings.

How does Hosea come to stress the masculine role of God so much? One is tempted to think of conditions in patriarchal society, where the father has unrestricted control of his family. Is the father figure of this stage of civilization being projected on to God? But the prophet's polemic points in a different direction. God's masculinity results from his relation to the practices of his adversaries. Yahweh is husband, not because of his patriarchal authority, but mainly because of an erotic connotation: he is contrasted with another power, conceived of in feminine terms.

The nature of the religious rites which the prophet execrates and the view of God bound up with them can be deduced from the saying about the high places in 4. 11–14. This saying shows clearly how the symbol of marriage and Israel's real relation to God merge into one another.

> Harlotry and wine and cider / take away the understanding.
> My people – they enquire of a thing of wood / and their staff gives them oracles.
> The spirit of harlotry seduces them / and they left their God to play the whore.
> They sacrifice on the top of the mountains, / make burnt offerings upon the hills,
> under oak and poplar and sacred trees, / because their shade is pleasant.
> That is why your daughters play the harlot, / your daughters-in-law commit adultery.
> I shall not visit it upon your daughters, . . . / and on your daughters-in-law,
> For they (the men) themselves go aside with whores, / and sacrifice with *qedēšōt* ('cult prostitutes').

Every settlement of any size possessed a sanctuary, a piece of high ground with an altar, a sacred tree, generally a stone pillar *(maṣṣēbē)* and a wooden post *(ʾᵃšērā)*, which were supposed to be the abodes of divine powers. Hosea is attacking what was common practice in the local sanctuaries at his period. Sacrifices, designed to serve sacramental communion with God, were celebrated. This involved drinking wine to the point of drunkenness; and also *qedešōt*, ritual prostitutes. But daughters and daughters-in-law were taken to these sanctuaries too. At the culmination of the feast, which lasted far into the night, the barriers of everyday morality broke down and promiscuous copulation was practised. The male community did not meet only to perform an act designed for a particular occasion, some casual act because of one or several girls of marriageable age. It gathered to celebrate the New Year Festival. Consequently oracles were sought from the wood of the terebinth, perhaps from its rustling; but perhaps too (since 3.4 mentions the ephod) an oracle bag was used, out of which the little 'yes' and 'no' sticks fell, saying – in answer to enquiry – what was to happen in the coming year. On this occasion the wombs of girls of marriageable age were opened. But the ceremony aimed at more than that. Its purpose was to bring about a new, fruitful year. Acts of sexual union performed at the feast were probably designed as symbolic actions (or sympathetic magic) aimed at strengthening the power of procreation and generation in human beings, animals and plants.

Hosea associates the sanctuary rites he objects to with the divine title Baal, which he uses three times in the singular and three times in the plural. He is not using a proper name here; *ba'al* is a functional term, meaning 'lord' over wife, slave, fruitful land, and domestic animals – that is to say, mastery which utilizes and channels the co-operation of others.

The Yahweh whom the Israelites praised as Baal at the sacrificial offerings was presented at celebrated cultic places such as Bethel and Samaria as a bull figure made of cast-iron (10.5–8; 13.2), which the people did not hesitate to kiss. But the god depicted in this form was also reverenced at local sanctuaries, where there is no evidence of statues of this kind. Hosea relates all sacrificial offerings in the land to this monstrous figure. If the adulterous Israel is locked in, all the sacrifices will cease (3.4; cf. 8.13).

How does Hosea come to describe the Israelite cult in this way? The Books of Kings tell us that the first king of the Northern kingdom set up a national sanctuary in Bethel, about 920 BC. There Yahweh, the God of the exodus from Egypt and the foundation of Israel's existence, was associated with a bull set up on a pedestal (I Kings 12). Probably the king was going back to an ancient tradition about the bull god *('ābīr)* of the patriarch Jacob. As might be expected, this bull god of Jacob's was a god of battle (Gen. 49.24; Num. 23.22). The animal was thought to be particularly aggressive, as we can see right down to the bull-fights of our own day. So when the nabi Zedekiah wanted to promise the North Israelites victory in the military campaign, he carried iron horns on his head (I Kings 22.11). But in many ancient oriental civilizations the bull was also the quintessence of fertility, and this characteristic was undoubtedly more important for the Israelite farmers. The god represented by the animal figure is a Baal who gives grain, wine, oil, wool and water (2.5ff.). Here it is assumed that there is a relationship between the bull-Baal and the fertile land – the earth, his wife. The farmer was unable to explain the changeable opening and closing of the soil (which does not merely change according to the seasons, but also from year to year) except by the influence of mysterious divine forces. Because fertility depends on rain in Palestine, it seemed obvious to imagine a huge Baal as husband over the mother earth, a god connected with winds and clouds, and with rain which he let fall on the earth as his sperm. This interpretation of climatic and meteorological interactions was quite logically thought out, and deduced from observations which seemed obvious to common sense. The ancient Israelite God seemed to have little to do with all this. But had not clouds and winds, lightning and storms belonged to him ever since the days of the exodus? Must he not then be identical with the Baal who gave the rain? Did he not once promise cultivated land to the patriarchs? Was this not the supreme goal of salvation history? Must he not then be elevated to the figure of a fertility god, who in this way continues, as it were, the story of salvation history? If Hosea's contemporaries associated Yahweh with fertility rites, rain, and the characteristics of a Baal, this was in accord with their world-picture. Yahweh revealed himself as Baal, the husband of the earth, he was showing himself to be the focal point for Israelite farmers and their economic needs.

The modern reader will ask himself in surprise how sexual orgies like this could take on a religious colouring, and how they could be considered to represent religious truth. Were these not merely gossamer-thin religious pretexts for the satisfaction of people's own sexual desires? Schooled by Christianity, we have become accustomed to a deep cleft between religion and sexuality. But for the Semitic peoples of the ancient world, whether they were Canaanites or Israelites, procreation was part of the mystery of life, and life was God's supreme gift. And human life was intimately connected with the earth and its produce. Everywhere on earth we find sexual polarity, in animals and plants as well as in human beings, and life is inconceivable without it. Is not everything male and female on earth linked together in a mysterious, inter-communicating cohesion? Is not the man's sperm that falls into the woman's womb in some way similar in essence to the seed of the plants which falls into the furrows of the earth? Since this was generally accepted, people could encourage the fertility of their environment by their ritual actions, through sexual rites, imitatively supporting the God who fertilizes the earth.

In this way the baalized religion of Yahweh seems to confer a perfect unity between man and nature. Is this not a positively ideal form of religion? Without any moral narrow-mindedness?

Old Testament scholars are accustomed to see the baalized Yahweh religion which Hosea attacks as an aberration which can be traced back to the Canaanite surroundings of the otherwise morally strict Israel. But it must be noted that Hosea never suggests that the impetus to the practices he talks about came from an alien religion. We must be careful not to identify the Baal of Tyre whom Elijah fought a century earlier with the rites attacked by Hosea. There is no doubt that Baal was a universal Canaanite god, whom we already come across in early Ugaritic texts. He is depicted there as the lord of lightning and clouds, but never as a bull. He has to do with rain and fertility, is sometimes swallowed up by Mot, death; and when this happens, fertility disappears from the earth. But as far as we can see, Ugarit was not familiar with any sexual rites. It is true that we are told about a sexual incident in connection with Baal: he copulates with a cow in the underworld – or we are told that a bull calf is born to him as a result of this union. But in all this there is no talk of special fertility functions, and even less of co-operation by human beings. The Ugaritic Baal expressly hates sacrificial meals involving the misuse of young girls.[13] So, while assuming an ancient Canannite root for the rites attacked by Hosea, we must also presuppose a very specifically Israelite development. It is hardly possible to attribute the conditions of eighth-century North Israel lock, stock and barrel to an imitation of Canaanite practices. Here it is not a matter of an external imitation of foreign rites. It is a question of a whole concept of the Yahweh cult which was undoubtedly thought through theoretically in itself.

Surprisingly enough, *the monarchy* also belongs within the orbit of the cult which has been estranged from Yahweh. Just as Amos identified the sanctuary at Bethel with the royal house (7.13), so – through the name of his first child – Hosea identified the monarch with the city (and sanctuary?) of Jezreel. Jezreel was not only the winter residence of the Israelite king. A hundred years earlier it had been the place where Jehu's revolution had taken place:

> Call his name Jezreel! / For yet a little while
> and I will visit the blood aura of Jezreel / on the house of Jehu,
> and put an end to the kingdom / of the house of Israel.

No other saying uttered by the literary prophets of the eighth century shows as cogently as this the difference between them and the pre-literary nabis. For Jehu's extermination of the Omrids in Jezreel (II Kings 9f.) was undertaken at the instigation of the nabi Elisha. When Jehu, a faithful follower of Yahweh, resorted to bloody extermination, he was turning against cultic institutions set up by the previous dynasty for the Baal of Tyre. Yet this revolution was not only abhorred by Hosea, but was interpreted as bringing an aura of blood over the country which now, so many years later, was finding its fulfilment in the catastrophe of people and state. Compared with the earlier nabi movement, therefore, moral standards had become much more refined. The conscience of Yahweh's convinced adherents had become keener. A blood bath within the community of the covenant could not be excused by insistence on the purity of the service of Yahweh. Hosea is penetrated through and through by a sense of the validity of the link between action and destiny; and where there is blood guilt this has particularly appalling effects. The time factor, which is set by Yahweh through his 'visitation', is added to this. (At this point Hosea leaves the level of marriage symbolism and turns to the action-destiny complex and its implementation through the approach of the deity.) By giving the first 'child of whoredom' a name pointing to the house of Jehu, he connects this link between action and destiny with Baal. The wickedness committed at Jezreel was the flagrant result of the debased religious practices into which Israel had gradually slid. It is probably not by chance that Hosea took up the name of Jezreel, 'God (El) sows (inseminates)', which was apparently seen by supporters of the royal house as being the expression for the heart of the country (cf. 2.22) and included the monarchy among the powers which bring about fertility. In Hosea 3.4 the king is regarded as the firstfruit of the marriage between God and people, while in 7.3f. pleasure in the king counts as adultery. And the king was chosen, according to 8.4f., with the help of the bull of Samaria. These passages are based on the view that the king is the guarantor of the country's fertility, not primarily its political head.

Not only does Israel's own monarchy appear to be the product of a false view of God and a disastrous cultic practice. The ties of Israel's foreign policy are also conditioned by these things. The mighty Assyrian king, for whose favour the rival political groups in the country compete, is a lover who is actually given additional gifts (8.8f.; 10.5f.) and with whom Israel enters into a covenant which conflicts with the exclusive covenant with Yahweh (12.2).

So Yahweh appears again and again as the deeply loving, shamefully deceived husband and father. His 'family' surrounds him with hypocritical devotion *(kāḥaš)*, as Hosea likes to put it (4.2; 7.3; 10.13; 12.1). Yet the Israelites trick one another in the same way (4.2); and because of what they do they will soon meet with the appropriate fate and will be cheated of threshing floor and wine press (9.2). Hosea can elaborate the father's role to such an extent that Yahweh seems at the mercy of his refractory children:

> Whenever I would heal Israel, the burden of Ephraim's guilt was revealed (all the more) (7.1; cf. 6.4).

In another passage the prelude to eschatological salvation is the seduction of his bride by Yahweh the lover (2.14). We do not find anthropopathic features like this in the description of God in any other of the literary prophets.

Hosea is perfectly well aware of the visible level of political and military events. He takes up a particular position in a fratricidal war between Israel and Judah (5.8ff.) and is convinced that for Israel disaster will certainly not come from Judah, but that Judah is also on the road to destruction. He explicitly names the great power of Assyria, knows its king Shalmaneser, is aware of the approach of this dangerous enemy from the east, and expects it to fulfil the prophetic prediction at Yahweh's behest. Since certain groups in the country also play with the idea of Egypt as ally, Hosea knows, in addition, that some of the people will emigrate to Egypt. These prophecies of Hosea's, like the predictions of Amos, proved accurate. He condemns the incessant revolutions of the final phase of the Northern kingdom, and again certainly rightly. But for Hosea, even more than for Amos, this external level of history is merely the non-essential foreground for deeper factors – for what I have already called in the case of Amos supra-history, which is grasped metahistorically.

Hosea's scheme of metahistory is primarily determined by the image of marriage. Even Israel's history of salvation (which plays a considerable role in this prophet) is understood by means of the metahistorical prototype of Yahweh as husband and father. Hosea several times extends his range, referring to the patriarch Jacob (ch.12) and the service he did for a wife, or to the exodus from Egypt as the beginning of the ties between Yahweh and his people: 'Out of Egypt have I called my son' (11.1f.). The wanderings in the desert from Egypt to Canaan are regarded as an ideal period of betrothal (12.10f.; cf. 2.14f.). Admittedly Hosea never names Sinai. But for him salvation history no sooner reached its peak than it turned into a history of disaster. At the very threshold of the promised, land, Israel already dedicated itself to a strange lover for the first time, at Baal-Peor (9.10). The history of unfaithfulness goes further by way of Gilgal, the first stage in the promised land, where 'all their wickedness' was concentrated and where Yahweh began to hate Israel (9.15), down to the days of Gibeah, where Saul resided (9.9; 10.9) and where, with the beginning of the monarchy, the deeds already began which now make the end seem inescapable. It is only when Hosea describes how Yahweh releases himself from his ties with Israel that he drops the marriage symbolism, and Yahweh is described demonically, as one who transforms himself into wild beasts (13.7f.).

5.4 Divine marriage as common ground for prophet and opponent. The covenant

Although Hosea so passionately contests any association of Yahweh with the sexual rites practised in his name, and although for him the human imitation of the supposed divine fertilization of the earth represents idolatry *par excellence*, this same Hosea nonetheless knows no other way of comprehending the true relationship of Yahweh to Israel except in terms of love, marriage, betrothal and having children.

This is where we find the great riddle in the interpretation of Hosea. The story of the prophet's marriage is centred on a relationship with God which is determined by masculine love and expects feminine surrender and devotion; and Hosea's sayings remain largely along these lines. The land is seen as God's unfaithful wife, and the people as his sons. Yahweh has shaped salvation history with a fatherly hand. He has loved the child Israel ever since Egypt, taught him to walk, drawing him with 'bands of love' (11.1–4). (The Septuagint, spiritualized in tone as it is, uses the word *agape* at this point; but there is no doubt that what Hosea means is *eros*.) Where the individual phases of salvation history are illuminated, in order to call their wasted achievements to remembrance, the language of love poetry is used. So Hosea calls Israel a vine – in Hebrew a favourite image for the beloved; the inhabitants are grapes (9.10). There is even talk about the cow – for Israel – and the calf – for Ephraim – although the closeness of these designations to the divine bull is grist to his opponents' mill (4.16; 10.11). It is true that in the last passage the ox is associated with 'ploughing' and 'sowing'; but 'ploughing the woman' can also be a marriage metaphor (cf. Judg. 14.18). The pasture (of the oxen) also belongs here, as a metaphor for supra-historical divine rule (13.6; 4.16), as well as liberation from yokes which strangers have laid on them (11.4). Expressions drawn from family law describe divine behaviour – when, for example, there is talk about the proof of family solidarity (*rāḥam*, 1.6; 2.4,23; inexactly translated as 'have pity'); or when the betrothal or marriage is associated with the bridegroom's gift to the bride after the wedding night (2.19ff.). The same applies when preservation from passing over into the power of death is described as ransom (ransom being the duty of members of the clan, according to Israelite law, 13.14).

One is tempted to say that for Hosea Yahweh was just as much a fertility god as the baalized Yahweh was for his opponents. For Hosea, too, Yahweh comes and makes it rain (10.12), giving corn, oil, wool, but also wine – gifts, that is to say, which go beyond what is directly necessary to preserve life (2.2ff.). And Yahweh also shows himself in storm and wind (13.15).

Hosea's imagery therefore moves in the same world of thought as that in which the opponents he attacks are also at home. The theoretical background is largely identical. It is difficult to determine the point where the practical conclusions diverge and develop into deadly opposition. Why must Yahweh on no account be called Baal, although he has so many features in common with that almighty lord and master? The cultic imitation of the divine fertilization of the earth was the subject of contention. And yet it must not be forgotten that

Hosea himself saw his own marriage as a kind of imitation of the relationship between Yahweh and Israel.

Why does he not set himself more firmly apart from his opponents? Why does he not apply attributes to his God which are less open to misinterpretation? Why does he not represent him as a king, perhaps, ruling over his subjects?

As far as I can see there is only one concept which can explain why Hosea follows his opponents so far that it seems almost impossible to turn away from the conclusions they draw. And that is the notion of *covenant*. The word *b^erīt* (translated in our Bible as 'covenant') occurs five times in Hosea. At present there is a kind of covenant phobia among German-speaking Old Testament scholars. They are inclined to see *b^erīt* as a late concept (nebulously termed Deuteronomic), and would like to replace the translation covenant by a more abstract rendering, such as 'obligation'. But to deny Hosea passages like 2.18, 6.7 or 8.1, or to restrict the meaning of *b^erīt* – the word used there as the total term for the relationship to God, and the very heart of the history of Hosea's own people – is not convincing in the context. In addition, the interpreter is robbed of any chance to explain the astonishing consensus between Hosea and his opponents over supra-history, which both see reflected in the duality of man and woman. There is no doubt that *b^erīt* was understood in varying ways in the religious history of Israel. The North Israel of the prophet, and Hosea himself, understood it as being a bond similar to that of marriage. It is true that evidence that *b^erīt* was also used in a secular context only turns up a good two hundred years later (Mal. 2.14). But the relatively early references which use *ba'al* for the husband and *b^e'ūlā* for the wife (Gen. 20.3; Ex. 21.3), together with the connection between *ba'al* and *b^erīt* in Judg. 8.33, Jer. 21.32, suggests that it is probably legitimate to put the view of marriage as *b^erīt* much earlier than the actual written evidence we have for this usage. Because the *b^erīt* between Yahweh and Israel is understood as a conjugal relationship, it allows room to introduce a wealth of emotional implications. No one was able to describe God's love as the foundation of the covenant as clearly as Hosea. As husband, Yahweh dissolves the bond, rejects the people as his kindred, and will no longer be available to them (1.9), since the people themselves have neglected the bond for so long. Significantly enough, it is at the cultic places that *b^erīt* is transgressed *('ābar)* – in Gilead, Shechem and Samaria (6.7–10; 8.1–14).

5.5 Torah, knowledge of God, a correct view of nature and future salvation

Hosea does not see himself as an innovator. What he expounds are long-familar conclusions drawn from the covenant given by Yahweh. A necessary part of this covenant is the *tōrāh* (8.1), a precept which as yet has nothing in common with the later meaning 'law', but focuses on the distinction between clean and unclean in dealings with the divine. This is the task of the priest (4.6). But the large number of Yahweh's *tōrāh* precepts is greatly exceeded by the number of altars in the country (8.11f.); every priest should have known that. And the priests above all have failed. Unlike Amos, Hosea attacks them as a class more than any other social group in the nation. For *tōrāh* feeds the knowledge of God; and for Hosea this is *the* concept which provides the guide for conduct. Here knowledge, Hebrew *da'at,* is not interpreted as detached, objective investigation, but as an understanding, with emotional and sympathetic connotations and practical consequences, which is possible only as a result of close personal community with what is known. Anyone who knows God avoids bloody deeds, deceit, theft and adultery (4.1f.); but he will also avoid the senseless slaughter of sacrificial beasts and all idolatrous worship of Yahweh, which brings him down to the level of images of bulls and sexual practices. *Ḥesed,* attachment and faithfulness to the covenant, then determines behaviour, not only towards God but also towards human beings, who are ruled by God. This is made especially clear in the imitation of the divine response to the sacrifice (6.6):

> In *ḥesed* have I pleasure, and not in sacrifice, / in knowledge of God rather than in burnt offerings.

But for present-day Israel, all chances of positive action have been thrown away. Disaster is coming upon the people unconditionally and inexorably. Hosea does not exempt himself. It is true that on special days of repentance the people occasionally behave as if they were ready to repent; but these are passing, useless emotions (6.1–6), for the Israelites are too closely imprisoned in the sphere of their evil deeds (5.4). The prophets of the eighth century – as part of their conception of fateful spheres of action – believe that there is a point at which an evil-doer can no longer draw back from the slippery slope on which he has put his foot.

And yet from the very outset Hosea expects the great *new beginning* after the catastrophe (3.5). Whereas Amos was only able to speak about this fresh start, *šūb,* as a possibility belonging to the past, Hosea shifts a *šūb* on the part of the whole people into the future. *Šūb* is both a turning away from something, and a new start and self-examination. Such an act of turning away from one's own sphere of evil-doing to God does not as yet mean any substantial act which builds up a new positive field of action. Yet *šūb* is the presupposition for every new sphere of good acts or salvation. The book today closes with a discourse exhorting the people to *šūb*, to this fresh start, and with a subsequent oracle assuring them that they have been heard. What is demanded is the renunciation of security in foreign policy (Assyria), as well as self-made and self-devised manifestations of the deity. As soon as this movement begins, God intervenes, lending his support. He heals the estrangement *(mᵉšūbā)* and converts his anger to love, just as at the same time he converts men and women so that they may remain in his shadow and enjoy the fruits of the earth. The passage is important for prophetic eschatology. When considering future salvation, too, men like Hosea do not merely proclaim a destiny that simply descends on people, to which they have to resign themselves. The materialization of Yahweh's utterance, anticipated in history, is certainly not to be prevented by anyone. But it does not aim to do more than prepare possible conditions for fruitful human activity. For the future, too, the order based on the connection between action and outcome remains valid, and with it the structure of the person who is tracing out his own design of what he is and will be.

None the less, the essential turning point will be brought about by Yahweh. He will set up a new *covenant* (or will extend the renewed covenant in undreamed-of ways). It will be beyond anything that has existed hitherto, bringing peace between man and beast, and making the use of weapons unnecessary. Through active divine forces, Israel will then be endowed with the capacity for moral action which it has at present lost (2.18ff.):

> I have to make for them a *berît* ('covenant') / with the beasts of the field,
> with the birds of the air / and with the creeping things of the ground.
> The bow, the sword and war / on earth will I break.
> I will let them lie down in safety, / I have betrothed her to me for ever.
> I will betroth you to me in *ṣedeq* ('righteousness') and *mišpāṭ* ('justice')/ in *ḥesed* ('steadfast love') and in family solidarity,
> betroth you to me in faithfulness, / and you (woman) shall know Yahweh . . .
> I will (then) react *('ānā)* to the heaven, / it will react to the earth,
> the earth will react to the grain, / the new wine and the oil, and they will (all) react to Jezreel.
> (So) have I to sow you for myself in the earth, / to show myself as solidarity to Not-Solidarity;

I have to say to Not-My-People 'You are my people' [. . .] / and he shall say: my God.

Knowledge of Yahweh as it will be in the future is said to be the final and supreme benefit among the gifts received by the eschatological bride after her wedding night. This knowledge includes perception of the way Yahweh and 'nature' interlock. It abolishes the estrangement between man and his environment, animals and plants. Yahweh reacts (*ʿānā*) within the cohesion of an intricate word order. (The word *ʿānā* is usually translated 'answers', but for Hosea it is an important word of relationship, which means more than a purely oral utterance; cf. 2.15.) Through a sixfold chain of causality by way of natural forces (beginning with the heavens, proceeding with the earth and its produce and ending with Jezreel), he guides the history of men and women; and yet does so in such a way that its outcome remains the result of their acts (cf. 10.12). But the acts, for their part, are based on a past sixfold chain of active divine forces.

The covenant saying which I have quoted here (and which was perhaps put together out of two oral units at the time when it was committed to writing) provides the key to Hosea's thinking in general. The individual levels of metahistory, which in Amos seem to cleave apart, are here welded together by the idea of covenant. It is when we take this as our starting-point that we can understand why Hosea had good reason to reject the cultic practices of his time. He could no longer conceive of his God as a sexually characterized, male giant, who lays himself on the earth, letting his sperm fall on her as rain. Any such idolatry is a diminution of the divine activity, and quite simply absurd if it is applied to the one God.

Here an important step has been taken towards the perception of a transcendent God – and towards the concept of a coherent natural law as well. Yahweh is no longer one potency among others in the natural process. He does not bring about fertility in any direct sense. Between heaven and Jezreel there are indispensable natural forces, which cannot be controlled by cultic orgies, but which remain bound up with God's *ṣedeq* and the perception of man. There begin to be traces of an independent natural order, which has its proper place in the design of a moral world order. What Hosea stresses so polemically is the beginning of a new picture of the world and nature. But through the anthropopathic features of his presentation of God, Hosea avoids allowing the God who is the ruler behind this world-picture to become remote from the individual Israelite.

6. Micah of Moresheth

6.1 Mišpāṭ *Violated. Social criticism*

Hear this, you heads of Jacob, /rulers of the house of Israel!
A Is it not your affair / to understand *mišpāṭ?* . . .
You who tear the skin from them, / the flesh from their bones.
They eat the flesh of my people / . . . they break their bones,
spread them out as in a cooking pot / like meat in the cauldron.
B One day they will cry to Yahweh, / but he will not answer them,
will hide his face from them . . . because they will have let the auras of their deeds become evil (3.1–4).

The person who cries out these words is a younger contemporary of Amos and Hosea, a man from the province of Judah: Micah. We know nothing about his life. In the Israelite south, critical prophecy had probably begun some years earlier, with Isaiah. But Micah is far closer to the North Israelite prophets. He restricts himself to social criticism; so it seems best to treat him before the great Jerusalem prophet. Like Amos, Hosea and Isaiah, Micah's prophetic vision extends to greater Israel. If we may see the present arrangement of the book as a chronological one, he actually begins his proclamation with a tremendous poem attacking Samaria, the capital of the brother kingdom (1.2–7; cf. 6.16).

What is happening to the land of his fellow citizens disturbs him as it does Amos, and convinces him – again like Amos – that Yahweh is bound to surrender his own people to their downfall. Micah's God is embittered because numerous Israelites are being driven out of home and land, are losing their *naḥ^{a}lā* – their inherited homeland – which assures people of a peaceful free life and self-determination, *m^{e}nūḥā*, rest (2.1–5, 8–10). They will even snatch his cloak away from a peaceful citizen. False weights are used (6.9f.; cf. Amos 8.4–6). Prophets, priests and ministers have become venal (7.3). They do not even shrink from shedding blood if it is for their own advantage (3.10; 7.2). Within the family, the bonds linking one to another are growing slack (7.5f.). There is not a single person in the country who is leading a straightforward *(yāšār)* life, in line with the correlation between action and destiny (7.2; 3.9; cf. 2.7). What is happening in the country seems like crypto–cannibalism (3.1–3). Micah reduces all this to the idea that *mišpāṭ* is no longer being upheld by the ruling classes (cf. Hos. 5.1). Instead, it is being perverted into 'what is hateful' (3.9; cf. Amos 6.12). What God expects from man above all is this, *mišpāṭ* – the preservation and promotion of institutional ordinances which are vitally necessary to the community. God does not see this as payment in advance for some reward to be given by him; *mišpāṭ* is the natural echo of his own faithful acts in salvation history (6.1–8). Micah discovers with indignation that he is at present the only person who is filled with *mišpāṭ*: this has the result that he tells Israel of its rebellion and sin, so as to activate, through an effective word, the correlation between sin and disaster and to make it disappear, before it erodes everything round about it even more (3.8f.). To put *mišpāṭ* into practice can therefore very well include acts of punishment against a community, if this is a way to liberate it from an impurity penetrating ever more deeply.

Whereas in Micah *mišpāṭ* stands by itself as a positive goal of action (he hesitates to talk about human *ṣᵉdāqā),* the negative spheres of misdeeds and disaster are generally expressed by a pair of concepts, *pešaʿ* and *haṭṭa't,* which, though they mean 'rebellion and sin', also signify the means of atonement to which in certain circumstances the spheres of action can be transferred (6.7). Spheres of activity (both positive and negative) which involve the whole country proceed from the capital (1.5f.), the stronghold Lachish (1.13), or from the leaders and heads of the country. Micah speaks more strongly even than Amos, calling the groups responsible, if not by their names, at least by their titles. Whether addressing minister or *šōpēṭ* ('judge' – is the king meant? 5.1; 7.3), he appeals to them as the people who gather the tribe together (for war or religious rites, 6.9), twice calling them heads and 'leaders' (3.1,9); the last word, *qāṣīn,* seems to designate a military rank (Josh. 10.24; Judg. 11.6,11; Isa. 22.3). The little book frequently talks about military organization ('units a thousand strong', 5.2; 'armed shepherds', 5.5f.). Did Micah himself belong to this sphere of life (perhaps as leader of the Moresheth militia?).

At all events, he distinguishes himself from the nabis (3.5–8; 2.6–11), denouncing this group without exception. Their task is to penetrate into things by way of visions, more deeply than the normal person can, and to lead the people by means of the anticipatory speech event of Yahweh's word. But instead they are leading the people astray. They proclaim a favourable or unfavourable future, depending on how much they are paid. So Micah has to come forward as seer, though this is really the nabi's function (7.7f.). The conflict between the critical prophet and the prophet of unconditional salvation (which a hundred years later was to lead to severe conflict under Jeremiah) already shows its initial traces here. Since we are not told anything about Micah's life, much remains obscure, with regard to both his own interpretation of his mission, and the place he gives himself. Astonishingly often he appears as accuser, raising cries of lament or funeral dirges over the community of his people (1.8; 2.4; 7.1). He goes about naked, rolls in the dust (1.10), and calls others to lament (1.16). There may perhaps be customs in the background here about which we know nothing.

Micah does not meet with any more sympathy for his message of unconditional doom in the south than Amos and Hosea did in the north. His Judaean listeners are so sure of their God that they indignantly reject what he has to say.

> 'Stop this venom', they venomously cry, / 'stop this venom.
> He will not let disgrace come upon us. / May one say (this at all) (in) the house of Jacob?
> Has the *rūaḥ* of Yahweh perhaps become short of breath, / or are his deeds of this kind?' (2.6f.).

A modern reader imagines that antagonists like this must have been people who were indifferent to religion, unbelievers. But this is an anachronistic misunderstanding. The people who rejected Micah were maintaining the 'orthodox religion' of ancient tradition, which assumed that Yahweh would intervene under all conditions on behalf of the only people on earth who belonged to him. Moreover the nabis supported Micah's opponents:

> Is not Yahweh active in the midst of us?
> No evil shall come upon us (3.11).

A God such as Micah proclaims, who insists uncompromisingly on *mišpāṭ*, who lets the whole society perish because that society is not properly maintained, seems to them a new-fangled God. Aren't men like Micah narrow-minded moralists who vastly exaggerate? As Christians we have been indoctrinated for centuries with the idea that critical prophecy was always right, and its opponents wrong. But the historian ought to try to be just to both parties. When, after the long years of the Aramaean wars, Amos found disruption in the north, in which the exploitation of the weak had become normal practice to so shameless an extent that the break-up of the whole society was threatened, an unconditional proclamation of disaster may have been justified. But the Aramaean wars had little or no effect on the Southern kingdom. Did Micah's society really look any worse than other societies throughout human history? If unconditional disaster were always the consequence, humanity would have ceased to exist by now. But then why talk so unrelentingly in the Israel of the eighth century BC?

6.2 Devastation as the doom to come

What does the sombre future look like which Micah conjures up as a result of social conditions which have become intolerable? Like Amos and Hosea, he maintains the view of a sphere of action which determines destiny. Anyone who covets the fields of another man will one day lose his own to a foreign conqueror (2.1–5). Anyone who fills Jerusalem with blood guilt and unjustly gained wealth ultimately makes it unlivable in; he undermines even the places of worship, so that the temple on Zion becomes a wooded hill-top (3.9–12). The rich, who are full of acts of violence *(ḥamas)* – a negative power which does not entangle people outwardly but penetrates their hearts and minds (Amos 3.10f.) – will eat without being satisfied; will sow without harvesting; press out oil without becoming fat, and grape-juice without drinking wine (6.12–15; cf. 7.13, referring to foreign nations). The consequences of shameful deeds will one day have to be endured (6.16). The nabis, who can see further than other people, will see only blackness round them, because they have led the people astray with false visions (3.5–8). All this has as its premise the common Israelite conviction that habitual human action will one day find its consummation in a corresponding destiny. What is unusual is only that the present aura of wickedness and disaster is accorded a preponderance which cannot be set aside, while divine counter-actions recede entirely into the background.

Military and political realities are merely hinted at. The lament over twelve devastated Judaean cities (1.10–16) presupposes a conqueror who marches through Judah to Jerusalem; but he only becomes the subject as the occupier in 1.15. Deportation is touched on only in 1.16. Assyria is expressly named for the first time in the 'salvation' oracle in 5.5ff.

Micah says nothing about active forces which flow invisibly from God to human beings and evoke meta-historical movements. Perhaps we can still find in him an older view, since Yahweh himself is immediately involved, where there is a search for profounder motive forces. But what he does is ambivalent. On the one hand he turns away from the people, who are burdened with sin beyond the point where salvation is possible; he hides his face, no longer answers (3.1–4,7), and does not accept atoning action any more (6.1–8). On the other hand, God is himself injured, and approaches in order to strike.

> Can I remain uninjured *(zkh)* besides scales of outrage / beside bags
> with deceitful weights?

He therefore has to strike the sinful people and make them sick (6.11f.); he has to give up the sinners to desolation (6.16). For those who plan other wicked deeds he plans evil too (2.1,3). The impending dispute is publicly announced before the forum of the mountains, which from time immemorial have witnessed to Yahweh's saving history with the people (6.1–8). The whole force of Yahweh's glory marches (in the form of the foreign aggressor?) against one Judaean town (1.15); Against Samaria there will be a mighty theophany, so that destruction will be total (1.2–7). (Nothing is said – perhaps by chance? – about a theophany against the country of Judah.)

6.3 The riddle of the announcement of unconditional downfall and the prophetic experience of God

In none of his prophecies does Micah suggest that the disaster forecast and brought about by Yahweh is meant in any conditional sense; there is no talk of possible repentance. But in the disputation in ch. 6 – the only passage where he reverts to salvation history, in order to show that Israel's failure is incomprehensible – the partner shows signs of relenting: The national 'self' begs the prophet for a *tōrāh*, an oracle:

> With what shall I come before Yahweh / and bow myself before God on high?
> Shall I come before him with burnt offerings, / with yearling calves?
> Shall I give my firstborn as my (embodied) sin, / the fruit of my body as the aura of sin surrounding my vital powers?

The prophet's answer sounds strange, and is not quite clear to us. He takes up the entrance liturgies sung at the great annual festivals, which were well-known to his listeners (Ps. 15):

> You have been shown, O man, what good is / and what Yahweh requires of you
> – to do *mišpāṭ*, to love faithfulness to his covenant / and to walk thoughtfully with your God.

Is Micah pointing to a missed opportunity, which is gone for ever? Or does he see the way to a turning point here?

We are told in Jeremiah 26, not in the book of Micah itself, that the most radical saying which Micah uttered against Jerusalem (3.9–12) moved King Hezekiah 'to entreat the favour of Yahweh' (by cultic means), whereupon Yahweh was sorry for the evil which he had announced. This sounds in English as if Yahweh had taken it all back. But we have to remember that the Old Testament knows nothing, anywhere, of simple forgiveness on God's part. Since sin builds an inner-worldly sphere of power, it cannot be set aside just because God decides to let 'two and two make five'. When Yahweh is sorry for some evil he has intended, it can only mean that the disaster means death merely for part of the corporate personality (II Sam. 12.13f.), so that the greater part goes free – i.e., God accepts precisely what the spokesmen offer Micah (6.6f.). This probably means that Hezekiah carried out some extraordinary act of national humility and self-depreciation, with expiatory animal sacrifices or something of the kind. Perhaps the huge losses which the Judaean state suffered in 701 under Hezekiah through Sennacherib's campaign were viewed as part of this absolutely essential vicarious atonement. So Jeremiah 26 by no means proves that Micah only intended to announce *conditional* disaster – that he only threatened catastrophe for didactic purposes, in case no moral repentance followed. For Micah, as for the other eighth-century prophets, the disaster he prophesied was unconditional. But it is certainly not seen as *total* downfall. Certainly, Jerusalem will be put to the plough – a terrible thought. But there will still be people in the country who will plant the fields there afterwards.

But even if the announcement is not of total extermination, the disaster remains appalling and of hitherto undreamed-of dimensions, for both the prophet and his listeners. How can we explain the fact that the eighth-century prophets suddenly seem able to present their listeners only with compositions in these minor keys? The common view is that this is only an expression of what the Yahweh of the Old Testament had been for his worshippers from time immemorial – a strict law-giver and judge, a supernatural authority who saw to it that his commandments were strictly observed and that every transgression was punished without respect of persons. It cannot be too emphatically stressed that this view is not supported by the slightest historical evidence. Neither Amos, Hosea nor Micah talks about God as judge, nor does any one of them have recourse on any single occasion to a commandment (except perhaps Hos. 4.2, which is a later interpolation). It is true that Israel had for centuries been convinced of the correlation between action and destiny. But this was not the only law determining history. Parallel to that law, and running counter to it, are continuing divine aids to salvation, which are just as efficacious and which come into force when Israel has strayed from the proper way. 'Yahweh is a God who is gracious and is one with his kindred, long-suffering and rich in faithfulness to his covenant, and at all times ready to take upon himself the sins of his people' (Ex. 34.6f.). That is pre-prophetic religion! The prophets turn away from it, seeing the correlation between action and destiny and the active forces belonging to it as the essential scaffolding which gives metahistory its meaning. How do they arrive at this conclusion?

For the last hundred years scholars have tried to find sociological answers. It has been supposed that the prophets belonged to a particular repressed social group and clothed its ideology – perhaps in all honesty – with the nimbus of the word of God. But Amos, Hosea, Micah, and even more Isaiah show such a high standard of education and move so freely and independently in their society that they certainly did not belong to the peasant-farmer class. The Assyriologist Hugo Winckler has put forward another, even more venturesome theory. For him the prophets of doom who prepared the fall of their nation were a fifth column of the imperial Assyrian power, the agents of the eastern emperors. But the condemnation of Assyrian expansion which we find in Micah (5.5f.) and Isaiah is in itself sufficient contradiction of this hypothesis.

So the only explanations left to us are theological ones. A favourite solution is that the prophets experienced an ultimately inexplicable divine word, a kerygma, which allows no further questioning. The reader of the Bible has to 'actualize' this for himself. But it is difficult, especially if one is concerned with actualization, to dispense with the question of the sufficient foundation for the message, provided one is not prepared to be content with an inscrutable, capricious God. Moreover, can the God described here be equated with the Christian God? Can the God in whom Christians believe let sin on earth gain the upper hand to such an extent that he cuts himself loose from his chosen people, preferring from that time onwards to exist alone, without any ties with men and women? The Jesus of the New Testament proclaims a God who is ready to forgive without limit. And it is just this that the God of the unconditional prophecy of doom is not prepared to do. Why not?

It seems to meet the facts best if we deduce that the men of the eighth century had *a new kind of experience of God.* New, not in their subjective opinion but in our retrospective view of history. Their experience is not that Yahweh moves further away from the world, becoming – as transcendent God – holier and stricter. It is rather the very reverse that is true. The area of reality which was open to experience expanded in this period. Foreign nations which hitherto had been merely legendary had now become imperial powers that determined events in Israel's own personal area. Social orders which had seemed made for eternity collapsed. Even the worship of Yahweh was threatened with disaster. The God of Israelite tradition himself was affected by this complete upheaval and corruption. The super-dimensional correlation between misdeeds and doom touches him too (6.11), and he becomes sym-pathetic in the literal sense involved in the suffering (Hos. 6.4; 11.8).

Anyone who at that time became drawn into the total movement of all reality, behind the visible everyday world, anyone who looked for wider perspectives in place and time, became aware of a God even 'greater' than the religion of the patriarchs presupposed. If the real world is not to decline into chaos, this God is bound to insist on *mišpāṭ*, and to translate *mišpāṭ* into action, or create it anew, even after human failure and human *pešaʿ*. This made reality, as well as the God that rules it, infinitely wider and more comprehensive than the average Israelite had hitherto assumed. At the same time, God's moral will and his present activity also had to be greater, and his shaping of the future more flexible and more extensive. According to what these prophets experienced, the meaning of God is more closely woven into the mighty movement of all reality, and in many more different ways than had hitherto been assumed. God is not further away; he is nearer. The beginning of an ethical and futuristic monotheism make themselves felt. But this does not move God 'theistically' into the beyond. It links him metahistorically with world events through a thousand different threads.

If this explanation is on the right track, it follows that none of the prophets thinks that everything is going to come to an end with the coming catastrophe. Even if the sayings they formulated for their contemporaries are determined by unconditional disaster, every one of these men remains a prophet of salvation in the sense that they presuppose that life will go on in an undoubtedly positive sense, for both God and the world. Even Micah perhaps talks explicitly about a continuation of this kind (see below).

Surprisingly enough, Micah sees Yahweh in much more strongly *cosmic* terms than his North Israelite predecessors, and less limited to the land and civilization of Palestine. The book as we have it today begins with a splendid description, showing Yahweh setting forth from the palace of his holiness, striding in theophany over the earth, so that the mountains melt before the white heat of his appearance, and with them all spheres of sin – including sinners. After the beginning of the third part of the book (6.1–6), Yahweh calls on heaven and earth to be his witness as he justifies himself, describing what he has done for Israel in salvation history. Convicted by these world-wide vistas, Israel is forced to its knees before the God of the heights, as the book significantly calls him. For Micah, Yahweh is not associated with *ᵃdāmā*, as he was for Amos and Hosea. Yahweh dwells in heaven, but in such a way that he utterly fills the whole universe as its king. His royal powers of activity rule not only *over* Israel but *in* Israel too. Here even the babies are a part of his honour (*hādār*, 2.9). The sovereignty of God envelops the future ruler (5.4). The monarchy is therefore not understood as the confrontation of ruler and ruled; instead, those involved in the process of rule are embedded in the king's power as far as it extends. If it is infringed, the king himself is affected. But where there is rebellion, *peša'*, those responsible move out of the sphere of the divine-kingly glory and run the risk that this glory *(kābōd)* will turn against them through the agency of foreign nations.

6.4 *Messianic future*

About a third of the sayings in the Book of Micah do not proclaim downfall, but prophesy a state of salvation which will again come into being after the terrible disaster. These sections (except 5.3–6) are not composed in the genre of prophecy which is usual elsewhere. They have different oracle forms. Micah scholars are divided as to whether a prophet who lashes out more bluntly than any other at the intolerable state of affairs, prophesying a devastation of the cities during which even Jerusalem will be erased from the earth, could at the same time have drawn so bright a picture of a better future. Do not the proclamations of disaster perhaps derive from a later revision and correction of the visionary with his uncanny presage of disaster on the basis of a more developed perception of God? Moreover, the condition of salvation is never described in such a way that it simply presents a contrast to the degeneracy of the present. The book never prophesies that the peasant farmers who have been driven from their own acres will get back their fields and homes again, or that *mišpāṭ* will be gloriously restored (except in 7.9).

On the other hand, a good many of the prophecies of salvation sound so fresh and individual that it is hard to put them down to the generalizing trend of later centuries. It is also surprising that in a passage like 7.14–17 Yahweh is associated solely with North Israelite landscapes like Carmel, Bashan and Gilead. Elsewhere, too, Micah thinks only of the Northern kingdom. Is the later reviser supposed to have done so equally explicitly? The scholars who dispute that there is any hope of salvation in Micah (or Amos or Hosea) are forced to construct a messianic eschatology of salvation for the post-exilic period, (from which the revision allegedly dates); and this is hard to reconcile with other texts which are indubitably post-exilic (e.g., Chronicles). Since linguistic criteria have hardly been developed for the investigation of the prophetic writings, Old Testament scholars all start from the content – questions such as whether the use of 'judgment' and 'salvation' in one and the same prophet does not involve a contradiction in itself. But since the eighth-century prophets never in fact explicitly use both terms, the decision is usually based on modern judgments of taste. According to the biographical note in Jeremiah 26, after Hezekiah yielded, Yahweh was sorry for the evil prophesied by Micah. This raises the question of how, then, the partial divine withdrawal could be perceived with any certainty unless the spokesman of doom, Micah, had also become the spokesmen of God's magnanimity. But this in its turn means attributing some prospects of salvation to Micah.

The problem emerges particularly clearly from the sayings about extermination in 5.10–15. This is a *bayyōm-hāhū'* oracle, i.e., one of those beginning 'In that day', which always have a special structure. It prophesies the end of an army with chariots (which had already appeared in a shady light in 1.13), together with the extermination of cities (1.8ff.); but it also proclaims the end of sorcery and the conjuring up of the dead (cf. 3.7). Cultic objects like pillars of stone and wood (cf. section 1.7 above), which were supposed to house the god, will also be blotted out. This is not a 'salvation' saying – especially if the application to the nations at the end (v. 14 with 12b), which does not fit the context, is assigned to an editorial hand. Is the prediction then Micah's, or does it derive from a later 'Deuteronomic' pen?

The argument comes to a head in the famous messianic prophecy in 5.1–6. Scholars tend to call texts messianic which announce a future king who will bring salvation to Israel after a catastrophe (following the Aramaic word *m^e^šīaḥ*, 'the anointed one'; but the word is not found in the prophets).

> Now make breaches in the walls, rapacious daughter. / A siege is laid (by him? by God?) against us.
> With a rod they strike upon the cheek / the *šōpēt* (ruler) of Israel.
> But you, Bethlehem/Ephrathah, / [small] among the companies of Judah,
> from you will come forth one / to be ruler in Israel.
> His origin is from old, / from ancient days.

In the present context of the book, this is linked with the prediction in a second saying, which was probably originally independent:

> Therefore will he give them up (originally: behold I give them up?) / until the time when she who is in travail has brought forth.
> The rest of his brethren shall return / to the Israelites.
> He will arise and feed his flock in strength [. . .] / in the *gā'ōn* ('majesty') [. . .] of his God.
> For now he shall be great / to the ends of the earth.
> He will become the embodiment of *šālōm* ('peace').
> (6b) He will save from Assyria / when it comes into our land . . .
> (5b) He will raise up for us seven shepherds over him (Assyria), eight leaders of men.

The 'rapacious daughter' probably meant Jerusalem (a continuation of 3.12? Or is the reference to Samaria?). While a siege is impending there, a new ruler is born in the little town of Bethlehem. It was from here that David came, the famous founder of the dynasty; for all Judaeans the age of David represented the brilliant close of the salvation history shaped by God. That a person should come forth from Bethlehem, and that his 'outgoing' should belong to the primal period of salvation history *(qedem)*, offers hope for a rebirth of David, who is now born anew through a mysterious mother-figure at the place whence his family came. The achievements of salvation history, which have been totally erased by the behaviour of contemporaries, will be created anew by God after the fall of Jerusalem, at a time which has already been determined. Afterwards North and South Israel will be united, and the ruler's fame will spread far over the earth (cf. II Sam. 7.9; Amos 9.11f.). He will feed his people, veiled in divine majesty; the word *gā'ōn* is a play on the idea which we also find in Amos and Isaiah, but whose background is still unexplained. The result will be general well-being – *šālōm*, which means more for the Hebrew than political peace and contentment. The *šālōm*, which the nabis misleadingly already promise for the present day (3.5) will thus at last be reality. Isaiah (9.6f.) also finds the culmination of messianic rule in the establishment of *šālōm*. Both passages undoubtedly include the notion that the people who have hitherto been oppressed will receive their rights again, and that there will once more be *mišpāṭ* in the land.

Compared with the messianic prophecies in Isaiah 9 and 11, which we shall be considering later, this text, with the prophecy of a reborn David, undoubtedly seems more archaic. Whereas in the Isaiah passages the saving king appears only after the Assyrian army has been eliminated, through a miraculous theophany, here he is given the task of actually defending the country against the Assyrians. Archaic ideas about the victorious king show through; we are even told that he will set up his military administration in Assyria, i.e., that he will extend his power that far. Nevertheless, here as in Isaiah the ruler is not given the title of king.

I cannot see any sufficient grounds for denying Micah's authorship of the passage. If the sayings do go back to Micah, were they proclaimed when Assyrian troops invaded Judah under Hezekiah in 711 or 701? Or is the background the North Israelite capital Samaria in 722/1?

When proclaiming future salvation, Micah contents himself with brief indications – much more so than in his prophecy of disaster. Does the future intervention of God for the establishment of salvation – an intervention totally new in kind – mean the restoration of what had been before, or does it surpass this earlier condition? It is not the function of a prophet to point the details of this new turn of events, for he is talking to listeners who will no longer be affected by it, since by then they themselves will have perished. But there is certainly a point in establishing assertively ('but you', adversative), parallel to the statements about the downfall, that things will not come to an end either for God or for his chosen people. The prophet himself may draw the assurance from this that with the *dābār* (word) he is proclaiming he is not merely evoking a chaos that will swallow everything up, even if he cannot cherish any further hope for his own individual salvation.

7. Isaiah

7.1 The four periods of his prophecy

Amos and Hosea proclaimed their message in the days of King Uzziah (= Azariah); and according to the heading of his book this was also the first period of Isaiah's activity. Isaiah was the son of a man called Amoz, who is otherwise unknown (and who is not to be confused with Amos), and he preached the *dābār* he had received from Yahweh in Jerusalem. Here the prophetic movement first began to announce unconditional disaster a few years later than its counterpart in the north, Israel. Judaean prophecy, too, proclaimed the downfall of state and nation, the foreign rule of Assyria, and also renewal – one day. Thus critical prophecy spread to a place that was politically less important than Samaria but which, ever since David and the building of Solomon's Temple, had possessed a far greater dignity than any of the cult places in the north.

Isaiah was married to a *nᵉbīʾā* (8.3) – that is to say, a woman who acted as a seer, probably at the Temple. It is all the more surprising that Isaiah *never presents himself as a nabi*. He uses their literary genres, such as prophecy and the vision, as Amos had already done; he is filled with the lofty awareness that he not only prophesies the future but actually brings it to pass; he does not doubt that he can move his God to set a sign in the heavens or in the underworld (7.10ff.). But for all that, he is evidently a prophet without being a nabi. As well as the nabis (whom he frequently attacks), he also mentions the *ḥōzeh*, the seer (29.10; 30.10). Can one perhaps assign Isaiah to the same group as Amos, and see him as a man who divines the future, endowed with divine inspiration, but without any institutional ties? It is possible that there was a special royal *ḥōzeh* in Jerusalem, who had a confidential position as a kind of privy counsellor, without being a court official (II Sam. 34.11). That would explain how Isaiah came to have the right of direct access to the king (ch. 7). Unlike Amos in Bethel, he was still able to go on preaching publicly, even after he was accused (8.12) of preparing the ground for a *qešer*, conspiracy (also like Amos in the North). He unmasks the king, Ahaz, as unbelieving and hence as condemned to downfall with all his dynasty; yet he is not forbidden to speak. In order to underline his message, he takes liberties which go far beyond what must have been thought customary and decent at that time. For three years he ran about Jerusalem naked, as a sign and foretaste of the Egyptians, on whom his fellow countrymen were relying too much and who in a short time are going to be dragged away naked as prisoners of war, in accordance with the harsh customs of war at the time (ch. 20). If one remembers that, according to the Hebrew view, a naked man was even more scandalous than a naked woman (Gen. 9.21ff.; II Sam. 6.20), it is clear to what extent Isaiah was disregarding public opinion in Jerusalem. (Some scholars accordingly presume that the prophet wore at least a loin cloth during his demonstration.)

It is no wonder that there were people who mocked at Isaiah's talk about the work of Yahweh, which was going to break in on the country in a disastrous way (5.19). Yet no one dared to lay a hand on him. It has occasionally been suggested that Isaiah came from the aristocracy, and was perhaps related to the royal house; but this cannot be proved. There is more evidence for the view that he had been educated in Hebrew Wisdom. This is suggested, not only by the breadth of his culture, but also by his anthropology, which is particularly directed towards knowledge (*yāda'*) and reason (*lēb*).

Isaiah proclaimed his message over a period of about forty years and under four different kings (1.1). What he left behind him far exceeds what we have from Amos and Hosea. Of all the prophets known to us, Isaiah is the most powerful in his language. The wealth of the images he uses and the impressive force of his prophecies have continually elicited cries of admiration even from scholars who are otherwise sparing in their praise. Yet it is not easy to fix unequivocally the texts in Proto-Isaiah (ch. 1–39) which go back to Isaiah himself. His versatility and the many facets of his message continually moved his later adherents to interpolate their own interpretations and topical allusions. How can we chisel out the original rock of Isaiah? Unfortunately the results arrived at by individual scholars differ widely. Since modern literary criticism has not yet worked out its methods in a complete and comprehensive way, criticism of this kind rests more on the subjective feeling of the interpreter than on provable textual facts – and this is especially true in the case of the prophetic books. In addition, the Western obsession with a God who judges is also attributed to the Old Testament prophet as a matter of course; with this as the starting point, the divorce between an Isaiah who preaches judgment and an Isaiah who preaches salvation becomes the essential criterion. Yet in none of the thirty-nine chapters is there a concept which points with sufficient certainty to a divine act of judgment. I am therefore rejecting the usual alternative and will try to determine what is authentic simply on the basis of form-critical and semantic observation (which of course has to be tested). And where authenticity is concerned, I prefer to trust the transmitted text too much rather than too little.

Scholars studying Isaiah are at one in the conviction that the texts which have been preserved for us are not distributed equally over his long period of activity, but derive from *four particular periods*:

1. The period of social criticism (chs. 2–5). According to the prevailing opinion, this begins with the death of Uzziah, between 747 and 735 BC (ch. 6). According to my own view (which I shall be expounding below) it ends with this date.
2. The Syro-Ephraimite war of 734–732 BC (chs. 7–9). Following his lack of success, Isaiah falls silent (for a number of years?) (8.16–18).
3. Anti-Assyrian rebellion under the leadership of Ashdod, 713–711 BC (chs. 10–23).
4. Anti-Assyrian rebellion after the death of Sennacherib until the siege of Jerusalem, 705–701 BC (chs. 28–32; 36–39).

Between the second and the third period there is an interval of almost twenty years. We should certainly not suppose that Isaiah completely ceased to prophesy in the meantime; but what he said was evidently not worth permanent remembrance. He is again inspired with sayings of weighty significance once the political and military scene begins to move. As soon as the storm signals for the state begin to fly, he makes his voice unmistakably heard. Not only does he comment on events with the word of Yahweh that has been given to him, he actually directs the events themselves. During the reign of Ahaz he failed, but he succeeded under Hezekiah.

Isaiah lived in unsettled times, in which, after various attempts, the superior power of Assyria finally extinguished the independence of the small states of Syria-Palestine. When the prophet finally retired from the scene, the little state of Judah had to all intents and purposes been reduced to the capital, and was completely dependent on its mighty Assyrian overlord. Forty years before, Isaiah had divined and prophesied that this was what would happen to Judah. His political or meta-political involvement is considerably greater even than that of Amos. Like the literary prophets of the north, he sees historical developments conditioned by movements on meta-historical levels. Yet he finds it important – even more than his predecessors – to discover an anthropological foundation for what takes place supra-historically and is therefore only comprehensible in metahistorical terms.

Anyone who visits the ruins of Babylon today can only enter the site through the Ishtar gate, which the Iraqi Office for Antiquities has had removed from the centre of the city and made the commanding entrance. This archaeological example occurs to me as I note how Old Testament scholars all make the vision in ch. 6 the only possible approach to an understanding of the prophet. They take it from its actual place in the body of the book and make it the preface to all understanding of Isaiah – as the vision of the call which they claim was all important to the prophet. It is essential for us to examine the reliability of this premise before we enter into the other aspects of Isaiah's thought.

7.2 The Temple vision

In chapter 6, Isaiah gives an account of a *vision* in which he sees Yahweh enthroned in majesty, towering over the Temple of Jerusalem, and hears his tremendous voice. The chapter has been the subject of more exegesis than any other chapter in Isaiah. The very opening is splendid:

> In the year that King Uzziah died,
> I saw the Lord of all sitting upon a throne high and lifted up, and the fringe of his garment filled the temple palace.
> Seraphs stood round him. Each of them had six wings. With two they covered their face, with two they covered the nakedness of their loins, and with two they did fly. One began to call to the other:
> 'Holy, holy, holy is Yahweh Sabaoth, / the fullness of the whole earth is his *kābōd* ('glory')
> Thereupon the posts of the doors shook in their foundations through the voice of him who called, and the house was filled with smoke.

Yahweh's throne towers above the Temple, so high that only the hem of his garment reaches the earthly building and fills it. Before the prophet's eyes, God towers high into heaven, where sacred beings (like the Egyptian sacred asps) hover round, waiting to serve him. The prophet is silent about the form in which he saw Yahweh. Even for him it remains unutterable, indescribable. All he is able to describe are the supernatural servants, and above all the liturgy which they begin to sing at this very moment. The tremendous God, before whom the proud and noble building of the Jerusalem Temple below seems like a nutshell, is holy to the highest power of holiness. What holiness means is shown by the next scene. Holiness evidently exists in this upper region, whereas all that is earthly is his *kābōd*. What Isaiah experiences therefore is not merely a transcendent God, but a God who also dwells completely within the world, even though inner-worldliness only represents one of his manifestations – that is to say, his *kābōd*. The word is usually translated as 'glory'. But in the original Hebrew it means force, weightiness – what impresses outwardly but also radiates splendour and overpowering beauty. The raising of the heavenly hymn of praise makes the Temple below shake on its foundations.

The picture in the first scene is self-contained. The content is not specifically characteristic of Isaiah. It is in accord with the piety of the Jerusalem cult which the prophet shares, and which provides the framework for his experience. It can equally well be found in the Psalms. There the Temple is the centre of the earth and the site of the footstool of the divine throne, the ark (Ps. 99.5, 132.7), the place of a theophany to which Yahweh comes in a rushing wind and which – after he ascends his throne over Zion – causes him to be celebrated as the king of *kābōd* (Ps. 24.7–9). Every participant in the Jerusalem cult was convinced that at the autumn feast on Mount Zion he himself experienced what Isaiah describes here. The only difference is that the prophet's gaze penetrated further than the gaze of the ordinary Israelite. The ordinary man perhaps perceived flames above the altar in the forecourt, and smoke inside the Temple; he was aware of a *trisagion* – the threefold invocation of God's holiness – which was echoed by the Temple singers, and he 'believed' in the God who was present above all this. Isaiah, on the other hand, *sees* through the smoke the very garment of God; he sees seraphs above and hears celestial singing. The text makes clear in exemplary fashion what prophetic visions were considered to be, according to the prophets' own interpretation. They do not tell of seeing forces *beyond* this world. What they claim is a *profound* vision, a seeing into *the depths of the one human and divine reality*, a reality in which earth and heaven, far from cleaving apart, belong together in an inseparable unity. A fourth dimension opens up beyond everyday perception.

Because of this profound vision of reality, Isaiah is more deeply affected by his encounter with God than his fellows:

Then I cried:
Woe is me, I must fall silent (?), for a man of unclean lips am I,

And in the midst of a people of unclean lips have I my dwelling. For my own eyes have seen the King, Yahweh Sabaoth.
Then flew one of the seraphim to me, having a burning coal in his hand which he had taken with tongs from the altar. He touched my mouth and said:
'Behold, this has touched your lips.' / The aura of your sin has left you and your sin is expiated.

The prophet utters his cry quite spontaneously. Under the spell of God's holiness he becomes aware of his impurity as human being. His spontaneous feeling is marked by a semantic opposition quite common in Hebrew. For pre-exilic Israel lived in a cultically determined polarity between holiness on the one hand and impurity on the other. Between the two lay the sectors of purity and profanity[14]. Here holiness does not mean moral irreproachability, or the highest form of morality, as we assume it does in the case of the Christian saints. In the modern study of religion Rudolf Otto's view of holiness[15] has generally been followed: in the holy we meet the wholly other, remote from everyday experience; the holy is at once *fascinosum* and *tremendum*. This approach comes very close to the meaning of the Hebrew word. For pre-exilic Israel, however, holy in the sense of *qādōš* is above all the main concept of a cultically centred religion. Holiness is not merely something above this world; it is an active divine power which falls from above upon the world and is manifested in holy places, seasons, persons and texts. Its opposite pole is found in the unclean or impure. Filth in its foulest form belongs to this category, as do conditions that damage life, such as death and disease. Uncleanness is caused by sin and by any behaviour which is unfavourable to the community. Anyone who is touched by impurity will be drawn into a negative field of force. But if holiness then comes up against impurity, the holy becomes an electric spark which burns up the impurity, thereby putting an end to it.

Appalled, Isaiah becomes aware that he is impure. Since by virtue of his profound prophetic vision he experiences God's presence more intensely than others who, like himself, are in the Temple, he also becomes more intensely aware of the dangerous consequences. The 'fourth' dimension, which only a prophetic eye perceives, does not merely link the world of real life with the divine powers; it puts its mark on worldly life, showing it to have a moral basis. Isaiah's impurity is conditioned both individually and collectively: 'In the midst of a people of unclean lips have I my dwelling.' He is imprisoned in the solidarity of collective guilt.

But at this moment God's concern is not to make an example of

Isaiah for the whole of Israel. On the contrary, the divine world reacts graciously to him, forgiving him his sins. This was entirely in accordance with the traditional temple religion of Jerusalem: 'To thee all flesh comes on account of the burden of its sins. Greater than we ourselves are the auras of our rebellion, but thou dost set them aside through atonement' (Ps. 65.2f.).

In accord with this conviction, Isaiah's sins are expiated from the altar, and he is enabled to go on living and speaking, although – as the continuation shows – he is to be spared only for a limited time. For a decisive, third scene follows:

> I heard the voice of the Lord of all: 'Whom shall I send and who will go for us?' I answered: 'I am ready, send me.'
> He said: 'Go and say to this people:
> Hear so intensely that you do not understand anything (*bīn*).
> See so intently that you do not perceive anything (*yādaʿ*).
> Make the *lēb* ('heart') of this people unreceptive / and its ears hard of hearing,
> and seal up its eyes / so that it does not see with its eyes
> and (does not) hear with its ears / and with its *lēb* ('heart') does not understand / and repent (?) and bring about healing for itself.

This is the famous *hardness of heart* which Isaiah has to bring about. In English, hardness of heart sounds like 'obduracy' – acting contrary to what one knows to be right. That is also part of the meaning of the original text. But according to the traditional Israelite conviction, this obduracy, brought about by God, was conceivable only in the case of non-Israelites, who had committed some act of violation against Yahweh's own people. (A typical example was Pharaoh, in the story of the exodus from Egypt, Ex. 8.15,32; 9.34f.; 10.1). Isaiah, on the other hand, perceives that God can withdraw to a hostile distance like this, even in the case of his own people.

The prophetic statement set a precedent. According to Mark 4.11f., Jesus applied it to the Israel of his time and, following Jesus, Paul does the same in Rom. 11.8f. From this, Christian dogmatics developed a doctrine of double predestination, maintained pre-eminently by Augustine and later by Calvin. According to this, God, in a decree resolved upon before time began, predestined men as yet unborn either to faith and eternal salvation, or to disbelief and eternal torment. (Behind this stands the enduring experience of religious men and women that, however cogent the pointers to belief may be, there will always be a great number of people who close their minds to faith and to religious questions in general.)

In Isaiah, however, the statement is not meant in nearly such a fundamental sense. This became an acute problem for his generation for the first time; up till then no generation had failed so completely. What he proclaims touches on a divine act, but not one taking place before time; it is an act fulfilled in history. And it is not aimed at individuals but at a whole people. This resolve does not spring from any divine inscrutable decree. It is sufficiently justified by Israel's behaviour. However, there is one assumption; God cannot ignore human spheres of evil or disaster to an unlimited degree, because these have a formative effect on history. Nor is God's preparedness for the atonement of guilty human beings infinite. There is a gulf between this view and Christian ideas about God's infinite love. But this is an assumption which Isaiah shares with all the other prophets.

For Isaiah, obduracy affects the *lēb* (the 'heart'), which for the prophet is a central concept. In our modern European languages, heart is used in a transferred sense for feeling and the capacity for emotion. For the Hebrew it was different. For him, *lēb* was the seat of thought and will; it corresponded to what we call understanding and reason. *Lēb* is the organ that enables a person to find his bearings in the world, through *yāda*ʿ or *bīn*. Both verbs mean 'to know'; but this is not knowing in the sense of a detached analysis. It is involvement in persons and things which directs subsequent action and furthers the gaining and enhancement of life. If Yahweh 'hardens' a person's heart (*lēb*), he becomes insensitive and incapable of receptiveness in his reason, incapable of receiving impressions or of interpreting what he perceives. The *lēb* is dependent on information which reaches it through eyes and ears, and these organs will then fail to perform their proper function.

But what is it that Israel is going to misunderstand in the future? If we think in terms of what has to be *heard* intensively we may think of Isaiah's own message – his exposure of the real face of the Israelite life of his day, and his presentation of what was impending in the future. It is true that what Isaiah revealed was based on prophetic vision. But the prophet presumed as a matter of course that the content of his message was open to subsequent insight. What God reveals is completely in accord with reason, even if human beings often grasp what he has to say only at a later stage. But where truth appears in such naked form as in Isaiah's vision, it is bound to seem unconvincing. What the people *see* is the history in which Yahweh acts, and in which their own activity is such a failure. But they will only become aware of superficial, momentary constellations of events. They will think that quantity is quality and fail to remember the 'fourth' dimension. Orientation in the world goes missing at the same time as orientation towards God. Historical events are rushing meaninglessly past them. For Isaiah there is no opposition between faith and knowledge (as the Middle Ages later postulated). For him the world is simply the supra-history woven and interpenetrated by Yahweh, the supra-history proclaimed and evoked by the prophetic *dābār*. Consequently, true knowledge of the world also conditions knowledge of God and vice versa. On the basis of its special contact with Yahweh, the primal ground of all reality, Israel had hitherto been able to see true reality better than other nations. But that is now at an end. The people are threatened with 'hardness of heart', which excludes the possibility of conversion, and leads to an idiocy of the spirit, a blunting of the intellect.

This statement about hardness of heart has therefore to be understood in the light of Isaiah's own anthropological insights. It is connected with a criticism of Wisdom which we shall be considering later. Hardness of heart is not a chance or arbitrary matter. It is the regrettable end-product of a long prophetic and divine experience with these people.

There is therefore nothing in the chapter which necessarily points to an initial call, to an act through which Isaiah – hitherto untouched by prophetic experience – is now drawn into the orbit of a profound vision hitherto unguessed at. At any rate, the people who put together the book of Proto-Isaiah did not see ch. 6 as the beginning of his activity. Had they done so, they would have put it at the beginning of the book. In the same way, the person who split up the poem about the Northern kingdom (9.8ff.), with its refrain, putting the final stanza (5.25ff.) before ch. 6, clearly felt that the vision was the culmination of previous prophecies of disaster. The vision of Micaiah ben Imlah in I Kings 22, which is in many respects similar, is not an initial vision either. And when, during his vision, Isaiah comes forward with 'Here am I, send me', he shows that he is familiar with the procedure by which someone was commissioned or sent by God. He shows no signs of the resistance which people display at their *very first* call by God (cf. Jer. 1.6; Ex. 4.10). So my own supposition is that this vision came at the end of Isaiah's period of social criticism, and that the statement about a hardening of heart is not something that suddenly came over him one day, for which he was completely unprepared; it has to be understood as the summing-up of a profound disappointment over the people listening to him.

7.3 Social injustice and the arrogance of the mighty: the early period

Before we develop the basic structure of Isaiah's view of man and God, the different periods of the prophet's activity must be described.

What Isaiah found important in his early period is clearly expressed in the Song of the Vineyard in 5.1–7:

> I will sing a song about my beloved, / a love song concerning his vineyard.
> A vineyard grew up for my beloved / on a fruitful hill.

The singer then describes the trouble his friend had taken over the vineyard, but

> He hoped it would yield grapes / and it yielded sour ones.

The words sound as if they came from the song of a ballad-singer. For Hebrew ears, 'vineyard' was an ambiguous word, because in the language of love it meant the beloved woman. The fact that Isaiah is playing on his second meaning becomes clear from the refrain, in which the friend himself takes up the tale:

> So now, inhabitants of Jerusalem and Judah, / judge between me and my vineyard . . .
> Why did I hope for it to bring grapes, / although it brought sour ones?

The speaker does not wait for an answer. The injured lover gives the answer himself:

> So now I will tell you / what I will do to my vineyard.
> I will remove its hedge, so that it will be ransacked, / break down its walls, so that it will be trampled down . . .
> I will command the clouds / that they rain no more rain on it.

Scholars dispute whether the last line already reveals the friend's identity. Is the rejected wooer playing with primitive rain magic, in order to express his future contempt for the beauty he has hitherto courted? Or is the listener already supposed to get the uncomfortable feeling that the friend can only be Yahweh himself? In the final verse, at least, the riddle is solved by two word-plays:

> Yes, the vineyard of Yahweh Sabaoth / is (was) the house of Israel.
> The man from Judah / a planting for his delight.
> He hoped for goodly rule *(mišpāṭ)*, / but behold a rule of blood *(miśpaḥ)*;
> For faithfulness to the community *(ṣᵉdāqā)* / but behold a cry for help (*ṣᵉᶜaqā*).

This is not the place for an appreciation of the poetic beauty of the song. What we are concerned with here is the social criticism it contains. As in Amos, the paired concepts *mišpāṭ* and *ṣᵉdāqā* and their incomprehensible reversal through the behaviour of Isaiah's contemporaries are at the centre. Yahweh possesses an undeniable claim to human acts which will build up and sustain the community. He can hope for these acts in the way that the vineyard owner can hope for grapes, once he has intensively cultivated the ground. Like Amos, Isaiah believes that the capacity for doing good grows up in the framework of certain historical presuppositions which are determined by the correlation between action and destiny. Human beings are not 'by nature' able to be truly faithful to the community. For that they require certain preconditions which are both religious and economic. It is only after the land has been given, after the ground in the land of Canaan has been sown – that the vines (the Israelites) can become fruitful: can shape salvation by producing the appropriate soil where it can grow.

Some light is shed on the song of the vineyard by the saying about the city of the *ṣedeq* (1.21–27). For Isaiah, the divine weft of early salvation history found its culmination and its conclusion when Israel became a state under David, and when Zion was chosen as the leading sanctuary: and it was part of this salvation history that God should imbue the holy city with *mišpāṭ* and *ṣedeq*. The people of Judah, however, had shamefully squandered these positive, active forces, so their downfall was inescapable. All the same, Isaiah hoped for a state of salvation still to come, in which Yahweh would again send down his *ṣedeq* upon Jerusalem and the people seized by it would redeem themselves by means of their *ṣᵉdāqā* (which meant the practical implementation by men and women of the divine *ṣedeq*). According to the close of the Song of the Vineyard, Yahweh had been intensively active in history, again and again protecting Israel after it had taken possession of the promised land, in order to create a people which lived in harmony with itself and its God. But the people showed no inclination to lay hold on what their God had prepared for them or, for their own part, to play an active part in implementing it. The divine salvation history had no human successor. Now the primal foundation – the source of *mišpāṭ* and *ṣᵉdaqa* – is making an end. The vineyard, no longer tended, will undoubtedly wither and die.

But where in Judah is existence being undermined and faithfulness to the community ignored? Isaiah, too, never points to any divine laws or commandments. Rather the vineyard is laid waste when the mighty exploit the poor and store up their gains in their own homes (3.14f.). For Isaiah also, the increasing enclosure of the land in large estates was the worst injury of all. The ruling classes were robbing their fellow countrymen of home and land (5.8). But Isaiah does not merely concern himself with the peasant farmers, as Amos does. He is even angrier about the ill-treatment of the people who are without any rights at all – widows and orphans, who have no voice in the local community (1.17,23; 10.2). Townsman as he is, for him *mišpāṭ* (as unendangered, healthful existence, borne up by the community) is not so much connected with the possession of agricultural land as with the building up of society and the judicial organization of the state. He is angry about the way the law is misused, when everything can be achieved by bribery (5.20–23).

Since this is his standpoint, Isaiah too sees himself compelled to criticize the cult. Like Amos, he imitates the priestly *tōrāh* and (ironically?) the divine rejection of the appeal made in the cult (1.10–17 [or 20?]). In the words he puts in Isaiah's mouth, God goes even further than in Amos' polemic and condemns, not merely the communal offerings, but burnt offerings as well: 'I am sick of the blood of young bulls and goats.' He even rejects the ultimate possibility open to religion – prayer: 'Even though you intensify your prayers I will not listen. / Your hands – they are full of blood.' What robs the cult of all the effectiveness for people and makes it merely harmful is the Israelite notion that there is no problem about appearing at Yahweh's sanctuary, even if one has violated one's fellow-countrymen and is therefore introducing an aura of iniquity – perhaps even going round with unjustly shed blood on one's hands. But Isaiah maintains that Yahweh cannot endure 'festering iniquity *('āwen)* and solemn assemblies together'. Unlike Amos, however, it does not occur to Isaiah that the cult itself evokes a false sense of things, merely increasing the outrages of the wicked by relativizing the gift of the land and the election of the people. In Isaiah there is never any indication that Zion will be deported (cf. Amos 5.5), or will even be affected. On the contrary, for him Yahweh's presence on Zion is beyond question. It is 'my forecourts' which the Israelites 'are trampling on', his 'eyes' which he is hiding from the people who are offering sacrifices. So for Isaiah criticism of the cult is merely a continuation of social criticism. It is not an independent theme, as it is for the like-minded North Israelite prophets.

Like Amos and Hosea, Isaiah is aware of a possible alternative:

> Wash yourselves; make yourselves clean; / remove the evil of your doings.
> End your evil deeds away from my eyes / learn to do good.
> Seek *mišpāṭ*, / make the oppressed happy (?), raise up the orphan, plead for the widow.

In making these demands Isaiah is evidently thinking of cultic ceremonies of expiation. It was only at the sanctuary that auras of evil could leave the evil-doer (6.7); it had to happen before Yahweh's eyes, which probably meant at Zion. It is only when people are freed from this burden that affirmative social behaviour will be possible again.

If we compare Isaiah's early period with Amos, we discover that, in spite of their individual peculiarities, they agree fundamentally in their criticism of the social scene and the cult, or in their lament over the loss of *mišpāṭ* and *ṣᵉdāqā*. These points of agreement emerge even more clearly when we consider the genres used. The early Isaiah also takes up the new types of text occurring in Amos for the first time which, cannot be shown to have existed earlier among the prophets: lament, *tōrāh,* the divine response to a cultic appeal. Since Amos had been expelled to Judah (Amos 7.10ff.) and had probably arrived there some years earlier, before Isaiah began to prophesy, historical probability suggests that it was from Amos that Isaiah received the essential impetus. How otherwise can we explain the fact that unconditional prophecies of disaster – till then unheard of in Israel – crop up at almost the same time in North and South alike? But Isaiah is so independent that he takes over no single *motif* unaltered.

This is shown by his *predictions about the future* among other things. Like Amos, Isaiah proclaims unconditional disaster for the country, but in chs 2–5 (or in the older sections of ch 1) he does not say a word about deportation, and mentions no foreign occupation. It is true that the fence round Judah is torn down, according to 5.5–7; but the image is not developed into a factual statement that now enemies are going to invade the country. Isaiah sees death ahead for the people responsible, and he therefore already cries out a horrifying *hōy* over them (5.8ff.). In addition he sees the complete collapse of the internal political order. He enumerates the classes which are going to be affected: generals, soldiers, judges, nabis, soothsayers, elders (3.2). Children will become ministers, women will be rulers, no reasonable person will take over an office in 'this corruption' any more; seven women will snatch at one man, simply to have someone who can give them a name (3.4ff.). The renegade ministers, the accomplices of thieves, will disappear in a mighty process of purification, in which Yahweh will again refine the precious metal of the people from the impure alloy covering it at present. Then he will again give Jerusalem 'judges as at the first, / counsellors as at the beginning' (under David).

It is astonishing to what degree in this early period the prophet who, more than all the others, later takes his bearings from foreign policy – seeing it as a field where good and evil are decided – confines himself entirely to his own country, at most extending his range to take in the sister state in the north as well. Disaster comes unconditionally; conversion is talked about only as a future possibility (1.27).

Yet the disaster is not conceived in such all-embracing terms as in Amos. The king is never touched on in chs. 2–5, either critically or in the prophecies about the future. Only the people below him – people belonging to the court, the ministers and judges – come off badly.

Even in these very first statements, Isaiah enquires about the *anthropological* presuppositions for the conditions which have become so unbearable. Since pre-exilic religion knew of neither devil nor demons, the question of the origin of so much evil in history becomes acute. God reveals to Isaiah that man's overweening opinion of himself is the root of all evil. This is impressively described in the splendid poem about the fate of the vainglorious (2.6ff.):

> Truly you have left your people a free rein, house of Jacob.
> They were filled with people from the east, / with exorcists like the Philistines, / they struck hands with foreigners.
> The land was filled with silver and gold, / there was no end to the treasures.
> The land was filled with horses, / there was no end to the chariots . . .
> Then people were cast down, / men were brought low.
> Enter into the rocks, / hide yourselves in the dust before the terrors of Yahweh, / before the glory of his majesty *(gā'ōn)*!
> The eyes of the haughtiness *(gabhūt)* of man were cast down, / brought low the loftiness *(rūm)* of men.
> And lifted up *(niśgab)* was Yahweh alone in that day.

As so often, Isaiah points first of all to history. During the decades of peace round about the middle of the eighth century, Judah, like North Israel, enjoyed an economic heyday, which then underwent a severe setback. Perhaps the poem refers to the tribute which a certain Azriyau of Ja'udi (= Uzziah?) had to pay to the Assyrian emperor in 738.[16] This would explain the reference to treasures and chariots. Both were a reason for pride and both belonged to the tribute that had to be paid. But what the people here experience as a severe blow is merely a harmless prelude to what is before them in the future. The present humiliation will be multiplied in the humiliation to come (vv. 12ff.):

> Verily, a day for Yahweh Sabaoth (is ahead)
> Above all that is proud and lofty, / above all that is lifted up and [high] . . .

After this, the passage describes how all that is lofty in the world will be affected, from the cedars of Lebanon down to the ships on the sea. The new paragraph closes with the refrain from the first verse, expanded by some decisive words, because the future catastrophe is going to be many times greater:

Humbled shall be the haughtiness *(gabhūt)* of every man / brought low the loftiness *(rūm)* of men.
Yahweh alone shall be exalted *(niśgab)* / on that day.
They will go into the caves of the rocks, / into the holes of the ground, before the terror of Yahweh, / before the glory of his majesty *(gā'ōn)* / when he rises to terrify the earth.

Why this second, worse catastrophe is imminent is not explained in the poem, unless the reproach levied against the house of Jacob (perhaps a cultic title for the court?), that it has left the people to themselves, applies to the whole text. The poem programmatically precedes the earliest collection of Isaiah sayings (2.1ff.). In fact the opposition shown here between the arrogance of human vainglory or pride (which is expressed in the roots *gbh, g'h, rūm)* and true divine majesty, *niśgab* or *gā'ōn* (also deriving from the root *g'h*), will echo again and again in the prophet. The theme of human *superbia,* pride, as the ultimate cause of all sin – an idea which later plays so great a part in Augustine and Luther – is anticipated. But in Isaiah's view, pride is reduced to absurdity, not through the still and secret rule of God and by historical development, but through events which cut through everything perceptible, changing history and nature. The proud will be brought low by way of a divine revolt and driving terror on the day for Yahweh, which is imminent. Again a phrase from Amos turns up in slightly altered form. The Day of Yahweh *(yōm yhwh)* becomes a Day *for* Yahweh *(yom l^e yhwh,* cf. 22.5). The vision ahead is a theophany of Yahweh, which will come rushing upon the land from the north (Lebanon). What Amos and Hosea call a visitation, becomes in Isaiah a theophany. In this way he picks up the viewpoint of the Jerusalem cult, according to which, at the great Autumn Festival (every year, or every seven years), Yahweh 'rises' from some mysterious place and storms towards Zion with clouds and fire, in order to bless anew with *ṣedeq* the cultic community which has remained faithful to its bond with him, but to destroy evil doors (Pss. 50; 68; 97). This theophany of Yahweh leads to a division among men and women: to the sudden end of the wicked (because the auras of their misdeeds catch fire from the divine holiness); but also to the blossoming of those faithful to the bond with Yahweh, because the auras of their acts turn into a favourable destiny. This division between people, and the sudden completion through a theophany of the auras of their actions, means the establishment of a new world order, a divine *mišpāṭ.* Here Yahweh intends to raise up mankind *(dīn/špṭ,* Isa. 3.13f.; Ps. 50. 4–6; 96.13; 98.9). It is to be the victory of the divinely desired order of being which had existed once upon a time in the primordial era. For this, God needs no judicial proceedings and pronounces no judgment. To this degree the word 'judgment' can be used only in a highly figurative sense; though it is understandable that in the late Israelite period the idea of a divine forensic day of judgment could grow up out of this context.

What Isaiah expects is an extraordinary theophany – a day for Yahweh on which there will be no unscathed cultic community on Zion capable of receiving Yahweh in hope. Israel will then rather be numbered among the great powers of the earth, which are inwardly hollow and break down on the divine impact.

The theme of pride is taken up by Isaiah in other sayings of the early period, too, for example in the saying about the daughters of Zion who 'walk with outstretched necks, throwing seductive glances round them', and whose beauty will soon be put to shame (3.16ff.). The same idea can be heard in the great poem about the divine hand stretched out against the Northern Kingdom, with its refrain (9.8–10.4 + 5.25–30); this still presupposes prosperous conditions and must therefore date from the period before 732. Arrogance and pride of heart *(ga'āwā, gōdel lēbāb)* are attacked as the reason for the social repression and the unjust laws. Yahweh is not preparing for a theophany against North Israel. There it will be sufficient if he lets his hand fall upon them and whistles up a military opponent who will lower, roaring, over him like a hungry lion, as only the uncanny sea can do (similarly 28.1–4).

Isaiah would not be a Hebrew if individual and collective spheres of action were not a matter of course for him – spheres whose fateful workings make themselves felt in historical events. He points to these especially when he raises the *hoy* lament for the dead over the living. The people who draw the *'awōn,* burden of guilt, with ropes of nothingness are inwardly dead (5.18). Downfall inevitably faces them *(šeber,* 1.28; 30.13; cf. Amos 6.6); and this downfall will be accelerated where there is a powerful attack from outside. Isaiah expects that everyone who is weighed down by the correlation between misdeeds and disaster will burn away simply by themselves, leaving nothing but ashes behind them (9.18; 1.31; 5.24; for the whole context see also below).

7.4 The Syro-Ephraimite war and the move towards foreign policy

Assuming that the collections of Isaiah's sayings have been put together chronologically (and up to now no cogent evidence has been put forward for any other arrangement), the vision about the hardening of heart marks the close of the early period. According to this vision, Yahweh's social criticism and that of his prophet met with so little response that the clouding of the listeners' perception which has to be presumed has now been determined and fixed from God's side. This happened in the year of King Uzziah's death (ch. 6). The compiler of the book of Isaiah has linked this with two accounts (one in the third person, ch. 7, and one in the first, ch. 8) describing the activity of the prophet during the Syro-Ephraimite war of 734–732. According to the book in its present form, the disputes that went on at the time between Isaiah and his opponents bring out the effect of the hardness of heart imposed on the people.

Under Uzziah, prophetic criticism and predictions of the future are uttered unequivocally but in general terms, without the names of those who act or are acted upon, and without specific examples. When the war between Syria and Ephraim breaks out, this changes. Suddenly Isaiah becomes very much alive to political developments. Criticism and prediction both switch over to the level of military affairs and foreign policy. He learns, and wants to teach other people, everything that takes place between kings and armies, in order to penetrate and illuminate its anthropological and theological background. A theory about the moral forces that move political events begins to develop, and this is not confined to political terms. I therefore propose to talk about metapolitics as well as about metahistory.

First of all, let us recall the external circumstances of the day. In the second half of the eighth century BC, powerful Assyrian kings had attacked Syria-Palestine from Mesopotamia. In 738 the minor states of Israel and Damascus were forced to pay tribute to the mighty Tiglat-Pileser III. But in 734–733, while the king was busy in the eastern part of his empire, a coalition was formed between the Aramaean state of Damascus and the part-state of North Israel, whose centre was Ephraim. The aim of the alliance was presumably liberation from Assyria. If rebellion against the superior power of Assyria was to be successful, the participation of all the little states in the west seemed necessary. So the demand was made that Judah, under Ahaz, should join the coalition too. But Ahaz refused, being afraid of Assyria's superior strength. The Syro-Ephraimite coalition thereupon decided that its first attack should be made on Jerusalem, in order to install a king with anti-Assyrian sympathies there. Ahaz, on the other hand, prepared to defend his capital. At the same time he thought of calling on Assyria's help, even though this implied both political and religious subjection to Assyrian hegemony and subsequent vassalage.

It was in this situation that Isaiah intervened, at the instigation of his God. Neither rebellion nor an appeal to Assyria have any point. The prophet therefore seeks out the king and tries to make him understand the background of the situation. The beginning of the third-person account in ch. 7 describes the helplessness of the Jerusalem leadership. 'The *lēbāb* (the 'reason-heart'), of the men responsible 'has begun to shake as the trees of the forest shake in a strong wind'. Isaiah begins with an exhortation to the king: 'Do not let your *lēbāb* fear, do not let it weaken!' Then follows an indication of the situation, which this time is a characterization of the enemy, not of Judah. This is the first time that we can detect a metapolitical way of looking at things. Although Syria and North Israel are superior in numbers and arms, they are in the end only two smoking stumps of firebrands, and what they plan promises anything but success. Yahweh will bring the planning to nothing; he will not allow the notions of men to find fulfilment, as the prophecy emphatically stresses at the beginning. The enemies were once great and the firebrands long, but their energy has long since been used up:

> For the head *(rōš)* of Aram is Damascus / but the head of Damascus is Razon [the king at that time, a usurper];
> And the head of Ephraim is Samaria / but the head of Samaria is the son of Remaliah [a usurper who is not even thought worthy of a name of his own].

The conception of *rōš* is significant for Isaiah's view of politics and the state (cf. 1.5; 9.15). The nation displays its special character in the 'head' – the capital city; but the capital in its turn has its own 'head' – the ruler. For Isaiah, both the rulers are illegitimate and the capitals, as everyone knows, are morally corrupt. (Is what Amos had already demonstrated in the case of Samaria being presupposed here?) So in these cities no plan can be conceived which has any prospect of success, or which finds Yahweh's support. But any human plan which is not in conformity with the ground of reality – Yahweh – is doomed to failure. Yet Judah should be alert. It can stray on to the same slippery slope and pursue plans that are totally absurd. Isaiah adds a conditional clause to the prophecy of salvation:

> If you (sons of David) will not believe (*'āman,* hiphil), you shall not be established (*'āman* niphal).

He is referring back to an ancient divine oracle proclaimed to David, according to which the throne of his dynasty was to endure and be established eternally (*ne'emān*, II Sam. 7.16). What Nathan told the king in unconditional terms, according to ancient tradition, is now subjected to a condition through Isaiah; the condition of faith. According to the context, 'believing' means believing implicitly in a prophecy – and hence in the future announced by God. But probably more than this is implied. If we are right in assuming a reference to the ancient oracle proclaimed to the king, then this is at the same time a pointer to the century-long historical experience of the Davidic dynasty. This provides the reason for trusting similarly in a prophetic saying about the future. This faith refers to political action. It assumes that politics cannot be pursued without metahistory.

Isaiah knows how difficult it is for a person whose eyes are fixed on what is clearly evident to detach himself from the foreground of superficial political and strategic constellations, and to build on deeper and hidden metahistorical trends. His God therefore comes to meet the king half way. He offers him a sign of his own choice. At this point we can see how different Hebrew belief is from the faith of the New Testament, where the person who believes without seeing is praised, and the demand for a sign counts as proof of lack of faith. For Israel, signs belong to faith. Faith, *he'emīn*, does not mean a leap, an absolute risk. It is based on the experience of the individual and the people as a whole. It has a reasonable connection with signs and wonders (Ex. 14.31; Gen. 15.5f.). This explains the offer to Ahaz: 'Ask a sign (*'ōt*) of Yahweh your God whether it is deep out of the underworld or from high heaven!' Ahaz could have asked for the spirit of a dead person to be called up, or for a star to fall from heaven if he had wanted. The interpreter's heart misses a beat; what unbelievable self-assurance on the part of the prophet! (Scholars are not lacking who say that Isaiah could think himself lucky that Ahaz did not accept the offer!) Ahaz refuses to believe the prophet. He produces a pious argument: 'I will not put Yahweh to the test.' But for Isaiah this is just a prevarication. He announces a sign to the king on his own account – not a sign from heaven nor one from the underworld, but one that is entirely earthly and human:

> Behold, a young woman is with child, bears a son and gives him the name Immanu-El ('Deity with us') (7.14).

The passage is famous in its New Testament context and counts as a prediction of the virgin birth of Christ. Isaiah is not, however, thinking of a virgin. What he has in mind is apparently a young but married woman. Up to this point the text is clear enough. What is disputed is whether Isaiah is thinking of the birth of a messianic figure or of a normal man. In the latter case it was not the person's destiny which would have had symbolic character, but merely his name, as in the symbolic names of Isaiah's children (7.3; 8.3f.). At all events, the name 'the deity with us' is significant. The divine ground of all reality, Isaiah proclaims, dwells with greater intensity in Judah (in connection with the sanctuary on Zion, Ps. 46.7,11) than among the North Israelite kings, let alone in Damascus; within a few years this will show itself as a metahistorical factor in the course of events. I myself cannot quite avoid the impression that with this brief prediction in the form of an oracle about a mysterious birth, Isaiah is referring to an expectation which was familiar to Ahaz as well: the expectation of a mysterious future saviour-figure whom the people await and who was to grow up in rural seclusion. He will be fed on curds and honey (cf. Micah 5). We should then have to presuppose that in Jerusalem, too, there was a popular eschatology similar to the expectation of a Day of Yahweh in North Israel (Amos 5.18). But we may leave that on one side here. At all events, Isaiah goes on to proclaim that in the wake of the historical realization of the Immanu-El sign, the Davidic house will be drawn into the convulsion – a convulsion which will equal the greatest of all previous catastrophes in national history: the division of the kingdom after Solomon's death. The El power in Judah's midst will not display its potency merely against the present aggressor, but also against Judah's own royal house which, seen in the context of metahistory, has lost its foundation. Judah will first of all shake off the enemies before whom it at present trembles. But afterwards it will collapse through the very power that has destroyed these other opponents, the power on which Ahaz and his court particularly rely: the Assyrian enemy. Once on the march towards the west, the Assyrians will not stop at Judah's borders but will flood over its land as well as over the land of its neighbours (8.5–8).

In these particular years, Isaiah frequently uses symbolic actions to indicate future developments, so that 'the people really sees and yet does not understand' (6.10). So he sets up a sign with the inscription: 'speed spoil, hasten prey', and gives his own new-born son the same monstrous name. (Is he predestined to become the victim of gangsters?) This is a vivid way of showing his contemporaries that Assyria will carry away the riches of Damascus and the people of Samaria (8.1–4). Earthly signs like this (*'ōt*), given by the prophet at God's behest, *reflect a happening in advance*; thereby they actually evoke a train of events which no one can do anything to halt. To that extent these signs have a 'magical' effect.

Events were to prove Isaiah right, within certain limits. Tiglath-Pileser III appeared a year later. Within a short time he had conquered the Syro-Ephraimite coalition, made Damascus into an Assyrian province, and left only a rump state of North Israel. Judah was also forced to pay tribute and reduced to the status of a satellite, although the Assyrian armies did not actually push forward into Judaean territory, and the country's constitution was not infringed. All in all, the predictions which Isaiah drew and nourished from metahistory were fulfilled, not the superficial reckoning of the Judaean government.

But in this second phase, as in his first, Isaiah had prophesied that the country would be laid waste and depopulated (1.7; 6.11f.; cf. 5.17; 7.24); neither prediction came true. Had he unduly caricatured future developments? Or did he expect further disasters after 732? The saying in 8.16–18 (which is hard to fit into the framework of a particular genre, but may perhaps conclude a collection of sayings about the war) sounds like resignation, or a withdrawal into the private sphere. The prophetic testimony about the future will be 'sealed' in the prophet's disciples. Yahweh has 'hidden' his face, and the prophet accordingly expects further disaster. At the same time, together with his 'children', he waits for the God who is present in Zion. Is this not the brightening of a hope which goes beyond what the prophet had hitherto felt able to prophesy for the future?

Did Isaiah support a kind of military *quietism* or even pacifism during the Syro-Ephraimite war? He comes to meet Ahaz at the water conduit of the upper pool – which is usually interpreted as meaning that the king is just about to inspect Jerusalem's supplies, in expectation of a siege. Does the exhortation in 7.4, 'Be quiet, do not fear', mean letting all defence measures drop and leaving the protection of the country solely to God's miraculous rule? Is Judah expected to renounce all self-defence? And is this perhaps implicit in the demand for faith? Quietism like this is frequently ascribed to the prophet. His behaviour can then either be presented as exemplary for every believing community; or it can be disparagingly described as 'the religiously utopian character of prophetic politics', to take the title of a book by Weinrich.[17]

Now it is obvious that Isaiah views any alliance with a stronger foreign power with mistrust (e.g., 30.1–3), because any such alliance – in accordance with ancient oriental law – always involved religious ties; and this permitted the foreign gods to appear the stronger ones. At all events, the demand for faith in 7.9 is intended to hinder a possible coalition with Assyria. The prophet also lashes out at the people's trust in their own army (2.7; 31.1–3). Yet there is no passage which suggests that Isaiah would have considered that an army and the defence of the country were superfluous. His behaviour in the late period excludes any such assumption, just as much as the close metahistorical interweaving of divine and human workings which is always the underlying presupposition of what he says (see below). It is only the Isaiah school which later looks forward to an eschatological period in which swords will be beaten into ploughshares and spears into pruning hooks. But this is not going to happen because Yahweh himself takes over the military defence; it is because war among the nations is going to cease for ever (2.1–4).

7.5 The swing to an anti-Assyrian attitude in the late period

1. During the Syro-Ephraimite war, Isaiah had described to his people in graphic terms the way in which Assyria, once it had been called to their help, would really respond to the call: it threatened to flood and drown Judah altogether (8.5–18). But at that time the Assyrian emperor contented himself with a fixed tribute, in money and in kind. His troops did not enter the little state on the extreme edge of the Assyrian empire. So did Isaiah's prophecy merely mean that Judah was going to be swamped through political pressure, and reduced to a satellite existence?

Twenty years later (in 713 BC), the Philistine city of Ashdod rose against the Assyrian king. According to Sargon's annals, Hezekiah of Judah was also involved in this movement for liberation. In the background, Egypt (always delighted to support any anti-Assyrian attempts) added fuel to the flames. This time the Assyrian troops moved threateningly close to Judaean territory. Did the prophet now see the fulfilment of what he had prophesied long before as being imminent? He did not. What he had to say in the three years that led up to the crushing of the rebels – if we are correct in our chronological arrangement of his sayings – tended in two different directions. On the one hand he was concerned about Egypt. His symbolic action of walking about naked for three years was a demonstration that the great power in the south was going to be deported by the Assyrians (ch. 20). The influential position which he occupied in Jerusalem allowed him to sing a funeral dirge to an Egyptian delegation (ch. 18). In this dirge Yahweh visualizes Egypt as a vine whose shoots have now to be pruned. A positive attitude to Egypt seems to be implied here: if it is a vine, it is after all an important member of Yahweh's garden of the nations. (Later on Isaiah will judge Judah's southern neighbour more harshly.)

On the other hand, Yahweh is concerned with Assyria. Over this state too he now sings a horrifying *hoyj* (10.5ff.); for the rabble of the Assyrian soldiery – the cruellest army in the ancient east – has cut a bloody path through Syria as far as Samaria, and is now lusting after Jerusalem: 'For in his *lēbāb* is the lust to cut off nations not a few.' The arrogance of the Assyrian king knows no bounds. The reproach of having an overweening opinion of themselves, which Isaiah had levied against his own people in the early period, is now directed against the super-power which is crushing everything in its path. And yet it was Yahweh who first of all enabled the Assyrian to be victorious. 'Shall then the axe vaunt itself over him who hews with it? Or the saw magnify itself against him who wields it? As if a rod should wield him who lifts it!' Assyria is endangering itself; when it moves against

Jerusalem it is putting itself in a zone of extreme peril. This is not of course the case on the political and military level, where Assyrian superiority is unquestionable; but it is true on a metahistorical one. The empire is morally as dry as tinder and will take fire from the mighty power of 'holy Israel'. Yahweh plans to 'break the Assyrian in my land' (14.24–27). The yoke of Assyria – Isaiah uses a favourite word of the Assyrian annalists – will then depart from Judah (10.27; 14.25).

What Isaiah expounds in these three years is all orientated towards foreign policy. No reproach at all is levied against his own people. This may be connected with the fact that after 715 (or 725?) Hezekiah was ruling in Judah, a king whom – unlike his royal predecessor – Isaiah evidently supported in principle. Perhaps that is why in this period we find the prophecy about the salvation of the remnant, who will now soon be able to repent (10.20–22). The result of the war in 711 proved Isaiah right, in that the rebellion failed miserably, and from then on Judah was subjugated more severely than before. It proved him wrong inasmuch as the Assyrian certainly did not undergo defeat in Yahweh's land. And the war ended for the prophet with boundless disappointment because his people – in spite of the considerable defeat – gave themselves up to a completely unjustified ecstasy of joy after the withdrawal of the Assyrians – at least if we are right in assigning ch. 22 to this period.

2. In 705 Sargon II died. His son Sennacherib ascended the Assyrian throne. Once again Assyria's vassals in Syria-Palestine thought that the hour of liberation had come, and ceased to pay tribute. For three years Sennacherib was busy consolidating his rule in the east; but in 702–1 he set his army on the move towards the west. The minor states in Syria and East Jordan did homage to him as soon as he approached. Only the Philistine cities of Ashkelon and Ekron offered resistance – and above all Hezekiah of Judah. He was evidently the head of the rebellion and had made a firm alliance with the Egyptian Pharaoh. Sennacherib first of all pressed forward into the coastal plains, defeated at Elteke a makeshift Egyptian army which had hastened up, and then took forty-six Judaean cities, deporting most of the population. Finally he surrounded Hezekiah in his capital city 'like a bird in its cage'[18]. Shortly before the Assyrian troops stormed the city, Hezekiah surrendered. Sennacherib reduced the state of Judah to its capital, but left Hezekiah in office, although he had to send heavy tribute after the Assyrian. One is surprised at what was, by Assyrian standards, unusually lenient treatment of an obstinate rebel. According to II Kings 19, the reason was that the angel of Yahweh smote the besieging troops with an epidemic. According to

Herodotus, it was an appalling plague of mice which forced the Assyrians to lift the siege.

The collection of sayings in Isaiah 28–33 is generally attributed to this period; and scholars try to trace its basic material back to an 'Assyrian cycle' of sayings belonging to the years 705–701. Every sub-section begins with a funeral dirge over the ruling circles in Jerusalem, because they are making their plans without asking Yahweh, or taking any account of his *rūaḥ* (30.1ff.; 31.1ff.). Earlier (5.20) Isaiah had indicated that he was critical of Wisdom – at least he settled accounts with the self-assured attitudes which probably derived from education in the Wisdom schools of the court. The times were characterized, not only by trust in riches and ostentatious luxury (30.12; 32.9ff.) but, hand in hand with these, by a ridiculous culture of the intellect, in the superficial sense (29.14f.). It led to the cult's becoming mere lip-service, which no longer took possession of the *lēb* (29.13ff.). Another result was trust in the army instead of in Yahweh. But, Isaiah mocks: 'A thousand (of you) shall flee at the threat of one, and at the threat of five you will flee until the remnant of you is like a post on the top of a mountain' (30.17). This false wisdom exerts an influence on foreign policy, leading to reliance on Egypt – an unprecedented trust in the great power to the south. Under the conditions of the time (in which both sides appealed to their gods), Isaiah saw this coalition with a foreign power as a betrayal of Yahweh. But that was not the only reason for his attack. His prophetic vision also allowed him to see through the Egyptian power, as being militarily weak and inwardly hollow. Future developments were to prove that Isaiah was all too correct in his judgment.

> Woe to those who go down to Egypt for help, / they rely on horses.
> They trust in the corps of chariots, thinking they are many, / and on their drivers, believing that they are strong.
> They do not look to the Holy One of Israel, / they do not consult Yahweh.
> Yet he too is wise and brought disaster, / his word he did not withdraw.
> And he has to arise against the house of evil-doers, / against the helpers of *'āwen*-doers.
> Egypt is a man (*'ādām*), but not an *'ēl* (divine entity), / his horses are flesh and not spirit (*rūaḥ*).
> But Yahweh will stretch out his hand, / there the helper will stumble and the one who is helped will fall (3.1–3).

What is suggested here is an opposition between divine and political wisdom. But it is not an opposition which is interpreted ontologically, as if the human mind is bound to err. The divine wisdom could have been entirely accessible to the men in Jerusalem; and Isaiah is convinced that he himself possesses it. Nor is the contrasting of *'ādām* and *'ēl* intended to indicate a fundamental difference between this world and the world beyond. *El* is rather a mode of quiet divine presence in this world (cf. Immanu-El, 7.14); it is available to an Israelite if he trusts as he should and does not limit himself to outward appearances (the flesh).

The criticism of foreign policy in the saying about the foundation stone is more devastating. The prophet recalls that the Egyptians see Osiris, the lord of the dead, as the tutelary god of their country. The Twenty-Fifth (Ethiopian) Dynasty, which was then in power, laid especial stress on the worship of this god. Isaiah does not see Osiris merely as an idle product of the human imagination; for him the link between Osiris' people and Judah could only mean that Judah would be drawn into the realm of death;

A You have said: 'We have made / a covenant with death, with the underworld / have we an agreement.
The streaming scourge, should it pass through, / it will not reach us.'
For we have made lies our refuge (*maḥse*), / in unsteadiness (*šēqēr*) do we hide ourselves.
B Therefore, so has the Lord Yahweh spoken:
Behold, I lay in Zion / a tested stone.
A cornerstone of precious (?) foundation; / he who believes (*he'emīn*) in it, will not be anxious (?).
I have to set *mišpāṭ* (for him) as measuring rod, / *ṣ^edāqā* for the plummet.
Hail must sweep away the refuge of lies, / waters will overwhelm the hiding place.
Your covenant with death must be atoned, / your vision (?) with the underworld will not endure.
The streaming scourge, should it pass through, / will beat you too down to the ground.

The streaming scourge is the tool of the destructive weather god Hadad, with whose help the Assyrians carry out their campaigns. So to a limited degree Isaiah also recognizes this power as lying behind Assyria's political and military power, just as the Jerusalem politicians do. But what nonsense for them to flee from the god of the weather to the god of death! The prophet knows where a reliable, safe place is to be found: Zion. If anyone believes in this place, and that it will be founded anew – which means believing in the Lord of Lords who dwells there and 'making oneself fast' in him (*he'emīn*) – he has the prospect of *mišpāṭ* and *ṣᵉdāqā*; for Yahweh will again confer these things by way of Zion (cf. 1.26f.). But before that, Yahweh will himself bring up the scourge, in order to let the conceited Judaean politicians feel how empty has been their trust in superficial, momentary constellations of power.

Isaiah can also paint the imminent downfall of the state and its leaders in a different way: Ariel (a name for the capital city or for the Temple hill which is now an enigma to us) will itself be invested, besieged and so humiliated that it will only be able to cheep from the earth like a spirit from the dead (29.1–4).

If these poems, which introduce the subsections of the book beginning with chs. 28ff., are taken simply by themselves, they sound entirely gloomy and proclaim nothing but downfall. But in the present text in each case there is a turn towards salvation. Genre and semantics show that these 'salvation' sayings are in part later additions. It is therefore understandable that a number of scholars should see only the words of doom as genuine, drawing the conclusion that a positive attitude to the future of his people was as inconceivable for Isaiah in the later period as it was in the early one. But, on the other hand, there are statements about salvation in these chapters which are entirely in accordance with Isaiah's style and of which – when we consider the strength and vividness of the language – it is hard to believe an imitator would have been capable. We may take as an example the remark that Yahweh teaches the farmer to act differently at different times; he does not continually have to plough his fields, and does not have to thresh grain with small seeds as if it were corn. This is the way the teacher and guide of history himself acts – or so the listener is supposed to conclude (28.23–29). He does not go on destroying (threshing) for ever. The people who besiege Ariel will, after a surprising turn of affairs, be like the hungry man who dreams of the food he longs for but, waking up, is immeasurably disappointed (25.5–10). Yahweh will also 'stream up' in a theophany against 'streaming' Assyria; with his voice, as with a mighty staff, he will smite Assyria, which was till then Yahweh's staff on earth (30.27f.). Just as a snarling lion does not allow his booty to be snatched from him, so Yahweh comes down on the armed march to Zion and snatches it out of its deadly peril at the last moment (31.4f.).

It would hardly seem prudent to deny to Isaiah all these utterances about a sudden turn to salvation; nor do external linguistic characteristics justify such a rejection. Since even the so-called prophecies of doom contain scattered prospects of zones of refuge which will not be touched by the catastrophe (for example Zion, as the refuge of believers, 28.15ff.), Isaiah certainly seems at this time to reckon with a twofold development of affairs in the country. The city will no doubt be severely affected. But even in the Syro-Ephraimite war, the God dwelling on Zion is already the sole foundation of hope (8.18). Moreover, in the statements of doom, Hezekiah is never blamed for his defection from the Assyrian overlord. It is solely the fraternization with Egypt that is condemned (just as in the Syro-Ephraimite war it was probably not defence as such that was under attack, but simply dependence on Assyria.)

All in all, therefore, the material collected together in chs. 28ff. speaks in favour of the presumption that Isaiah, even in the final phase from which these sayings have come down to us, reckoned both with a severe catastrophe and with a sudden turn for the better. Perhaps he even put the sayings together himself in such a way that prospects of escape and a better future regularly follow the dirges (which are always directed only to the would-be wise, those who have authority over the people, or the capital city).

At the same time, we can undoubtedly discover certain changes in Isaiah's opinion about the future of Judah, compared with his earlier phases. However, his attitude to Assyria has changed even more radically. Initially Assyria was presented merely as the rod which Yahweh used to discipline his people. Later its downfall in Judah was predicted; while in the final phase Isaiah only prophesies that the Assyrian king will be forced to return to his own country.

This at least is the case if genuine Isaianic material lies behind the stories which close Proto-Isaiah (chs. 36–39). Most interpreters view these sections with deep mistrust, because here Isaiah seems to stand on the side of Judaean politics. This does not fit into the portrait of the uncompromising prophet of doom or repentance, which is generally the picture painted of Isaiah. Now without any doubt there are legendary features in these chapters. But the prophecies which are set in the narrative framework of the siege of Jerusalem coincide only in part with events as they actually happened; and this speaks in favour of their antiquity. In addition, there are two legends about the prophet which grew up independently of one another (36.1–37.8; 37.9b–35) and which are linked consecutively in this literary framework, stories varying in detail but, broadly speaking, describing events in the same way. In both of them Sennacherib commissions men to remonstrate with Hezekiah, to point out how stupid it is for him to trust in his own God (*bāṭaḥ*, 36.4f.; 37.10), and how little the gods of Hamath, Arpad and Separvaim had succeeded in saving their kings (36.19f.; 37.12f.). In both strands of the transmitted material Isaiah assures the king in his God's name that the Syrian attack will be foiled:

> See I will put my spirit into him, he shall hear a rumour, return to his own land and in his own land will fall by the sword (37.7).
> He shall not come into this city, or shoot an arrow into it . . . or cast up a siege mound against it. By the way that he came, by the same he shall return (37.33f.).

The second narrative adds other, independent oracles, including the splendid diatribe poem in 37.22–29. It is true that here we have third-person reports about Isaiah, but they are written in the same style as the accounts of the clash between Isaiah and King Ahaz in ch. 7. From the linguistic aspect, it is difficult to see why ch. 7 should be readily viewed by most scholars as historical, whereas chs. 36f. are rejected wholesale.

Incidentally, Isaiah changes his attitude to Egypt as well. Chapter 18 views the country in relatively benevolent terms, merely condemning its leadership. On the other hand, in 28.15ff. the country is regarded as being *the* power of death. It must therefore be conceded that Isaiah's attitude to the political and military powers on the world stage of his time altered in details. But the principles remained constant, since they were based on his metahistorical viewpoint. We must therefore now look at this viewpoint as a whole.

7.6 Messiah, understanding of God, eschatology

7.6.1 Among the first Christians, expectations grew up out of the Old Testament which clustered round a future Israelite king of salvation, who was to appear in a wondrous manner and who was later described by the (Aramaic) title 'Messiah'. And in Proto-Isaiah – more than in the other prophetic books – we find sections which prophesy a future king who cannot be compared with any other. The downfall which the prophet expects will precede the coming of this king, who will lead Israel to new heights. Although this figure as yet has no title, a new expectation makes itself felt in these chapters. In the usage of the church right down to the present day, Isaiah 9 and 11 are considered classic examples of Old Testament prophecies of Christ. And in fact the development of a christology in the early church is difficult to explain without this and other related prophetic impulses.

Most scholars believe that these particular passages come from Isaiah himself. Admittedly, reasons can be given for calling the prophet's authorship in question. The sayings seem to break apart the usual pattern of prophecy as a literary genre; they are longer than other utterances by the prophet. On the other hand the vocabulary is that of Isaiah, and the content can well be reconciled with the anthropology and metahistory of the rest of the book. I therefore propose to interpret the texts on the assumption that they are in fact Isaiah's.[19]

Before the accession of the future ruler, 9.2 refers to a people who are living in darkness, given over to the kingdom of the dead. This was more precisely described in the previous verse (9.1):

> As the former time (the time of the first one?) had dishonoured / the land of Zebulon and the land of Naphtali.
> So the later time will bring to new honour (the provinces) the way of the sea, / the land beyond Jordan and the circle of the nations (Galilee).
> The people who walk in darkness / will (then) see a great light.
> The dwellers in the land of the final darkness – / a light will rise and shine over them.

After the Syro-Ephraimite war, the tribal area of Naphthali and Zebulon was cut off from the rump state of North Israel and was reorganized into three Assyrian provinces. The inhabitants of this territory were being forgotten by those of their countrymen who had remained relatively independent. The same Isaiah who had so definitely announced downfall to the sister nation in the north is now concerned about the members of his people in the territories that have been separated. His God inspires him with the assurance that the misfortune will not be permanent. Yahweh himself will miraculously intervene as a holy warrior and will break the staff and rod which his divine hand had previously stretched out over North Israel. What is meant is Assyria (10.5). The mighty Assyrian army will be burnt away to nothing in a moment. At the same time, the people liberated in the north receive news from Jerusalem in the south that a new ruler has taken over the government there, and that he will unite the people. On the Egyptian model (and in accordance perhaps with the royal ritual of Jerusalem?) he receives four (or five) throne names, which proclaim abilities going beyond those of any previous king: 1. wondrous in planning; 2. hero filled with El, and hence (like Immanu-el in 7.14) filled with numinous power against his external enemies; 3. father for ever, i.e., true protector of his fatherland; 4. minister of *šālōm*, the personified state of salvation. He will rule over reunited Israel on the throne of David in *mišpāṭ* and *ṣ'dāqā*. These two active forces become supports to the throne; but, according to the ancient oriental view, it is the throne which guarantees the continuing existence of a country.

I would put the first messianic prophecy a few years after the end of the Syro-Ephraimite war, and before the fall of Samaria in 722–721. Here it is still uncertain how Isaiah sees the relationship between the disaster threatening Judah, his own part of the nation, at the hands of Assyria, and the coming saviour king in Jerusalem. It is only for the Northern kingdom that he prophesies a stage beyond the Assyrian disaster.

Isaiah probably uttered the messianic prediction of 10.27b–11.9 in his third phase, in the period between 713 and 711, when the Philistine city of Ashdod tried to rebel against Assyria, and was hesitantly supported by Judah. (At this point the division of the Bible into chapters – which dates from the Middle Ages – has torn apart a single, coherent saying.) Apparently at that time the Assyrian king had set a number of troops on the march against Jerusalem from the new military base of Samaria. Isaiah observed their approach from the north. They pushed forward over the subsidiary route from Michmash to Geba, taking village after village by surprise. The prophet expected that this time they would push forward to Jerusalem. In 732 he was evidently unduly hasty, in the short term, in his expectation of a march by the Assyrians against Jerusalem; but he now expects this march anew, in the context of the Ashdod rebellion. As the extended arm of the God who rules history, Assyria is going to set aside the corrupt rule in Jerusalem:

> Behold the Lord Yahweh-Sabaoth / tops the boughs with terrifying power.
> The lofty will be hewn down / and the arrogant will be brought low.
> He cuts the thickets of the forest with iron, / the Lebanon (palace) he will bring down through a mighty one.

The lofty are the rulers at the court, whose over-confidence had already been criticized in 2.6ff. The impending humiliation (*špl*) also echoes in that poem, too. But the tree which had spread out so luxuriantly to all sides and is now mercilessly pruned back represents the royal house which, elsewhere too, in the language of the ancient oriental court, is the tree of life for the whole people (Ezek. 17; Dan. 4). In the very near future, therefore, a complete deforestation is to be expected which will at long last bring down the men in Jerusalem, as Isaiah has expected for decades. But the destruction will not be a total one:

> There will (then) come forth a shoot out of the stump of Jesse, / a branch will break forth out of a root.
> Yahweh's *rūaḥ* ('spirit') shall rest on him, / the *rūaḥ* of wisdom and insight,
> the *rūaḥ* of planning and heroic power, / the *rūaḥ* of Yahweh-knowledge and Yahweh-fear.

The attributes which here describe the endowments of the future king fit the first throne names in chapter 9 (*yōʿēṣ* – *ʿēṣā*; *gibbōr-gᵉbūrā*; for *pelē'*, cf. 11.3b; for *ṣᵉdāqā*, v. 4f.). Perhaps this is not in fact a reference to the royal ritual of Jerusalem; it may go back to the ancient nabi practice of designating in advance a king who, through this designation, will be filled from above with the power of the extraordinary, the *rūᵃḥ*, which rests on him from then on (I Sam. 10.10; 16.13f.). But Isaiah reinterprets this. For him *rūᵃḥ* is the vehicle of wisdom. It no longer communicates warlike qualities. Isaiah 9.6 – wondrous in planning – already places a Wisdom predicate in the foreground. But now awareness, knowledge, reason are made pre-eminent in quite a different way and determine the nature of the new kingdom – though reason here means metahistorically perceptive reason, which reckons with the ground of history as the determining factor.

The ruler stands in an unbroken relationship to God; and through him *mišpāṭ* and *ṣᵉdāqā* are poured out over the whole land. Isaiah thinks of this ruler quite apart from any warlike deeds. He only emerges (9.6) after Yahweh's great victory over the Assyrians. His first purpose is to set up *mišpāṭ* and *ṣᵉdāqā* in the field of internal politics, to help everyone in the country realize the correlation between action and outcome in a fruitful way. The insights of Isaiah's early period, directed towards social criticism, which seemed to recede during the second foreign-policy phase now emerge once more. Earlier, Isaiah had attacked the royal house and the ruling classes for their lack of certain characteristics – *mišpāṭ* and *ṣᵉdāqā*. These same characteristics are now stressed again, positively, as the marks of the future king. The king will raise up the poor peasant farmers (*dallīm*): he will preserve their homes and prevent their fields from being snatched from them by violence. This is where his *ṣedeq* will be chiefly felt. The new kingdom that will dawn will not, however, be as yet a paradise of sinless human beings. There will still be potential evildoers, individuals who act in way detrimental to the community. But through the words of the future king their active force will soon be annihilated, as could only happen otherwise through a decree from the mouth of God himself. An incomparably positive sphere of good deeds and salvation will permanently surround the person of the king. Not only will he have *ṣᵉdāqā* as his sphere, as other men too can have it; *ṣedeq* will also become the girdle of his loins: this masculine noun is elsewhere used only of God (or of the holy city generally, 1.26).

Since the correlation between action and destiny never has a purely inward and subjective effect, least of all in the case of the king, the enduring sphere of *ṣedeq* will bring peace not only to human beings but also to animals. Even the wild beasts will become tame, the wolf grazing alongside the lamb. (To this degree paradisal conditions will in fact obtain.) The knowledge of Yahweh enjoyed by the king will overflow to his people and be the mark of his subjects as well (v.9). This last aspect will be more fully developed in a third messianic prophecy (32.1–8).

7.6.2 I must now make some general comments about the messianic expectation which in Isaiah emerges extensively for the first time.

1. Behind this expectation lies a massive *criticism of the king* – criticism not merely of the ruler's practice, but even of court ideology as such. What Nathan's prophecy (II Sam. 7) and the royal psalms had to say about the transference of divine forces to the royal office (Ps. 72) had either not been implemented in Israel or had borne no lasting fruit. At all events, if Isaiah's antagonist Ahaz was supposed to have received *rūaḥ* at his anointing, according to the account in ch. 7 he had no longer retained anything of its effect.

2. And yet, great though his contempt was for the volatile ruler of the moment, the prophet did not think of renouncing the concept of *a sacral monarchy* upheld by Yahweh. The future saviour king was again to belong to the Davidic dynasty, even though – instead of the degenerate Jerusalem line – recourse was to be had to a collateral branch of the same dynasty (9.7; 11.1) [which had apparently remained (?) in Bethlehem, Micah 5.2.]. The throne is promised eternal continuance (*kūn*), as in the traditional oracles (II Sam. 7.12, 16). The 'El' quality of what is prophesied reminds us of Psalm 45.7. What tradition had promised to the ruler of the day, Isaiah takes up and applies to the future ruler. But in so doing he is not setting up an antithesis to the present conception of kingship; it is merely a reinterpretation. He probably considered that even the nabi Naboth had not meant to prophesy the government of Solomon and his successors, but had in mind the rule of the Messiah. Perhaps Isaiah is here picking up an already current popular eschatology, which expected a mysterious boy Immanu-El (7.14). But his ideas go far beyond naive conceptions of this kind.

Isaiah's concept of the Messiah has *mythological* features. (The statements in Isaiah 11 are amazingly similar to the description of the saviour child whom Virgil celebrates in his Fourth Eclogue (*c.* 40 BC). There must be some kind of link here with the ongoing history of the tradition, though we still do not know what it was.) Judgment independent of appearances and any statements made by the king's hearers, peace in the animal world by virtue of the royal authority – were not the ancient nabis more realistic when they simply wanted to exchange one ruler for another by means of a revolution? Is anything of this kind conceivable among men and women: an unbroken awareness of God, a continual state of being filled with *rūaḥ*? At this point Isaiah's vision of the future goes beyond the traditional view of the king and shows unmistakably utopian features – features which we do not find in this form in either Amos or Hosea.

On the other hand, there is no visible sign as yet of a New Testament Son of God and Christ. There is no supernatural birth, and the Messiah (who is probably presumed to be the initiator of a new dynasty and will be only reigning over Israel and its country) does not enjoy eternal life. Moreover Isaiah expects an ideal ruler during his own lifetime. In another respect the prophet reduces the extravagant predicates of the cultic view of the king. Although he is endowed with the gifts necessary for success in war (*gᵉbūrā*, 9.6; 11.2), the Messiah only comes on the scene after Yahweh, as divine warrior, has himself destroyed the superior Assyrian power (9.4; 10.27ff. cf. 10.5ff.; 31.8f. cf. 32.1ff.). *Šalōm*, to the extent of peace in the animal world, is the ultimate end of his rule (9.6f.; 11.6ff.). An ideal of peace emerges here which finds no parallel in royal psalms such as 2; 18; 45 and 110. Nor is the prophet interested in the world rule radiating from Jerusalem, which these psalms presuppose. At most we find the idea (if 11.10 is genuine?) that since the Messiah is filled with God, as Solomon in his wisdom once was, he becomes the ensign for the peoples. It is probably not by chance that Isaiah (like Amos, Hosea and Micah) avoids applying the title *melek*, king, with its autocratic, overbearing overtones, to the future ruler.

3. Isaiah therefore remains more closely bound to the ideas of his environment than does the critical prophecy of North Israel. Yet Amos and Hosea in their hopes for salvation also reckoned with a monarchical constitution (Amos 9.11f.; Hos. 3.4f.). Why do not the seers, who see the monarchy as the root of the whole people's ruin, promise a return to the peasant democracy of the prenational period? It was not so remote in time that no remembrance of it would have existed.

The insistence on having a king at the country's head is probably connected with a Hebrew 'concentric' anthropology, which sees the single person, not as an isolated individual, but as a branch on the tree of his group, as an inseparable member of his people. Man is only viable as part of a corporate personality. But the 'total self' of kindred and people is not equally developed in all its members. It requires a representative, visible embodiment in *the central individual*, in the father of the family or the 'father' of the nation (9.6). To identify himself with this father is ideally the wish of every subject, every other member. On the other hand, the ruling head remains a genuine embodiment only when he is concerned about every member of the total body and identifies himself even with those who have few legal rights. The king's power of discernment conditions the state of discernment in the people (11.9; 32.1ff.). It is only from the king that loyalty to the community, fertility and success can spread over the whole country and the rest of its inhabitants, who for their part offer loyalty to the community in response to the king.

Because of this community pattern (see below), these prophets cannot dispense with a sacral monarchy. *Šālōm*, as the welfare of the whole people, remains tied to the personal centre. (In the figure of the Son of Man, apocalyptic later extended this relationship of correspondence between individual and collective to mankind as a whole. What the New Testament says about Christ as the saviour for all mankind takes this line of thinking further in a different way.)

7.6.3 Through his reflections about the present defective constitution of his people, and the better one he expects in the future, Isaiah seems to have arrived at a new *concept of time*. The lament over the whorish city in 1.21ff., which probably dates from the period of social criticism, and in which the monarchy is still excluded from the impending disaster, already contains a pointer to a future revival of the primordial period:

A Oh, how the (once) faithful (*neʾāmān*, cf. 7.9) city / has become a harlot.
She was full of *mišpāṭ*, / so that *ṣedeq* ('righteousness') lodged in her [. . .].
Your silver has become a base alloy, / your beer adulterated with water . . .

B I will turn my hand against you again, / I will purify you as potash purifies the base alloy.
I will let your judges return as in the first time (*rišōnā*), / your counsellors as at the beginning.
Afterwards you shall again be called / city of *ṣedeq* ('righteousness'), the faithful city.

The prophet sees a return of the first, primordial era after a period of tremendous decline. *Rišōnā* means the 'head' of a period of time, a normal state of things reached at the beginning, which proves fruitful in its results (Gen. 13.4; I Kings 13.6). With Isaiah the expression begins to be the term for the eras in which Yahweh created the fundamental presuppositions for a prosperous life (Gen. 28.19; Josh. 8.33; Ps. 89.49: Jer. 33.7, 11). It is the primordial period which was celebrated as salvation history at cultic festivals, a time different in quality from the present, which had become grey and flat, a time full of wonders and unmistakable acts of God. 1.21ff. evidently refers to the period of David and Solomon. At that time Jerusalem became Israelite and filled with the divine *ṣedeq*, which the people were to realize again in themselves. For Isaiah this era was also *the* climax of all previous times (9.7; 28.21; 29.1; 37.35); it was prepared for through unique divine victories on the day of Midian (9.4; perhaps also through the 'victory of Egypt' = the Egyptian episode, 10.25f., a later interpolation?). That period culminated in the founding of Zion as the permanent centre of the divine presence on earth (14.32). The division of the kingdom and the death of Solomon therefore constituted *the* national disaster (7.17). The words which Yahweh had since then uttered into history were like dynamite and had an appalling effect on the people, who had destroyed the achievements of the *rišōnā* and its *ṣedeq* through their growing arrogance (9.8ff.; 2.6ff.). The present time was marked by an inner hollowness and was drifting inexorably towards the great debacle (*šēbēr*).

The messianic prophecies look beyond the catastrophe to a new beginning of God's work in history, through which *mišpāṭ* and a new order of existence will be attained once more. Here for the first time (1.27) Isaiah introduces the equation between the primordial period and the end-time which was later to become a theme of apocalyptic. It is not expressly repeated in the statements about the saviour king. Chapter 9, verse 1 shows how Isaiah is still struggling with the concept and its terminology. Here 'the early time' (*rišōn*, used adjectively, not as a substantive) is the time of present humiliation. The coming time is clearly stressed as a time when Israel will receive new honour. (Isaiah calls it literally 'back' time, *'aharōnā*, because the Hebrew visualized the past as being spread before him, whereas the future was invisible – still 'behind his back', so to speak). Isaiah's view of history can therefore be compared with a line broken in two places. *Rišōna* begins with the warrior days of Yahweh, which led to the glorious era of David. There followed an intermediate period of progressive deterioration, caused by human misdeeds. The day for Yahweh will soon bring about a turn of events which will lead to a new era of salvation. However, this era is not conceived of in terms of a static point outside time. It is to be the beginning of a new and better national history. Yahweh's new work will surpass even the achievements of the early history of salvation (11.9; see diagram).

For Isaiah, therefore, time represents a kind of doubly broken line. It runs purposefully and irreversibly, but not homogeneously. Here we find the roots of what theology calls eschatology. Whether one can already term Isaiah's 'late time' an eschatological category depends on one's definition of the term. At all events, for this prophet stress lies on the continuity: in spite of theophany and the day of Yahweh, there is no sharp break between the time of the present and the impending 'late time'.

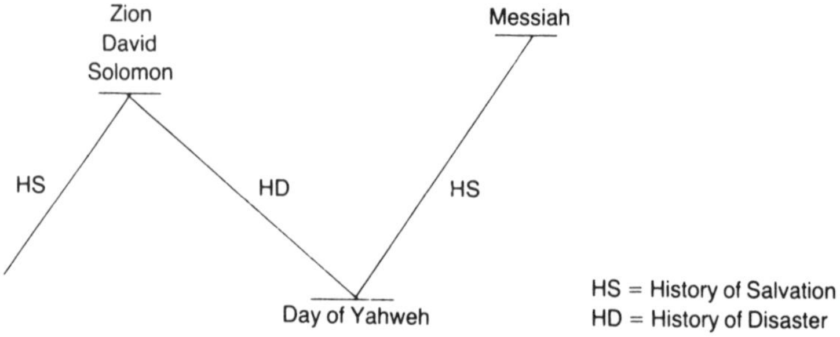

The land, Mount Zion and the people all remain the same. The very structure of the relevant passages makes this abundantly clear. The transition from predictions of disaster to predictions of salvation takes place in 9.1ff. and 10.27bff. within one and the same unit. Isaiah never utters an isolated prophecy of salvation. The driving motive for his conception of time, however, lies in an ethical futurism which was already evident in Amos and Hosea. Isaiah sees everything that surrounds him in a state of movement, in a mighty process, driving towards events such as there have never been before. The positively revolutionary upheaval in the times is inescapable in view of the divinely willed *ṣedeq,* and new conditions which make loyalty to the community possible and make the effects of salvation felt among the people.

7.7 The salvation of Zion? Hope for the remnant?

Mount Zion, with Solomon's splendid Temple, had long been seen as the centre where Israel and its God encountered one another. Consequently Zion plays an essential role in Isaiah's metapolitical reflections. It was here that he received the charge to harden the people's hearts. When Isaiah withdrew from his vain attempts to change the mind of the royal house during the Syro-Ephraimite war, he sealed the testimony to the future in the group of his disciples, and did not allow his witness to be heard outside it any more. He underlined this decision emphatically with a confession of faith in Yahweh, who was present on Mount Zion and who would evidently remain so in all the turbulence of coming military entanglements (8.17f.). The theme of Zion comes even more to the fore later, the more Isaiah begins to criticize Assyria. Yahweh's universal plan, *ʿēṣā,* means that: 'I will break the Assyrian in my own land, / and upon my mountains I will trample him under foot' (14.25). The description of the theophany in 30.27–33 (which von Rad calls 'one of the most powerful passages in the book of Isaiah') has a similar trend: the cultic community will assemble on Zion, and will hallow the feast and sing hymns. Then Yahweh will suddenly let his voice be heard, and let his arm strike:

> Before the voice of Yahweh will Assyria be stricken, / with his rod he lets him be slain.

Isaiah 31.1–9 is similar. Here Yahweh descends in order to march on Zion, and Assyria dies through the sword 'not of man'. (10.12 is therefore a summing up – perhaps by a later hand? Yahweh will bring the whole of his historicial work, in so far as it involves Assyria, to a conclusion on Zion, cf. 17.12–14.)

There is no dispute among scholars about the importance for Isaiah of the actual *contemporary* sanctuary on Zion. But the position of the sanctuary in the future is another matter. Whether Isaiah cherishes a *hope* for Zion or not has been termed the central question of present-day Isaiah exegesis. Is Zion merely the place where a decisive stroke against Assyria is to fall, after Judah has previously been completely exterminated? Or is it the place of survival as well? Does the decisive battle on Zion take place before the total annihilation of all Judaeans, and does it mean that a little group of Yahweh worshippers will be saved? Is only the city of Jerusalem destroyed, and not the Temple to the north of it? Isaiah's announcement of downfall would then not be meant as radically as the prediction of his contemporary Micah (3.12). The hope for Zion is the centre of von Rad's presentation of Isaiah. He sees Isaiah as being from the very beginning penetrated through and through by the belief 'that Yahweh would protect Zion from the Assyrians in all circumstances'.[20] He can appeal to passages such as 14.28–32, where the poor find refuge from the Philistines on Zion. Why not from the Assyrians too? Or to 28.16f., according to which Yahweh has laid a corner-stone on Zion and whoever believes – believes in the significance of this stone for Israel's future – will never give way.

Most Old Testament scholars, however, are inclined to see Isaiah as an uncompromising prophet of disaster, for whom even Zion is doomed to destruction. The main argument is provided by the close of the Temple vision (6.12f.):

> Yahweh will remove mankind, / mighty will be the forsakenness in the midst of the land.
> And though a tenth remain in it, / it will again fall victim to the extermination . . .

Doesn't this second extermination (both of them by the Assyrians?) mean a final end of the people? If ch. 6 is seen as a vocational vision containing the germ of all that Isaiah has to say in the years that followed, it is difficult to conceive that the prophetic vision saw any Judaean as being saved on Zion. On the other hand, when Amos 5.3 talks about a people twice reduced to a tenth it does not necessarily mean total extermination. The rejection of any positive hope for Zion is given further support by the Ariel poem in 29.1ff. The worst of fates is predicted for dwellers in the cities:

> Your voice shall come from the earth like the voice of a spirit from the dead; / from the dust you will only be able to cheep out your words.

Unfortunately it is still not clear whether Ariel – a place where cultic festivals are celebrated and where David once camped – refers to the city of Jerusalem or to the Temple mount. The following verse describes a turn of events – 'in an instant, suddenly' – in which the enemy army is scattered. But this may be excluded as a later interpolation. If the name Ariel is applied to Zion, then here too no one is left. For Isaiah there was no preservation in the face of judgment; there was only, afterwards, a completely new, divine salvation, unrelated to what went before. 'It is only the continuity of the word that is preserved', as W. H. Schmidt puts it.

Yet another problem is connected with the Zion hope: the meaning of *the remnant of Israel*. Isaiah's first son is given the symbolic name *šᵉʾār-yāšūb*. This was earlier translated as 'a remnant repents', and interpreted as referring to the preservation of a minority of the nation in spite of all coming catastrophes. The remnant can then be associated with the figure of Immanu-El (7.14), and means the people of the future saviour king. 'When the Messiah appeared he was surely intended to have people round him; and nothing is said about a completely new creation out of dust and the divine spirit,' as Procksch puts it.[21] The remnant is connected, too, with the saying about faith in 28.16f., and with Isaiah's disciples as a sign and portent (8.18). Above all, the remnant is formed out of those who arrive at Zion and survive there during the last great Assyrian attack. All this gives a more or less consistent picture (see especially Procksch in his 1930 Isaiah commentary); and fits organically into an overall view of Isaiah which is not directed towards total disaster.

But exegetical common sense has since veered round in the diametrically opposite direction. Even scholars like von Rad, who adhere to a Zion hope, abandon every notion of a remnant of the people in the positive sense. According to their view, remnant means no more than the insignificant remainder of the population in the land, comparable with the ruins which will be all that is left of the cities. The name of Isaiah's son means 'only a remnant returns (from the battle)'. As justification for a purely negative connotation of *šᵉār*, reference is made to ch. 6, the tone of which is allegedly inexorable and intended in a totally destructive sense. In support of this view, it may further be said that some of the *šᵉār* (or *nōtār*) statements in the book were probably added by a later hand, and that it is in these later interpolations particularly that the positive character of 'the remnant' is stressed (4.3; 11.11, 16; 28.5). In addition there is talk about the remnant of non-Israelite peoples; and in Isaiah this cannot be meant in a positive sense. But it is a study by W. E. Müller, above all, that has brought about this change in opinion.[22] Müller attempts to prove that 'remnant' was a military term in the ancient East, describing a conduct of war which wiped out the enemy power 'down to the lees'. In this sense the remnant in Isaiah too would be meant as a melancholy reminder of past greatness.

But impressively though the arguments are marshalled, they are hardly enough to prove that the word 'remnant' should be given a totally negative definition. Hasel has investigated the ancient oriental parallels more fully,[23] coming to the conclusion that 'remnant' means the ultimate safeguarding of some kind of continuity in the social life of a population that has been invaded by a foreign army. Among many peoples under the yoke of a foreign power the idea of the remnant therefore meant the sustaining of a positive hope. It would seem that Isaiah's usage also points in this direction. When the remnant of the Philistines is mentioned, it is expressly added that this is going to be slain; so the concept of the remnant as such does not by any means already imply total disaster (14.30f. 17.6). The saying about repentence, *šūb,* with all its full and proper content, crops up in the Temple vision (6.10; cf. 9.13; 10.20ff.). Is the name *šᵉār-yāšūb?* supposed to have any other connotation? In the saying to Hezekiah during the threat in 701, a sign is given through the harvest which the fields yield during the following three years – the sign 'out of Jerusalem shall go forth a remnant *(šᵉērīt)* / of a saved company from Mount Zion' (37.32). All this is entirely in accordance with Isaiah's expectations for the future. The remnant provides the germ of the people to come, who are assigned to the Messiah. But it is only possible to talk about a remnant after the catastrophe (cf. 1.8). It is not yet certain who is one day going to belong to it.

So Isaiah does not see it as his function to missionize. How seldom we hear admonitory words from his lips! He is not a preacher of conversion. It is not his task to gather the remnant together. Yahweh himself will see to that, not prophetic preaching.

7.8 Suprahistory as Yahweh's work and its metahistorical analysis

7.8.1 History and suprahistory. For a number of years there has been a dispute among Old Testament scholars as to whether (and to what extent) Israel in general and the prophets in particular possessed or developed a sense of history. Von Rad, more than any other, argued passionately for the recognition that the prophets only become comprehensible when one knows the historical traditions to which they appeal and which (in their eschatology) they see as being recreated. According to his view, for the prophets history is *the* divine revelation. Other scholars have emphatically denied this, maintaining that the prophets nowhere show any interest in an inner-worldy causal link between human action and suffering; that they never make the dynamic force of history as such a theme; and that therefore there can be no question of history in the real sense.

Underlying this discussion is not only a varying evaluation of Old Testament statements but – whether implicitly or explicitly – the whole contemporary theological debate, particularly the discussion about the relation between God and history today. This is the only possible explanation for the fact that the basis of the argument is often shockingly narrow. We find arguments like 'The prophets never use a word which the dictionary would translate as history.' But there is no word in the Old Testament for marriage, or agriculture, or religion either. Is this supposed to mean that these areas of life were unknown in Israel? But sometimes the other side also makes things too easy for itself. If the prophets mention the exodus from Egypt, or King David, this is sometimes taken to support the claim that they show a sense of history – as if something of the same kind could not also be demonstrated in traditions of a mythical kind as well.

The Old Testament certainly contains historiography, which, in the so-called Succession Narrative (II Samuel 9–I Kings 2), shows events developing out of human causes and effects, which can therefore be interpreted in a historical sense. Yet it is equally certain that a view-point of this kind cannot be detected in any one of the prophets. It is true that I have used the traditional concept of salvation history in order to explain the prophetic interpretation of time. But salvation history is marked by the divine acts and decrees which precede every human deed. They no doubt develop stage by stage, but they do not amount to history in the sense in which we use the word. Isaiah is aware of that particular kind of movement on the part of God and the people who are bound to him. It is a movement running through time, from stage to stage. Isaiah is alive to it, not only in the era of salvation history (which for him ended with David), but in the present and the future too. It was a movement into which the prophet and his listeners knew themselves to be irresistibly drawn. So in what precise terms did he talk about it?

As in the case of Amos, I have chosen the term *suprahistory* in order to make clear a total cohesion which is alien to our way of thinking. With it, I am trying to reduce the whole complex of Isaiah's thinking to a common denominator, though this is inevitably conditioned by our modern ways of talking about things. Suprahistory means a 'total' movement running through time, which includes – and also impels – not only the Israelite people but everything that exists between them and the underlying reality of God. I shall call the theory of this supra-history *metahistory* in so far as in what he says Isaiah develops its bearings on the political behaviour of his day. In Isaiah, as in Amos and Hosea too, suprahistory is composed of various levels which cannot be clearly divided from one another.

7.8.2 I shall leave on one side *the political and military level,* because it only turns up occasionally (10.27bff.) and is self-evident. Closely bound up with it in Isaiah is *the level of national existence,* which he develops quite differently from his predecessors in North Israel. For him, the whole nation, as person, total self or corporate personality, is always in the foreground. Anything but an abstract power, the nation is a body which, though it is invisible, can certainly be experienced. This body is in itself hierarchically divided (1.4–6; cf. 37.29). The head is the capital city, and the king is in turn the head *(rōš)* of that (7.7–9; 28.1–4). The *lēb, lēbāb* or corporate reason of the people as a whole is bound up with the monarchy (29.13; 10.7; 19.1; cf. 1.5). The capital seems to rest on 'the neck' of the people (8.8; 10.7; 30.28). Deportation lays bare the genitals (20.4). Wars shave off the hair (7.20). What Isaiah experiences as the almost self-contained physical unity of his people springs from an experience of the common will which does not depend on the will of the individual – a public opinion which is not formed in the brain of the individual. Would it be permissible to compare this with what the nineteenth century AD called 'the national spirit'?

But an Israelite thinker denies any self-contained, purely spiritual entity of this kind, either in the individual or in communities. The nation can be grasped only in association with the land, which is not only its necessary economic foundation but also the factor that moulds the character of those who dwell on it. Consequently the metaphors drawn from the body slide into those of the national tree, or forest (14.30), the royal tree – the dynasty – embodying the centre of the national forest or vineyard (10.33f.; 11.1–9). In his own way the individual then forms a sapling with roots and fruit (5.24). From this apsect, Israel is a vine in the vineyard of its country (5.1–7). The same is true of Egypt-Cush (18) and Assyria (10.18). In the political events of the day Assyria reaches out to other trees, even to the wood and vineyard of the Lebanon, to which a position is assigned here which is not entirely clear (the centre of the earth? 37.24; cf. 10.34; 29.17; 33.9). With the image of the fruit tree, the body politic – the body of the people – is also presumed to be an active subject, with the purpose of bringing forth fruit for itself and others.

Significantly enough, animal metaphors are seldom used. When a people goes to war beyond its own frontiers it can no longer be seen as a tree; it is more like a beast. Assyrian and Egyptian troops are like the insects which are typical of those particular countries – bees and flies (7.18; 18). But when we are told that Israel bears the 'yoke' of Assyrian rule (9.4; 14.25), it is only the Assyrian as overlord who is being thought of: the image of an ox is not necessarily in the writer's mind. Assyria is once compared with a huge snake from which a winged seraph-serpent is to issue (14.29). The connection with water may have suggested the comparison of Egypt with a river monster (30.6–8, 28). Assyria is merely compared with a lion, and in addition is identified with the sea, which is apparently the more important point (5.29f.).

The link with sources of water seems to be essential. It allows the people to be described as branches of their main river. Judah depends on the narrow Shiloah, Assyria on the mighty Euphrates, Egypt on the arms of its Nile (8.4–8; 18; 37.25). Seen from Judah's strategically unfavourable situation, all her neighbours appear as a chaotically threatening sea of nations; Isaiah then takes up the tradition of the Jerusalem cult as well (Ps. 46) and talks about the roar of the nations (17.12f.; 37.29) or about the way the enemy nations overflow on to his own country (*seṭep*, 8.8; 28.2,15,17). This way of looking at things also suggests phrases about flooding and heavy rain, storm and sea (28.2; 30.28). Whereas the Psalms play on a myth about a great struggle in the primaeval waters, here the incoming tide dashes itself against a rock which is Yahweh himself and surrounds his mountain, Zion, which nothing will be able to knock down. Isaiah apparently assumes that Assyria also possesses a rock like this (31.9).

Every nation has its predetermined place in a mythical, three-storey world-picture. But by what it does and the way it develops its specific religion, it can reinforce these cosmic relationships. Egypt has bound itself to the underworld and the realm of the dead (28.15). The life of Israel and Judah, on the other hand, is centred on Zion, the coping-stone of creation, through which Yahweh has sealed up the mysterious subterranean flood (28.16; 14.32) and over which Yahweh's throne towers up into heaven (6.1). Assyria, on the other hand, occupies a relatively neutral position in the north. It only enters the cosmic zone of danger because it desires to rise up to the heights *(mārōm),* to elevation over the earthly sphere as a whole (37.23f.).

7.8.3 By conceiving the nature of the different peoples in terms of the body, Isaiah is able to presuppose the same underlying anthropology for both individuals and nations. For him, as for Amos, the sphere of action which creates destiny is a fundamental law of human history. Yet beyond that he also pursues the anthropological preconditions that determine human misdemeanour. He seeks human structures which explain why the correlation between action and destiny in his own generation is largely negative.

The sayings of the early period already express the conviction that man has to mould himself through behaviour which takes account of the community; that his acts encircle him with aura-like spheres, colouring him according to the moral character of what he does, and gradually being transposed into a corresponding destiny. *Mišpāṭ* and *ṣ'dāqā* are active forces deriving from God; they are both meaningful ordinances for the community and the capacity for preserving that community (1.21; 5.6f.). For Israel they are given beforehand since they derive from the divine decrees of the Davidic era and from the renewed actualization of those decrees at the great festivals. Isaiah's contemporaries, however, are binding their sinful acts to themselves as if with chariot ropes (5.18); they are unable to avoid acting in a way that damages the community, and are therefore destroying themselves. Their *'āwōn* (as Isaiah calls the massed auras of transgressions against man and God) becomes the crack in the walls of their existence (30.13). The evil doers lose their vital sap, wither inwardly, and will one day catch fire (1.31; 5.24; 9.18). They stumble, as Isaiah says elsewhere, and are shattered through their fall. This underlying order of things, which determines events, is summed up in the Wisdom axiom in 3.9f.:

> Woe to their vital powers *(nepeš),* for they bring evil on themselves *(gāmal)*. Say that (to be) *ṣaddīq* is good, for they shall enjoy the fruit of their deeds.

But in that case why has Israel nevertheless shaped its history in a predominantly destructive way? Why has it chosen the road to what is now inexorable ruin, having once had an unparalleled initial advantage? Prompted by his God, Isaiah becomes aware of the polarities which effect human structures. It is not enough to do spontaneously what the community requires at any given time for its benefit, as Israel had hitherto believed. If a person's behaviour is to be in accordance with the needs of a community, he must have some visible place, some position on which he can rely. Human existence is characterized by dependence, the need for support.

Whether as individuals or collectively, in addition to their own actions and before those actions are performed, people take their bearings from *beṭaḥ*, 'a power on which one can rely', from *māšʿen*, 'support', and from *maḥse*, 'succour'. If someone is to act fearlessly, he needs a secure base. This begins with the elemental supports of water and bread; it includes the social order with its different classes (3.1f.); and extends to military arms and the major power who acts as ally (31.1; 36.16). Isaiah often uses the verbs in question and a wealth of derived nouns (*biṭḥā*, *biṭṭaḥōn*, *mibṭāḥ*, *ḥāsut*, *mašʿēnā*, *mišʿenet*); the differentiation of meaning between these terms has yet to be investigated.

To take one's bearings from what is reliable is both necessary and good. But the Judaeans are giving a wrong direction to this endeavour because they generally look only at what is apparent at the present moment. But the present is transitory. The only things that retain their value are powers whose potency can hardly be glimpsed merely by the physical eye, above all the sanctuary on Zion and what exists round about it (14.23; 28.15–17). Trustworthiness must be sought, not in what is present for the moment, but in the divine *dābār*, the utterance which proclaims the future and brings it to pass (see pp. 151ff. below). Instead of hurrying to Egypt, what Judah should do is to enquire of Yahweh (31.1), rely on the portents he sends, and persevere in trust in a hidden God (8.18). It is in these contexts that the call to faith belongs. It is related to a particular prophetic utterance about future developments (7.9; 28.16). For Isaiah, faith is not an independent theme; it is only one of several ways in which the correct use of man's capacity for *beṭaḥ*, reliance, finds expression. Tranquillity and peace, which permit a successful and harmonious life even in unquiet times, spring solely from trust in the underlying reality (30.15; 7.4). Does this anthropological structure of *dependence on a primal ground of trust* not suggest the vague beginnings of what Schleiermacher, centuries later, was to call the feeling of absolute dependence? This condition must not be confused with lack of independence and heteronomy. It does not mean dependence on authoritative conditions of rule.

A second kind of striving belongs to the structure of man. This may be termed the pressure to heighten and enhance life. According to Isaiah's view, this kind of striving had degenerated even more among his contemporaries than the search for reliance. The song about the fate of the haughty (2.6ff.) had already castigated this fateful tendency towards an undue self-estimation. This remained one of the prophet's themes right down to his later period. Again and again he admonishes the *hybris* of the mighty; an over-valuation of property and means of power, an over-estimate of themselves which inevitably led to a fall. Here again we still need an investigation of the terms he uses in this context (*g'h, gbh, gdl, rūm*). Whereas the problem of reliance is considered only in the case of Judah in his later phase, Isaiah talks of the arrogance of foreign nations, and of the Northern kingdom as well (9.9; 28.1–4; cf. 16.6). Even the Assyrian king has a monologue on arrogance put into his mouth (10.8ff.; 37.24; 14.13ff.).

Do these views suggest that Isaiah was a small-minded religious fanatic, the kind of person who condemns anyone who does not lead a strictly religious life? Does it not even suggest hostility towards culture, if luxury is cited (3.16) as symptom of the rottenness of the court? Such a conclusion would be unduly hasty. Isaiah finds it quite acceptable that there should be many degrees among people and nations, and that individuals should stand out above the rank and file to a highly varying extent. For him, the term *kābōd*, which sums up the importance, respect and demonstrable splendour of a person, group or class, is an indispensable mark of human existence (8.7; 22.23f.; cf. 11.10). This becomes evident at the very point where *kābōd* is endangered (5.13; 10.3,18; 22.18; see also the related term *tip'eret*, 10.12; 28.1). Men need knowledge in their search for something to trust and their urge to enhance life. Knowledge is a human characteristic, but at present Isaiah has to say that animals are behaving more reasonably than the Israelites (1.3). It is true that in their arrogance and pride these people think they have a monopoly of wisdom. But since they hope that superficial, momentary constellations of power will provide sufficient security, and that the perversion of *ṣ'dāqā* into evil-doing is unimportant, their wisdom is hollow (5.21; 10.2) and their plans will inevitably be thwarted (7.5–7). They misjudge the standards of reality and they are making themselves the hub of the world. This of course also applies to the enemy, when the Assyrian boasts: 'Are my commanders not all kings? . . . By the strength of my hands I have brought about (victory) and by my wisdom, for I have a trained understanding' (10.8,13). Their reason-heart (*lēbāb*) does not reckon with suprahistorical powers and thereby shows itself to be foolish (10.7; 31.1–3). For Israel especially, it follows that the conceit of these sages will be 'fixed': 'Look closely, yet do not see.' The prophet has to ensure that their *lēb* does not perceive what is happening – that is what is meant by the famous hardening of heart in ch. 6.

Isaiah therefore does not content himself with accusations, but searches for the anthropological basis for the failure; and here he discovers a polarity of endeavours, which are inherent in all human beings but which they can pervert, either as individuals or in community. That is what has happened. The prophet does not go on to explore metaphysically how the tendency to evil in man comes about. He does not think even remotely in terms of a devil; nor does he make the creator responsible. Theodicy is therefore for him superfluous because, in spite of all his criticism of wisdom and arrogance, he looks forward to a time when human beings will acquire true trust and freedom from fear, the reliable wisdom that makes a person capable of true living, and a new, favourable correlation between action and destiny (11.1–9; 32.3–8,17). Before that, people and nations will have to be humiliated. But in the end Isaiah has an optimistic view of the future. One day there will be a new opportunity for his people to win life.

7.8.4 Between the sphere of God himself and the auras of human deeds which, invisible though they are, are known from experience to be efficacious, are forces which are neither abstract nor personal. They are more in the nature of 'things', and are of decisive importance for the fate of mankind. These active forces enter the community of men and women from the primal ground of life itself. They already played an important role in Amos. For Isaiah, too, *mišpāṭ* and *ṣᵉdāqā* belong here, as the foundations sustaining political, economic and religious life. That they should be lost to the Israel of his day is absurd, but nonetheless undeniable (1.21; 5.7). Yet he expects that they will be conferred anew through the Messiah (11.1–9; 10.22).

Isaiah names other forces as well, which Amos does not mention. The seraphim in 6.2, 6f. might be assigned to this group. They were probably taken over from the ideas of the Jerusalem cult, but for Isaiah they play a part only in this one passage. Otherwise he does not recognize the existence of angelic beings. What are important are extensions of divine power into this world. When in 31.1–3 he stresses that the Egyptians are 'men, not *'ēl*' and that their horses are 'flesh, not *rūᵃḥ*' he is introducing the concepts of *'ēl* and *rūᵃḥ* as metahistorical factors. For Isaiah, El – originally a Canaanite name for God and a predicate applied to Yahweh in the cultic language of the psalms – belongs on an 'inner-worldly' level. It might perhaps be described as the power of an impersonal divinity, which surrounds human beings and makes them unconquerable. This at least makes names like Immanu-El, Ari-El and El-*gibbōr* comprehensible (7.14; 8.8–10; 9.6; 10.21; 14.13; 29.1). (Yahweh himself is called *hā'ēl* in 5.16.) *El* is only used in connection with Israel; the other nations have at most weak *'ᵉlīlīm*, 'godlets' (19.1,3; 10.10f.). The wind of the spirit, *rūᵃḥ*, is even more an eminently metahistorical force for Isaiah. Success is guaranteed only when *rūᵃḥ* enters into strategic planning and human alliances (30.1). Yahweh can so breathe *rūᵃḥ* into a statesman that he goes against his own interests in order to save Judah, when it is unjustly beleaguered (29.10; 37.7)). *Rūᵃḥ* turns against the sea of the nations and works havoc there, letting them be dashed apart like spray (17.13). In the saving future *rūᵃḥ* will enable the Messiah to establish his rule on earth (11.2). (It is noticeable that Isaiah – unlike the earlier nabis – never puts down his own inspiration to *rūᵃḥ*.).

What is heard through Isaiah's lips is Yahweh's *dābār*, and for him this is without doubt the most relevant active force in the metahistorical process. By giving expression to Yahweh's *dābār*, Isaiah moves history. *Dābār* is translated as 'word', which necessarily narrows the meaning down; for it is not the individual word, but only meaningful speech which is *dābār* – and even then only when it is either based on undeniable facts, or actually creates a particular situation. Other talk is mere lip-*dābār*, as it is contemptuously called in 36.5. *Dābār* normally issues from the lips of God, the king or his messengers. But this is only one side of the matter. *Dābār* also means situation, circumstance, fact (39.2,6). If the two connotations are considered together, it emerges that the speaker is bound to do (*'āsā*) what he has uttered in the *dābār* (38.7). Furthermore, a *dābār* comes into being (*qūm*) by itself, and changes from a speech event into an actual event – is, as it were, materialized (8.10). This may take a considerable time, and may come about in stages. So the poem about recent history in the Northern kingdom, with its refrain (9.8ff. + 5.25ff.), begins emphatically: 'Yahweh had sent a *dābār* to Jacob. / It alighted on Israel.' Five or six stanzas then develop the theme: how the Yahweh saying (doubtless uttered by a prophet) has been realized through a series of catastrophes. The word of God as *dābār* establishes destiny. Yet where Yahweh's *dābār* issues in the form of *tōrāh*, it also contains alternatives. Consequently the saying in 1.10ff., with its criticism of the cult, points to rejection and downfall if the existing gulf between faithfulness to the community in everyday life and sacrificial feasts at the Temple continues; but it opens up the way to new *mišpāṭ* if the people are washed clean and a new orientation takes place. In the same way, Israel had always seen the blessing conferred for faithfulness to the community and the divine curse imposed for violation of that community as *dābār* powers – powers which, hovering over men and women, accompany history and only materialize where the presuppositions that have previously been defined are fulfilled (cf. the conditional clause in Isa. 7.9).

Dābār is therefore neither mere communication between an 'I' and a 'Thou', nor information about an 'It'. It is *dynamis* – effective word. It is a concept which still echoes in the New Testament (in Rom. 1.16f., for example). If Yahweh has had a *dābār* proclaimed, he does not let it escape from history any more (31.2). The dynamic aspect therefore outweighs the noetic one. When prophets appear before their listeners with the proclamation formula, 'Thus says Yahweh', they are not merely intending to predict history; they want to provoke it too – to bring it about through what they say. Consequently, though it is useful to ask about fulfilment, it would be foolish to expect it literally.

For Isaiah, *dābār* as a power that establishes the future is on the same level as a sign established by God, *'ōt*. *'ōt* occasionally takes the form of a verbal sign – for example in the names given to the sons, 'a remnant repents', and 'speed spoil, hasten prey', or in the child Immanu-El. In other places *'ōt* manifests itself as an inscription on a tablet (8.1), or the life of Isaiah's children (8.18). When the prophet runs about naked (20) or when there is a rich harvest after two poor years (37.30f.), this is *'ōt* as well. Natural and social events, things that can be heard and things that can be seen, can all be understood as *'ōt*. Isaiah is not thinking of selecting chance events and giving them a subsequent religious interpretation. From the very beginning these happenings, seen metahistorically, are not ends in themselves; they are the preparation for some decisive turn of events.

Theologians frequently appeal to the prophets' use of *dābār* when they are treating the relationship between revelation and history in the Bible. A view is coming to be accepted in present-day scholarship which Albrektson has reduced to the formula: 'Many of these divine messages do concern history. But clearly we ought not to call this revelation in history, it is rather a revelation about history.'[24] But statements of this kind neglect the foundations of prophetic thinking. To modern interpreters it seems natural to assume that history is a history of facts, and that the question of meaning can be asked only at a subsequent stage. But this is a positivist invention – and perhaps not even a true view of history at that. For men like Isaiah, the happenings round their people had from time immemorial been a series of *d^ebārīm*, circumstances which had another side – in word and therefore in meaning. Because a speech event cannot be distinguished from history (since human and divine acts are founded on effective words), for Isaiah there was no such thing as history-in-itself, but only metahistory. In this total process – or so it is axiomatically presupposed – everything has its meaning, and no event is in itself ambiguous. Admittedly, the whole context of the meaning in its totality is accessible only to God; but it is revealed to Israel by way of authorized spokesmen; and this revelation runs ahead of actual events. A *dābār* never subsequently 'interprets' an event that has already happened. Nor, however, does it ever announce 'everything under the sun'. The *dābār* sets itself in the *dābār* series which has been uttered in the past, and continues the logical sequence. One can call this concept of *dābār* 'belief in revelation' – though it may be better to dispense with the dogmatic concept of revelation altogether in the context of the Old Testament. But if the word is used at all, revelation then means the disclosure of the meaning of the world and reality, the driving power of supra-history. It is not a pointer to some specifically religious zone of salvation. All the people involved are called to subsequent insight which the development announced will confirm as reasonable.

7.8.5 What Yahweh proclaims points ultimately to Yahweh himself. People are not merely held fast in the aura of what they do, exposed to historical and metahistorical forces. They are dependent on God. It is only through Yahweh that human beings, earth and reality combine at all in a meaningful process of events. This God can be described by means of *transferred personal characteristics*. In Isaiah his rule corresponds to the different supra-historical levels which we described above. If, for example, the nations are described as physical bodies, Yahweh confronts them as a huge cosmic body, with a face and eyes which, through a correlation of sin and disaster, become bitter and hide themselves (1.15; 3.8; 8.17). His majesty rises up against human arrogance (2.6ff.). If nations are seen as trees, he goes to work like a woodcutter (10.33; cf. v. 15) or sends fire (10.17). The fire gushes out from the white heat of his wrath (*'ap*, 5.15; 9.19), which is in turn linked with his nose (*'ap*) and tongue (30.27; cf. 5.25). References to Yahweh's hand are even more frequent. Stretched out over all nations (14.26), it lies heavy on evildoers (and will not be withdrawn, 9.12, 17,21; 10.4; 5.25), so that the connection between their acts and their destiny is activated. But as soon as Yahweh, through a theophany, brings about his day, he emerges into the foreground from his usual concealment; he establishes universal *mišpāṭ* (3.13), freeing those who dwell in darkness by means of a miraculous victory (9.2,4), destroying the foreign power and trampling it down on his mountains (14.25; 31.4).

The impending theophany which is going to revolutionize history is celebrated by the prophet as *Yahweh's work* (28.21). This is an expression which corresponds best to a term taken from suprahistory. The work (*maʿase*) has long since been in progress. Isaiah's sayings point to its goal. He must have used this expression more frequently than the writings that have come down to us show; for the people who confront him sceptically, mocking him and thereby drawing a burden of sin after them with ropes, pick out this term as being particularly characteristic of Isaiah, saying:

> Let him make haste / let him speed his work, that we may see it.
> Let the purpose of the Holy One of Israel draw near and (finally) come about / that we may know it! (5.19).

The expression 'Yahweh's work' was probably taken over from cultic language, where it meant the great deeds from Yahweh's hand belonging to the past, in creation (Ps. 92.4f.) and salvation history (Ex. 34.10; Judg. 2.10). Isaiah extends its meaning to what already discloses itself in the present to the clear-sighted person as a course of events founded on suprahistory (5.12). Over against this work he sets the secret political intrigues which represent human *maʿase* (29.15f.), and which try to avoid being seen. Because human *maʿase* is degenerate, Yahweh's *maʿase* must also 'degenerate' – become an alien work. Just as earlier Yahweh carried out his work through a holy war against Israel's enemies, so he now leads Israel's enemies against Israel herself. But both acts belong to one and the same overriding divine work. The ultimate end of *maʿase* is then seen by the Isaiah school as being the final destruction of the Assyrian super-power and the new Israel (10.12; 29.22f.).

Yahweh's *plan* (*ʿēṣā*) runs through time parallel to his work. This plan was really meant to be taken over by the Judaean monarchy as the foundation of its political planning (30.1); but it is mocked at by the men responsible (5.19). And yet – so Isaiah proclaims – Yahweh will establish it in spite of them and will therefore have to destroy the plans of human beings (8.10; cf. 7.7; 19.2, 11, 17). Assyria will be just as much affected as Israel (14.24–27). And yet the secret plan of history points to an increase and decrease of divine activity, so that people may be brought to maturity. It does not involve any 'threshing' of Israel to the point of complete extermination (28.28). The harmony of human and divine planning will one day be reached in the rule of the Messiah, which will promote community (11.2; cf. 9.7). This divine plan or *ʿēṣā* does not mean (as it does in later Christian dogmatics) an eternal divine resolution formed before time. On the contrary, what God resolves and plans takes place within the sequence of time. And yet his new plans are concentrated into a total plan which corresponds to his total work for, on and with mankind. With Yahweh's *ʿēṣā* and *maʿase*, therefore, Isaiah reduces to Hebrew concepts what I have tried to sum up in a rather rough and ready way under the term 'suprahistory'.

Western dogmatics are accustomed to see a fundamental contrast between God's work (*opus dei*) and human work (*opus hominis*). It may perhaps be useful to stress that to incorporate this semantic opposition into Isaiah's concept of Yahweh's work is to block one's access to the prophet. For Isaiah, the divine work has to be realized through human beings. Even Yahweh's 'alien' work is put into action through human troops – the Assyrians.

Holy, *qādōš*, is the divine predicate that is applied to Yahweh's work and plan (5.19; cf. 5.24; 29.23). According to the Temple vision, Yahweh's beauty, greatness and glory (*kābōd*) are manifested in the visible spheres here below, i.e. in the fullness of the whole earth, which they therefore embrace and interpenetrate. This God is therefore not some theistic Supreme Being; he is Yahweh of hosts (the active forces) and *qādōš*, holiness (6.3). Holiness is not (purely) a heavenly property – even in the threefold invocation of the *trisagion*. In this passage it is associated with the Temple, but in most other places it is linked with the one people of Israel, who have been elevated from the midst of the peoples of the earth. As 'the Holy One of Israel' Yahweh does not so much rule *over* the people as rule in them. This makes him the secret centre of metahistory, whose backbone is Zion and this same Israel. When the Assyrians attack these powers they are therefore attacking the *qādōš* (37.23). Since Yahweh is the Holy One of Israel, he should be seen in the great deeds with which he intervenes on behalf of his people and through which he establishes his will. That is why the prophet sees Yahweh, who is shown to be Israel's *qādōš*, as the ground of all real trust (*bāṭaḥ*, 30.15; 31.1; cf. 10.20; 17.7; 29.19,23).

With these concepts – Yahweh's work, Yahweh's plan and the Holy One of Israel – Isaiah defines Yahweh's innermost nature. But in using them he is not intending to outline a metaphysical scheme. He is concerned with metahistory – a system of thought which both reveals and evokes events which are intimately linked with moral responsibility. Isaiah dispenses with specific political proposals. His arguments are drawn from metahistory and he expects that they will meet with assent. He does not only *maintain* that Yahweh is the Lord of politics, and that his commandments can claim validity in this field too. He does more: he proves cogently how the penultimate and the ultimate reality interlock.

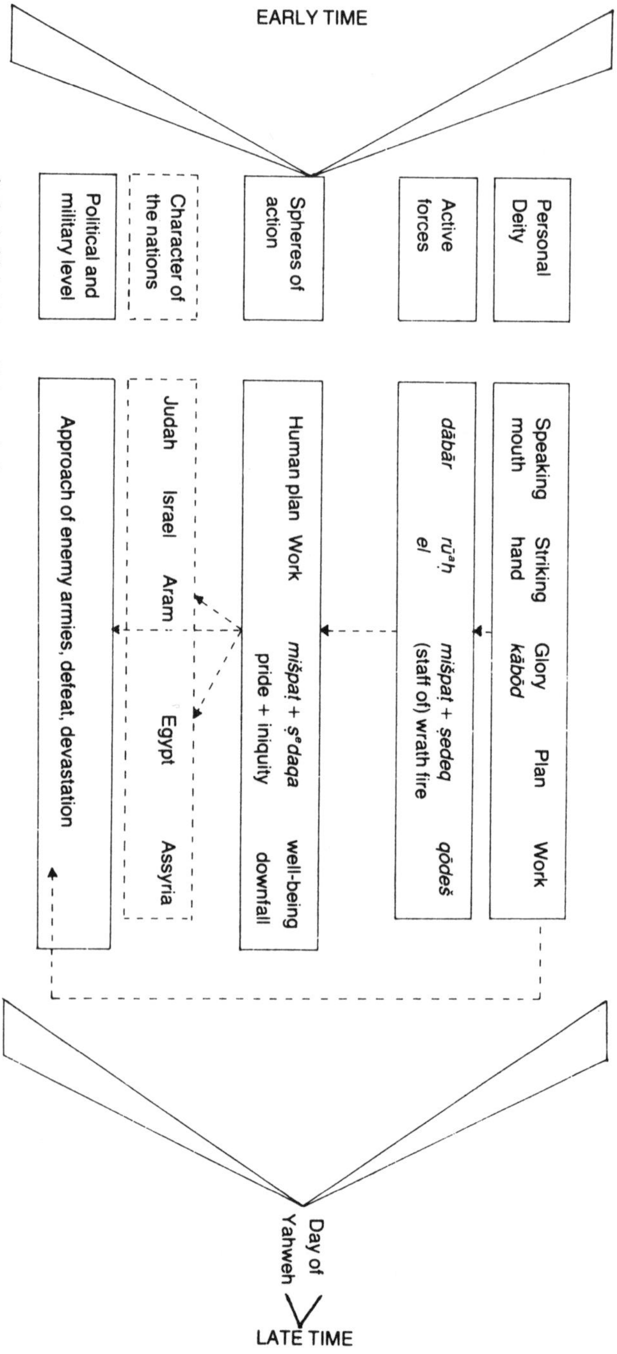

Isaianic Metahistory: Schematic Survey

IV

Prophets of the Day of Decision: The End of the Assyrian Period

8 The End of Assyria and the Growing Hope for the Day of Yahweh: Joel, Nahum, Zephaniah

8.1 The fate of Assyria and its satellites

After Isaiah departed from the scene, prophecy was quiet for about seventy years. It is as if the giant figure of Isaiah had stopped the mouths of any possible successors. Of course there will have been cultic nabis in the Temple in Jerusalem during these years. But what they proclaimed was meant for the immediate moment. They did not mould the expectations or fears of a whole generation. Otherwise traces of them would presumably have survived. The political situation may also have contributed to the silence. After the Assyrian king Sennacherib had withdrawn from Jerusalem in 701 and had received King Hezekiah's oath of allegiance, Assyrian rule was firmly established. For a long time, any attempt at rebellion was useless. Year by year, little Judah paid a considerable tribute to Nineveh. In the Temple at Jerusalem the altar to the god of the super-power, the god of Assyria, stood in the centre of the forecourt. Under the title 'Lord', Baal (the Judaeans were spared from having to use his proper name, Assur), he received regular sacrifices, as did the army of the heavens, the stars, on which the Assyrians laid great stress. The altar to Yahweh did, it is true, stand next to the Assyrian one, but it was pushed to one side, no longer in the central position. We can deduce from Zephaniah and Jeremiah that for many people Yahweh and Assur really blended into one.

When, round about 630, the first cracks appeared in the giant Assyrian empire, prophets once more arose in Jerusalem whose proclamations went beyond the events of the immediate future and opened up a new horizon of world politics. What they said was again thought worthy of permanent remembrance.

We can assign Nahum and Zephaniah ben Cushi to this period with some degree of certainty. Nahum came from an otherwise unknown place, Elkosh, while Zephaniah probably came from Jerusalem. Both of them proclaimed the downfall of Nineveh, the Assyrian capital. According to Zephaniah (2.13–15) Yahweh was going to make the metropolis a wilderness because the people there had arrogantly boasted, 'I, and there is no one else'. But enmity towards the great power is still subdued in Zephaniah. His proclamation against Philistia is almost more violent (2.4–7). His own countrymen are not spared, either. They are threatened with a worse catastrophe than any they had hitherto experienced. A funeral dirge is already raised in anticipation over the 'rebellious and defiled, the violent city' where, from the ministers down to the judges, nabis and priests, not a single class is what it ought to be (3.1–5). We may suspect Isaiah's influence in the social criticism, or when the cause of the decline is defined as being lack of trust (3.2) or human arrogance (3.11; cf. 2.15). Like Isaiah, Zephaniah sees devastation breaking over the city in the immediate future. But beyond the catastrophe there is still hope for a remnant of Judah, who will then succeed to the property of the neighbouring nations (2.7,9; 3.12f.), *š*^{e}*'erīt*, as in Amos and Micah, not *š*^{e}*'ār* as in Isaiah).

Nahum's polemics against the capital of the empire (perhaps a few years later) are incomparably more passionate. The king who has gone forth from Assyria (Sennacherib? Assurbanipal?) is the very embodiment of wickedness (*b*^{e}*līyya'al* – hence the New Testament name for the devil, Belial) and has devised evil against Yahweh and the whole of mankind. He will not return (1.11; 2.1; cf. 3.19). But the city belonging to him was filled with the same evil spirit: 'Woe to the bloody city / full of deceit, // robbery fills her, her booty she does not let go.' Dramatically and with a wealth of imagery, Nahum describes the attack of an anonymous enemy army, before which Nineveh soon collapses (2.4ff.; 3.1ff.). Where Judah's future is concerned, this prophet has only positive promises to proclaim: 'I have afflicted you / I will afflict you no more. // Now I will break the yoke from off you, // its bonds I will burst apart' (1.12). Nahum, too, picks up Isaianic concepts, calling Assyria a lion (2.12; cf. Isa 5.29) and promising that its yoke will be broken (1.13; cf. Isa. 9.4). But unlike Zephaniah, he extends only the positive lines in the picture of the future drawn by his great prophetic model. Because his picture of things is so black-and-white, Nahum has sometimes been condemned as a nationalist and as a dubious prophet of salvation. His contemporary Jeremiah was soon to strike a very different note in the attacking his own people.

If the Book of Joel is also to be assigned to the end of the Assyrian period (and we shall be discussing this point presently), the day of the holy war against the nations and the decisive battle in the valley of Jehoshaphat near Jerusalem (which is touched on but not developed in 3.9–17) are also aimed at the Assyrians and their numerous satellite peoples.

In the last decades of the seventh century BC, therefore, there was a growing sense of the impending fall of the foreign super-power. The external circumstances of the final years of King Assurbanipal allowed people to guess that something of the kind was imminent, even without visionary experience. That the prophets also proclaimed the Assyrian downfall was by no means as surprising as the announcement of the downfall of the prophet's own people had been in the early Assyrian period. Added to this is the fact that Zephaniah, like Nahum and – if he can be put here – Joel too, was able to fall back on Isaiah, who had already, decades before, talked about the catastrophic downfall of Assyria. All the same, the break-up of the Assyrian power in 612 was experienced by Israel as well as by the other nations of the ancient East as a decisive event, and as a mighty confirmation of the reliability of the prophetic proclamation.

8.2 The Day of Yahweh

Amos had already picked up the expectation of a coming Day of Yahweh, on which metahistorical events were to be concentrated and lead to a unique establishment of the divinely ordained order on earth (5.18–20). In the 'arrogance' song (2.6ff.), Isaiah had painted 'the Day for Yahweh', as he preferred to call it, with all its appalling effects. But the most impressive description of the impending culmination of world events is to be found in Zephaniah. For him, 'Near at hand is the *yōm yhwh*' becomes the watchword of prophecy in general (1.7,14). But this means a day of sacrifice for God (1.7) or,

> A day of overflowing wrath is that day / a day of distress and anguish.
> A day of thunder and of tumult, / a day of darkness and gloom.
> A day of clouds and veils of darkness, a day of trumpet blast and battle cry . . .
> I will lay oppression on mankind / they walk like the blind . . .
> Their blood shall be poured out like dust / the sap of their life (?) like liquid dung (1.15–18).

So this day will bring the whole earth into movement. It will be accompanied by a sinister warlike event, with trumpet-calls and cries. Is it supernatural powers who are this time rushing to battle, spreading horror and devastation on all sides? (It was this passage in Zephaniah which became the basis of the mediaeval *Dies Irae.)* How can the expectation of the future be so concentrated on a single D-day of this kind, on which the fate of mankind is to be decided?

Before I go into this, we must consider the dating of another 'minor' prophet – Joel ben Pethuel; for the *yōm yhwh* is just as central to his message as to Zephaniah's.

In the case of Joel, the book's heading gives us no information, either about his time, or about where he came from. Consequently the date assigned to him by scholars varies between the ninth and the second century BC. A devastating plague of grasshoppers (locusts) is the background of most of the sayings in the book, and is the occasion for complaint, petition and the subsequent assurance that the prayer will be heard. The basis seems to be a liturgy for a ritual of fasting and repentance *(ṣōm)* occasioned by this catastrophe, which had destroyed the harvest of a whole year. Grasshopper plagues of this extent were – and still are – not uncommon in Palestine; and this does not make the dating any easier. The onset of swarms of insects is described as Isaiah describes the onset of the foreign power. A strong nation, which can be compared with lions, has invaded the land and has laid waste the vine (1.6f.). What is imagery here, and what is fact? Nahum was to depict the Assyrians as grasshoppers (1.15–17). Is there a connection here? In 3.17 there is a promise that one day no foreigners will pass through Jerusalem any more. This is a reference to the troops of a foreign power, who evidently pass through the city in the presence of the prophet as if it were a matter of course. But since this was something that recurred continually, from the time of the Assyrians down to the days of the Romans, we again lack any chronological framework. So we are left merely with the connection at some points in the Book of Joel between the plight brought about by the grasshopper plague and an imminent Day of Yahweh. Grasshoppers are the harbingers of that incomparably greater catastrophe.

This connection is seen by most Old Testament scholars as sufficient reason for assigning the book to the post-exilic period. The line of thought is viewed as being already apocalyptic in outline, and this was only conceivable at a comparatively late period. At this point we see particularly clearly how fatal it can be to pursue any isolated method of literary criticism. For in fact statements about a Day of Yahweh can almost certainly be found only in writings of the seventh and sixth centuries – first of all in Amos, and then in Obadiah and a disciple of Isaiah (13.6ff.). In Zech. 14.1 there is again an echo of this expectation, though now in post-exilic times; but significantly enough the phrase occurs in altered form, in the style of Isaiah: 'A Day for Yahweh'. Otherwise not a trace of it is to be found in the whole of post-exilic literature. The whole of apocalyptic literature expects that the final event will be relatively long drawn out. To telescope it into a single day does not in any way fit into the apocalyptic scheme. So it is the pointer to the impending Day of Yahweh more than anything else which actually speaks in favour of assigning Joel to the late Assyrian period (as Rudolph does). In that case his strong dependence on Isaiah becomes explicable (Yahweh dwelling on Zion, hope for the remnant, return of the primordial period, 2.23). And so, above all, does the similarity between Joel and Zephaniah in the description of the Day of Yahweh (trumpets, cries of war, darkness and gloom, clouds and thick darkness, 2.1f.).

What, then, do the prophets of the Assyrian period really understand by the Day of Yahweh? In Christian theology this 'day' became the Last Judgment. For the prophets, however, the Day of Yahweh does not mean any exact forensic investigation; it is a day of war, on which God will come in a rushing theophany accompained by cosmic phenomena, such as storm and lightning. In a flash he will finally consummate the auras evoked by the deeds of all sinners and evil doers (i.e., he will utterly destroy the wicked) and then set up a new *mišpāṭ* which will endure for ever. Even if Joel includes the idea that Yahweh will forcibly gather together the enemy peoples in the valley of Jehoshaphat near Jerusalem, in order to dispute with them about the injustice that has been done in Israel, these proceedings end, not with the pronouncement of judgment, but with the consummation *(gᵉmūl)* of their misdeeds on the heads of those responsible (3.4–8).

The Day of Yahweh is thought of as a unique event. It is not a day which Yahweh will bring about within time, like other days. We are never told that he will bring it about, or cause it to come, or make it, or anything of the kind. This is rather a day which actually *is* Yahweh, in which his Godhead will take fully visible form. It is hardly possible to avoid returning here to a specifically Hebrew way of looking at time. For the Hebrew, words which we translate as 'day', 'year', and so forth, are not physically homogeneous units of measurement; they are temporal rhythms, filled with a particular content.[25] It is therefore quite possible for a Hebrew to curse efficaciously a day which returns in the course of every year (Job 3; Jer. 20. 14–18). Or he can separate out every seventh day as being by its very nature holy and belonging to Yahweh. But the actual semantic bearing of this complex of thinking on 'the Day of Yahweh' still requires elucidation. The disappearance of the expression from the whole of post-exilic literature (which develops a more comprehensive conception of eschatology) at least speaks in favour of giving a narrow meaning to the phrase, in the sense of 'the day on which Yahweh will take shape fully, as he really is'.

Biblical scholarship, instead of illuminating the content of this concept synchronically and semantically (i.e. from a contemporary context), has tried to do so diachronically (in the light of historical development). Two contrasting derivations are offered. The great Norwegian scholar Sigmund Mowinckel[26] wanted to trace back the phrase to a central cultic ceremony, as a 'day that Yahweh makes' – from which in his view all the important New Year and Enthronement festivals are derived. Von Rad, on the other hand, in his *Old Testament Theology* points to the ritual ceremony of the holy war, where Yahweh is conceived of as the One who casts down the enemy to the ground – for example on the day of Midian (Isa. 9.4).[27] Both explanations have the disadvantage that they merely postulate the 'original' use of *yōm yhwh* which they presuppose, without being able to produce any evidence for it. In the existing texts the expression is always applied to an upheaval in all existing conditions – to be brought about by God and to be expected in the imminent future. In 2.2 Joel cries:

> His (its) like has never been / from of old; nor will the like succeed it / through the years of the generations of generations.

Whether by this he means the day itself, or a mysterious people which will enter the scene then, at all events the day brings something that has never been before, and which goes beyond anything known in previous history. More is needed for its preparation than the proclamation of Yahweh's *dābār* by individual prophets. All Israelites, even the slaves, will be seized by Yahweh's *rūᵃḥ* and will be driven to prophesy (Joel 3.1–3), so that the day prepared by God in an anticipatory speech event will be utterly complete and successful.

This idea as expressed here does not yet include the end of the world or any fundamental alterations of natural laws. But it is obvious that after a day like this the world cannot simply go on as before. So *yōm yhwh* – so far as we can form any judgment about it all from the text – is from the very beginning a (pre-)eschatological concept. Consequently the hope for a remnant of Israel, which Isaiah still prophesies as something quite separate from the 'Day of Yahweh', is linked by the later prophets with survival after this turn of events (so still Obadiah 17).

The emergence of the phrase *yōm yhwh* to express an impending establishment of Yahweh's rule, surpassing everything that has gone before, marked a profound change in Israelite religion. Up to then, Israel had looked backwards to salvation history and creation both for its religious assurance and its cultic worship. From now on its leading spiritual representatives look forward. Like the civilizations surrounding it, pre-prophetic Israel lived only in the present and found assurance in this present in the light of a past which legitimated the present state of affairs as being the best possible. In order to experience God and the meaning of life and history, the cultic community gathered together at the New Year Festival. There the past was reactivated: the choosing of the patriarchs, the exodus from Egypt, the entry into the promised land, the commandments given on Sinai. Similar viewpoints are to be found in the other religions of the ancient world and still exist in most civilizations at the present day. The literary prophets make an end to the complacency of the Israel of their day – by no means consciously but, in the course of the years, all the more effectively for that. By criticizing social, political and cultic conditions as intolerable, they relativized the ultimate importance of the divinely given past, salvation history, and anything metahistorically connected with it. The achievements of salvation history and the realization of them in the cultic festival were evidently not, after all, so final and efficacious. Even there Israel could apparently turn *sedeq* into poison, put its promised land at risk, and in its arrogance create a sinister negative correlation between action and destiny. The prophets certainly do not reject the view of a history of salvation as such, but they do establish that Yahweh's work has still to be perfected; and they set this in the framework of a metahistory which strives towards monotheism and a monanthropology – that is to say, a (harmonious) fellowship of all men living within a nature designed for them. In order really to know God as he is, as Ezekiel was later to say (cf. also Joel 3.17), one must experience the future revolution.

It would seem that the prophets did not merely change Israel's religion. For the first time in the history of mankind, human beings dared to make hope the foundation of their ontology and their theology. The prophets therefore brought a futuristic turn into the thinking of following centuries, a sense of incompleteness and a further purpose to be found in the course of world events. This fed the eschatology of apocalyptic, and then Christian eschatology. From this too, however, came the secularistic transformations of the biblical hope for the future which we find in the ideologies of modern times.[28]

9. The Transition to Literary Prophecy in the Assyrian Period and the Problem of Transmission

9.1 Writing as an exception and an emergency measure

Before I continue the treatment of the individual literary prophets, perhaps some considerations about the concept of literary prophecy in general may not be out of place. As we have seen, unfortunately we hardly know anything about the circumstances and social conditions from which the literary prophets came. The evolution of their writings also poses a vast number of riddles.

Amos, who lived round about 750 BC, is the first figure to whom a book with prophetic content can subsequently be traced back; and his younger contemporaries Hosea, Micah and Isaiah evidently took up the custom of setting down sayings about the future in writing. After an interruption of several decades, this custom was continued in the post-Assyrian period. Scholars have become accustomed to describe these men and their successors as literary prophets, and to distinguish them from pre-literary prophecy. But the term 'literary prophet' is open to misunderstanding. For Amos and men like him are not aiming to be men of letters any more than were their predecessors. They remain the proclaimers of a divine *dābār* which above all has to be uttered publicly. If it is written down, that is a secondary process, which must often have been adopted as a temporary measure, or in an emergency. The literary prophets were largely writers against their will. Yet out of what was really a temporary expedient, a highly independent literary genre was born which soon acquired its own importance, documenting in its own way the dawn of a new phase of religious thinking.

But how were these sayings committed to writing in the first place? Isaiah reports in 8.1 that one day he supplemented his earlier prophecies about the fall on the enemy coalition formed against Judah during the Syro-Ephraimite war, by writing on a tablet (or a sheet of papyrus), 'Speed spoil, hasten prey', a riddling saying which was intended to summon Assyria to overthrow Aram and North Israel. Here the writing is nothing but a symbolic action. It sets a visible sign in history which calls for fulfilment, just like Isaiah's little son, who was soon afterwards to be born and who received the same name – or non-name (8.1–4). We find a similar event in Isaiah's late period. 'Come, write it on a tablet among them, inscribe it in a book', God calls to him, 'that it may be for the days to come / a witness for ever' (30.8). Unfortunately it is still not clear whether the charge to write applies solely to the preceding 'reproach' to Egypt, where the country is given the name 'Rahab who sits still' and is thereby compared to a primaeval dragon vanquished by Yahweh; or whether this is the conclusion of a more considerable 'Assyrian cycle' which provided the basic material for 28.1–30.7, and which the prophet is committing to writing at his God's command.

Equally uncertain are the statements in another passage. 'Bind up the testimony, seal the teaching in my disciples – (But) I have to wait for Yahweh, who is hiding his face' (8.16f.). The words sound like resignation, as if Isaiah would like to break off his public ministry, but had prevously impressed on a group of disciples the message with which he had been inspired. The section could be the close of a collection of sayings which provide the foundation for ch. 8. (Other scholars relate it to a 'memorandum' about the Syro-Ephraimite war.) Unfortunately we still do not know whether the sealing is meant literally (in the sense that an actual writing existed) or whether it is a case of 'closing up' in the memory of the disciples what has been orally transmitted. At all events, Isaiah must have committed to writing a whole series of sayings which were quite considerable in bulk. Otherwise the diversity of forms which the book displays today would hardly be explicable.

In the later Babylonian period, Jeremiah (ch. 36) reports that he was forbidden to speak in the temple and that Yahweh had therefore commanded him to write down all his words, so that they could be read publicly by one of the prophet's friends. This information may well offer a more typical reason for the rise of the first written prophecies than the occasional hints in Isaiah. Amos had already found himself in the same situation as Jeremiah did later. Banned as he was from North Israel, we are bound to assume that he had no other choice than to put his utterances into writing and to let them circulate in this form.

Probably none of the prophets of the early Assyrian period ('early Assyrian' as far as the Assyrian suzerainty over Palestine is concerned) composed even one writing. Even in the case of Amos there are certain indications that the book as we have it is based on a number of independent 'broadsheets', which the prophet himself wrote, or had written for him. They were only put together into a single book by a later hand. The same may be said of Isaiah, and perhaps of Hosea and Micah too.

9.2 Aphorisms and leading metahistorical ideas

Luther already complained that the prophetic books were unedifying, if read continuously, 'since they maintain no kind of order but leap from one matter to another so that a man can neither understand nor endure it'.[29] The apparent lack of cohesion is explained – as form criticism has meanwhile shown – by the fact that the prophets only committed to writing what they delivered orally. And the orally delivered saying was formulated tersely and poetically, so that the listener could easily commit it to memory. When, later on, it was given a fixed written form, individual sayings might be shortened to avoid repetition, or poetic lines might be expanded into prose, in order to make it easier for the uninformed listener to understand what was said. The repetition of the introductory rubric: 'Thus says Yahweh', or similar openings, at the head of what were originally independent fragments, is missing in many cases. But the basic structure of the relatively short oral genres, such as prophecy and funeral dirge, is generally preserved (Hosea is an exception).

Yet these recorded sayings are not as lacking in cohesion as Luther imagined, even though the principles of the arrangement do not follow thematic headings. They have a didactic purpose, conveying special prophetic points of view or metahistorical references and relations. The speech about the nations in Amos 1f. puts together what were probably independent oracles on the subject in such a way that it begins with the arch-enemy, Aram, and ends with the people of Israel. The song of the vineyard in Isaiah 5, with the sweep of its whole historical dimension, certainly does not follow the social criticism in chs. 2–5 merely by chance. It raises the individual sayings to a metahistorical level. The sequence of visions in Amos 7.1–9; 8.1–3 shifts the perspective from cosmic externals to the cultic heart that was Israel's centre. All four visions are perhaps a summing up and conclusion of what had been heard – ever since Amos 5.1 – as a series of *hoy* songs over doomed Israel (cf. the vision in Amos 9.1–4, which follows the collection of sayings in 8.4ff.; the descriptive passage in Isa. 6, following chs. 2–5). Since research into the editorial history of the prophetic books is still in its beginnings, the connections here have as yet hardly been investigated.

The fusing together of a sequence of sayings points to a new kind of prophecy. Unlike the earlier nabis, this does not content itself with individual aspects of the future of people and king, but develops comprehensive viewpoints from which to contemplate the total cohesion of divine and human reality and its movement. The fact that a considerable body of prophetic writing exists points to the attempt at putting together the principles of metahistory, which I have tried to show in more detail in connection with Amos and Isaiah. A critical prophecy is beginning, which differs from the previous investigations of the future in Israel, and not just because it has been committed to writing (which may in any case be secondary). Occasionally these men have been called reform prophets; but in applying that term to them we must always remember that their reforms were not programmatic in intent.

9.3 The breakthrough to literary individuality

The prophetic books are the only writings in the proto-canonical Old Testament to bear the names of particular authors from whom they do really derive. As a rule Hebrew writing, whether it be history (like the sources of the Pentateuch) or poetry (like the Psalms) is anonymous. It is surprising that it should be with the pre-exilic prophets that an indication of authorship seemed essential. (With later prophets such as Deutero- or Trito-Isaiah, or Malachi, this necessity is no longer felt.) What impulse prompted the disclosure of the prophet's name in the early Assyrian period? Might one not assume that it would be a matter of indifference who passed on a *dābār* of Yahweh, with its prediction of the future? The important point was certainly not a striving for intellectual originality or fame. This is all the more evident since biographical facts about the prophets are, regrettably, recorded only very fragmentarily, and only show through where the prophet's life has symbolic character. But apparently the man to whom Yahweh entrusts the disclosure of the future for the community of the people, is, by reason of that very fact, lifted out of anonymity, more than others of his fellow-countrymen. As a prophet with a special status, from that point on he is set apart from his social origin and his religious position, his name linked inseparably with the truth of the *dābār* of Yahweh that he expresses.

9.4 Disciples

Pre-exilic prophetic writings would certainly not have been preserved had there not soon been people who copied them again and again, preserving them for posterity. Nor did these people restrict themselves to copying down collections of Amos' or Isaiah's sayings word for word. They were editors, who very soon bound together heterogeneous prophetic jottings into a relatively unified genre: the prophetic book. Whenever possible, a heading assigns the particular prophet to a particular hour in Israel's history, which means the reign of a certain king of Israel or Judah; in addition, the name of the prophet's father and his place of origin is recorded. The conscientious way the editor worked is shown by the fact that in Hosea, for example, the place of his origin is missing; and, in the case of Micah, his father's name. In these instances the facts were apparently unknown to the editors. On the other hand, these people were convinced that they were endowed with the same authority as their prophetic master and were therefore empowered to supplement the material and expand it. Topical references are added, to bring the prophecy up to date (although it must be said that this was mainly a post-exilic practice). Every prophetic book as we have it today closes with prophecies of salvation or with hymns (Amos 9.7ff.; Hos. 4.2ff.; Micah 7.8ff.; cf. the positive or optimistic additions to the individual sections in Isa. 28–33). We have to assume that editorial work of this kind began relatively early on. But here, too, research is still largely in the dark.

The little we can discover about the lives of the first literary prophets suggests that initially they were isolated figures. But a glance at the process by which their books were transmitted makes us suspect that they did not remain as solitary as they appear at first sight. Perhaps it was Isaiah's disciples (8.16) who made a beginning here, forming a school in Jerusalem in which material deriving from Amos and Hosea was passed down, too. We may perhaps assume that for generations there was a kind of school of Isaiah followers. This seems likely because at the close of the Assyrian period Isaiah's, in particular, is the proclamation from whom a number of other prophets (Joel, Nahum, Zephaniah) pick up the threads.

BIBLIOGRAPHY

1. General

Surveys of more recent research on the prophets can be found in J. Limburg, 'The Prophets in Recent Study: 1966–1977', *Interpretation* XXXII, 1978, 69–83; W. McKane, 'Prophecy and Prophetic Literature', in *Tradition and Interpretation*, ed. G. W. Anderson, Oxford 1979, 163–88.

In recent years the genres used by the prophets have been a focal point of interpretation. I have given my own views in K. Koch, *The Growth of the Biblical Tradition*, ET London and New York 1969, 15–18. C. Westermann, *Basic Forms of Prophetic Speech*, ET London 1967, postulates a derivation of these forms from prosecutions at law. Other important studies are W. Janzen, *Morning Cry and Woe Oracle*, BZAW 125, Berlin 1972; G. M. Tucker, 'Prophetic Speech', *Interpretation* XXXII, 1978, 31–45.

We still need investigations into the origin and composition of the prophetic books. B. S. Childs, *Introduction to the Old Testament as Scripture*, London and Philadelphia 1979, presents a somewhat arbitrary interpretation in terms of 'canonical shape'.

Research into the psychological background to the way in which the prophets received word and inspiration was carried on by H. Gunkel, *Die Propheten*, Göttingen 1917; J. Lindblom, *Prophecy in Ancient Israel*, Oxford 1962; G. Widengren, *Literary and Psychological Aspects of the Hebrew Prophets*, Uppsala 1948. There has also been particular interest in the sociological conditioning of prophetic activity, including their relationship to cultic institutions and prophetic schools. This was stimulated by S. Mowinckel, *Psalmenstudien* I–VI, Oslo 1921–1926, and *Prophecy and Tradition*, Oslo 1946. The most recent discussion is R. R. Wilson, *Prophecy and Society in Ancient Israel*, 1980.

The prophetic view of the relationship between God and the nations has been investigated by N. K. Gottwald, *All the Kingdoms of the Earth*, New York 1964, and the problem of the so-called 'false prophets' by J. L. Crenshaw, *Prophetic Conflict*, BZAW 124, Berlin 1971. There is extensive literature on eschatology and messianic expectation; only S.

Mowinckel, *He that Cometh*, Oxford 1976, and the collective volume *Eschatologie im Alten Testament*, ed. H. D. Preuss, Darmstadt 1978.

Relevant literature on divination in the Ancient Near East outside Israel is given in H. B. Huffmon, 'Prophecy in the Ancient Near East', *The Interpreter's Dictionary of the Bible*, Supplementary Volume, Nashville 1976, 697–700. For *Ugarit-Forschungen* IV, 1972, 53–78.

Pride of place in comprehensive theological treatments must be given to G. von Rad, *The Message of the Prophets*, London 1968 (with a traditio-historical orientation); cf. also C. F. Whitley, *The Prophetic Achievement*, Leiden 1963 (concerned with the prophetic contribution to 'Hebrew religious thought'); A. Heschel, *The Prophets*, 1962 (a Jewish existentialist approach); J. Bright, *Covenant and Promise*, Philadelphia and London 1967 (stressing the idea of the covenant), and two books by R. E. Clements, *Prophecy and Covenant*, London 1955, and *Prophecy and Tradition*, Oxford 1975 (starting from prophetic forms of speech).

2. Individual books

Isaiah 1–39

O. Kaiser, *Isaiah 1–12, Isaiah 13–39*, London and Philadelphia 1983², 1974; A. Wildberger, *Jesaja*, Biblischer Kommentar Altes Testament X, 1–3, Neukirchen 1972ff. (the most detailed commentary). For the problem of the prophet's call see R. Knierim, 'The Vocation of Isaiah', *Vetus Testamentum* 18, 1968, 47–68; for the later phase, B. S. Childs, *Isaiah and the Assyrian Crisis*, London 1967; for Isaiah's relationship to Wisdom, see W. Whedbee, *Isaiah and Wisdom*, Nashville 1971.

Hosea

W. Rudolph, *Hosea*, Kommentar zum Alten Testament XIII 1, Gütersloh 1966; H. W. Wolff, *Hosea*, Hermeneia, Philadelphia 1974; J. L. Mays, *Hosea*, London and Philadelphia 1969. For particular problems see M. J. Buss, *The Prophetic Word of Hosea*, BZAW 111, Berlin 1969; W. Brueggemann, *Tradition for Crisis*, Richmond 1968; for the idea of the covenant, D. J. McCarthy, *Treaty and Covenant*, Oxford ²1978.

Joel

W. Rudolph, *Joel, Amos, Obadja, Jona*, Kommentar zum Alten Testament XIII, 2, Gütersloh 1971; H. W. Wolff, *Joel and Amos*, Hermeneia, Philadelphia 1977.

Amos

W. Rudolph and H. W. Wolff (see under Joel); J. L. Mays, *Amos*, London and Philadelphia 1969; K. Koch et al., *Amos, untersucht mit den Methoden einer strukturalen Formgeschichte*, Teil 1–3, Neukirchen 1967. For individual issues: H. H. Rowley, 'Was Amos a Nabi?', *Festschrift for O. Eissfeldt*, Halle 1947, 191–8; G. M. Tucker, 'Prophetic Authority', *Interpretation* 27, 1979, 423–34.

Micah, Nahum and Zephaniah

W. Rudolph, *Micah – Nahum – Habakuk – Zefanja*, Kommentar zum Alten Testament XIII, 3, 1975; H. W. Wolff, *Micha, Dodekapropheton*, Biblischer Kommentar Altes Testament XIV, 4, 1982; J. L. Mays, *Micah*, London and Philadelphia 1976. See also A. S. van der Woude, 'Micah in Dispute with the Pseudo-Prophets', *Vetus Testamentum* 19, 1969, 244–60.

NOTES

1. B. Meissner, *Babylonien und Assyrien* II, Heidelberg 1925, p. 297.
2. Letter A 15.
3. Letter A 1121.
4. A. Parrot and G. Dossin, *Archives royales de Mari*, X 9.
5. Letter A 4260.
6. In *Ancient Near Eastern Texts relating to the Old Testament*, ed. J. B. Pritchard, Princeton ^{3}1969, p. 26 (hereafter *ANET*).
7. In *Altorientalische Texte zum Alten Testament*, ed. H. Gressmann, Berlin and Leipzig ^{2}1927, pp. 443ff. (hereafter *AOT*).
8. *AOT*, pp. 281–3.
9. M. P. Nilsson, *Geschichte der griechischen Religion I*, ^{3}1968, pp. 546f., 625ff.
10. A. Weiser, *Die Profetie des Amos*, Giessen 1929.
11. Op. cit., pp. 310f.
12. J. Wellhausen, *Israelitische und Jüdische Geschichte*, Berlin ^{9}1958, p. 108.
13. A. Jirku, *Kanaanäische Mythen und Epen aus Ras-Schamra-Ugarit*, Gütersloh 1962, p. 42; *ANET*, p. 132.
14. G. von Rad, *Old Testament Theology* I, ET Oliver and Boyd 1965, reissued SCM Press 1975, pp. 272ff.
15. R. Otto, *The Idea of the Holy*, ET Oxford University Press ^{2}1950.
16. *ANET*, pp. 282f.
17. F. Weinrich, *Der religiös-utopische Charakter der profetischen Politik*, Giessen 1932.
18. *ANET*, p. 288.
19. According to the Hebrew Bible the prophecy begins in 9.2. This is 9.1 in the Hebrew, but the division in the English Bible is to be preferred (see p. 134).
20. G. von Rad, *Old Testament Theology* II, ET Oliver and Boyd 1965, reissued SCM Press 1975, p. 164.
21. O. Procksch, *Jesaja*, Kommentar zum Alten Testament, Leipzig 1930.
22. W. E. Müller, *Die Vorstellung vom Rest im Alten Testament*, rev. ed., Neukirchen 1973.
23. G. F. Hasel, *The Remnant*, Berrien Springs, Michigan ^{2}1974.
24. B. Albrektson, *History and the Gods*, Lund 1967, p. 119.
25. T. G. Boman, *Hebrew Thought Compared with Greek*, ET SCM Press 1960, pp. 129ff.; despite the severe criticism made by James Barr, *The Semantics of Biblical Language*, Oxford University Press ^{2}1962, some features of Boman's account can still be maintained.
26. S. Mowinckel, *Psalmenstudien* II, Oslo 1922; cf. id., *The Psalms in Israel's Worship*, Blackwell 1962, p. 116 n. 35.

27. G. von Rad, *Old Testament Theology* II, pp. 119ff.
28. K. Löwith, *Meaning in History*, ET Chicago 1949.
29. *Werke*, Weimarer Ausgabe XIX, p. 350.

INDEX OF BIBLICAL REFERENCES

II Samuel
6.20 106
7 11, 19, 30, 136
7.9 104
7.12 136
7.16 122, 136
9 144
11f. 19
12 28, 35
12.10 30
12.13f. 99
13.28f. 23
16.21f. 23
18.14 23
34.11 105

I Kings
1 19
2 144
2.13ff. 23
3 18
10.9 60
11.31–7 30
12 84
12.19 61
12.28 37, 52
13 18
13.6 138
14.7–11 30
15.25–9 30
16.1–13 31
17.1 32
17.17ff. 26
17.18 33
17.24 33
18 11, 25, 31, 34
18.12 26
18.17 33
18.22 33
18.31 35
18.36 33
19 35
19.16 33
19.19 35
19.19f. 25
19.21 32
20 27
20.3 22
21 34, 50
21.20f. 31
22 25, 26, 33, 41
22.11 84

II Kings.
1 34
1.3 33f.
1.6 34
1.16 34
2–6 25
2.12 29
2.16 26
3 26, 29
3.4 49
5 26
6.12 26
8.20 61
9 68
9f. 86
10.10 31
13.14 29
14.29 39
15.10 39
19 26, 127
22 26, 29
24.14 49

Job
3 161

Psalms
2 137
4.6 58
15 98
18 137
24.5 58
24.7–9 109
45 137
46 146
46.7 123
46.11 123
50 119
50.4–6 119
51.21 58
65.2f. 111
68 119
72 136

Hosea continued
13.7f. 88
13.14 89
13.15 89

Joel
1.6f. 160
2.1f. 161
2.2 162
2.21–3 59
2.23 58, 161
3.1–3 162
3.4–8 161
3.9–17 159
3.17 162

Amos
1f. 75
1.1 70
1.3 49, 71
1.3ff. 63, 64
1.3–5 71
1.8 70
1.11 69
1.14 71
2.3ff. 65
2.6 44, 59
2.6ff. 46, 50
2.6–16 44, 66
2.7 48
2.8 53
2.10 51, 74
2.13 64
3.1f. 74
3.2 63
3.6 73
3.8 68, 71
3.9–11 47
3.10 61
3.10f. 97
3.11 64, 65
3.12 44
3.13f. 63
3.14 54, 65
4.1–3 46, 50
4.2 53, 54, 71, 72
4.3 65, 68
4.4 51
4.4f. 50, 62
4.6ff. 55, 76
4.10 64
4.12 64
5.1 166
5.2 64, 65, 72
5.3 142
5.4ff. 61
5.4–6 51, 54
5.4–7 56
5.4–6.14f. 55
5.5 44, 116
5.6 57, 63, 65, 69
5.11 64
5.11ff. 48
5.12 44, 48, 59, 62
5.14 52
5.14f. 53, 54
5.15 59, 69, 70
5.16f. 44
5.18 124
5.18ff. 44
5.18–20 159
5.21f. 51, 54, 57
5.22 52
5.23–7 57
5.24 58, 69
5.25 74
5.26 53, 54, 58, 61, 69
5.27 65, 68
6.1ff. 44
6.1–6 76
6.1–7 47, 50, 54
6.6 120
6.6f. 50
6.7 65
6.8 55, 71, 72
6.8f. 65
6.12 58, 59, 94
6.12–14 56
6.14 44, 65
7 39
7.1–3 39
7.1–9 166
7.2 43, 55, 64
7.4 43
7.4ff. 64
7.4–6 39